RESEARCH AND POLICY IN ETHNIC RELATIONS

Compromised dynamics in a neoliberal era

Edited by
Charles Husband

To Barbara,
my friend, colleague and wife,
to whom I am incalculably indebted

Contemporary Issues in Social Policy

Series editor: Charles Husband

This exciting new series brings together academics, professionals and activists to link cutting-edge social theory and research to contentious issues in social policy, challenge consensus and invite debate. Each text provides a critical appraisal of key aspects of contemporary theory and research to offer fresh perspectives.

Research and policy in ethnic relations: Compromised dynamics in a neoliberal era
Charles Husband (editor)

New philanthropy and social justice and social policy: Debating the conceptual and policy discourse
Behrooz Morvaridi (editor)

Political disengagement: The changing nature of the 'political'
Nathan Manning (editor)

See more at http://bit.ly/1AWjClV

First published in Great Britain in 2015 by

Policy Press
University of Bristol
1-9 Old Park Hill
Bristol
BS2 8BB
UK
t: +44 (0)117 954 5940
pp-info@bristol.ac.uk
www.policypress.co.uk

North America office:
Policy Press
c/o The University of Chicago Press
1427 East 60th Street
Chicago, IL 60637, USA
t: +1 773 702 7700
f: +1 773 702 9756
sales@press.uchicago.edu
www.press.uchicago.edu

The image on page 113 has been kindly supplied by the Muslim Youthwork Foundation. The 'Skratch Punk' font in the image was created by Nik Coley.

British Library Cataloguing in Publication Data
A catalogue record for this book is available from the British Library

Library of Congress Cataloging-in-Publication Data
A catalog record for this book has been requested

ISBN 978 1 44731 489 9 hardcover

The right of Charles Husband to be identified as editor of this work has been asserted by him in accordance with the Copyright, Designs and Patents Act 1988.

Cover design by Qube, Bristol
Printed and bound in Great Britain by CPI Group (UK) Ltd,
Croydon, CR0 4YY
Policy Press uses environmentally responsible print partners

Contents

Notes on contributors

Yunis Alam is a lecturer in the Division of Sociology and Criminology at the University of Bradford. He is an active researcher in ethnic relations, social cohesion and mass media and has also written several works of fiction, including novels and short stories. His current sociologically driven research is a qualitative study of car culture in Bradford.

Ioannis Dimitrakopoulos is head of the Department of Equality and Citizens' Rights at the European Agency for Fundamental Rights. He studied social sciences in the UK and later lectured at the University of Ioaninna and Athens College in Greece. Since 1985 he has he worked in local and regional government, and conducted or coordinated national and transnational research projects. In 2003 he joined the Agency and has been responsible for several of its major publications.

Charles Husband is Professor Emeritus of Social Analysis at the University of Bradford (UK), Visiting Professor at the Sámi University College (Norway), and Docent in Sociology at the University of Helsinki (Finland). He is an interdisciplinary social scientist with a long history of seeking to apply social science research and theory to the formulation of equitable anti-discriminatory policy and practice in multi-ethnic societies.

Andrew Jakubowicz is Professor of Sociology at the University of Technology Sydney. His research focus covers cultural diversity issues in Australia and internationally, with a particular interest in mass media. He has recently completed work on three series of the TV and online documentary 'Once Upon a Time in', covering the development of the Vietnamese, Lebanese and Italian communities in Australia. His recent book *'For those who've come across the seas...' Australian multicultural theory policy and practice* collects key writings on contemporary Australian issues from terrorism to art. He has recently completed a project on creativity, cultural diversity and innovation, exploring the way in which migration creates opportunities for new synergies.

M.G. Khan is a tutor at Ruskin College, Oxford, and the author of *Young Muslims, pedagogy and Islam*, published by Policy Press. He was one of the founders of the Muslim Youthwork Foundation and has a history of engagement in youth and community work, where his contribution has been both in developing theoretical understanding of issues and in practical intervention.

Stan Kidd has been Corporate Strategy Adviser for City of Bradford Metropolitan District Council since 2007. He previously held senior positions as head of service improvement and interim director of corporate performance. He holds an honours degree in politics from the University of York and a public administration master's from the University of Warwick Business School. He began his career working with adults with learning disabilities, and worked for many years in local education authorities as a policy and strategic planning specialist. His research interests include governance, public management theory and public service reform.

Tony Reeves was Chief Executive of City of Bradford Metropolitan District Council between 2006 and October 2014. Prior to this he held a number of senior positions in northern local authorities in the fields of housing and urban regeneration. While in Bradford he worked closely with political leaders, public sector and business partners on addressing the district's long-term economic and social challenges and was pivotal in the development of the £24m City Park, Westfield's new Bradford Broadway scheme, the pioneering city centre growth fund, and the innovative Get Bradford Working programme. While chief executive, he was asked by Business in the Community to become HRH Prince of Wales's Ambassador for Yorkshire and Humber. He also led on housing, regeneration and planning within the Leeds City Region.

Emma Stone is Director of Policy and Research at the Joseph Rowntree Foundation and Joseph Rowntree Housing Trust. In previous roles at JRF, Emma managed programmes on social care, disability, immigration and inclusion. Outside JRF, Emma is a trustee of Y Care International and DORS (Development Organisation of Rural Sichuan). Emma's doctoral thesis was on disability and development in China.

Acknowledgements

This book is the outcome of an international seminar organised by the Centre for Applied Social Research at the University of Bradford. We are indebted to our colleagues who made this such a successful meeting, and to the participants who, under the Chatham House rule, spoke so directly and extensively about the issues addressed in this book. Thanks are also due to the many colleagues, in the United Kingdom and internationally, who have responded to drafts of this book with a strong affirmation of the concerns expressed here.

The team at Policy Press have been truly supportive and efficient in aiding this book's transit to publication: specifically we would like to acknowledge our indebtedness to Susannah Emery, Laura Greaves, Rebecca Megson, Laura Vickers, Emily Watt, Dave Worth and to their editing and proof reading staff, Dawn Rushen and Ruth Harrison, who have so efficiently scanned our text and helped to reduce the flaws in the book.

Introduction

Charles Husband

This book is an expression of concern. It arises from an experientially based anxiety about the use and abuse of social science research in informing policy in relation to issues of equity, respect and anti-discriminatory policy in multiethnic societies. The foundational basis for this concern does not rest in one institutional location or with one category of actors. Inevitably, at one level, it does address the motivations, institutional locations and actions of individuals, but the core issue to be addressed in this text is in essence the nature of the relationships between categories of actors within the contemporary dynamics of the multiethnic United Kingdom, and elsewhere. The focus of the argument and the majority of the concrete examples are based in the UK, but the scenario sketched here has a much wider relevance. The cumulative story that emerges from the chapters that follow is one of a significant dysfunctional tension between university-based social scientists, research funders and those who make use of the resultant policy-relevant research. More importantly it will be argued that the key elements of this critical dynamic are known to the actors involved, but that it has not been in their interest to explicitly name the malaise and address its sources and routine reproduction in their interdependent professional practice. There is a collusive denial of the inherent flaws in the current relationships, and of the damaging consequences of contemporary politics and ideologies on their shared endeavours to promote equity and civility within multiethnic societies.

Political context

Of course one key issue is the framing political environment within which this research and policy milieu operates. The assumption that in contemporary Britain there exists a consensual commitment to the promotion of an equitable and congenial civility across the multiethnic demography on this nation state is far from being substantiated in reality. At a very basic level, many people are resistant to acknowledging the veracity of the fact that the UK is already a de facto multiethnic society, with a demography that non-negotiably guarantees the sustained reproduction of ethnic difference among our citizenry (see Dorling and Thomas, 2004). The reality of ethnic diversity is paralleled by the growth of what Fekete (2009) has called 'xeno-racism'. In contemporary Britain there is a deep undertow of anxiety that has fed a neurotically defensive xenophobia that is expressed, for example, in the growth of support for UKIP (the UK Independence Party) and the expressive politics of anti-Europeanism. In Britain, and across Europe, we have seen a political collusiveness in constructing asylum-seekers as an out-group that all nation states may comfortably shun. The generic politics of dissuasion, identified by Weh in 1987, whereby states developed harsh regimes for treating would-be asylum-seekers in order to deter their arrival, has, by the second decade of the 21st century, achieved a robust viciousness that mocks the generosity of spirit that characterised the treatment of asylum-seekers in earlier decades. Immigration control has become a highly visible and recurrent core theme within party political rhetoric, as politicians seek to win popular electoral support: particularly as the next general election approaches. This has provided a discourse in which racist sentiments have been capable of unembarrassed public expression, coded in ways that have deflected the condemnation that they merited (on discursive deracialisation, see Reeves, 1983).

In addition, since 9/11 the eruption of Islamophobia in Britain has provided a further out-group against whom the majority population have felt enabled to express strong stereotypical and hostile views. Building on long established deeply embedded cultural beliefs and values (Halliday, 1996), the British population has digested news and drama presentations of Islam that have been highly stereotypical and negative (Poole, 2002; Poole and Richardson, 2005). The emotive politics of the 'War on Terror' and the long traumas of Iraq and Afghanistan have fed a wide felt hostility to Islam, and a permeation of public life by the insidious proliferation of the ideology and practices of *securitisation* (Noxolo and Huysmans, 2009). In the name of security, and under the amorphous threat of terrorism, a commitment to fundamental human rights principles has been eroded at the level of government and popular opinion (Wilson, 2005; Gearty, 2007). Enhanced interrogation techniques (torture) and extraordinary rendition (kidnap and removal from your country) have become negotiable concepts and practices. States across Europe have found the building of mosques to be highly controversial, and the wearing of the veil has been made a sign of non-Europeanness. The processes of dehumanising and depersonalising 'the other' have become too familiar and too easy (Tileaga, 2007).

Additionally, over recent decades in Britain, as elsewhere, there has been an erasure of racism from the political agenda of national government. Ironically, convinced of their progressive achievements in human and civil rights, through post-Second World War domestic policy, states have, through what Giroux (2010, p 2) has called a 'national commitment to historical amnesia', displaced a concern with the nature and grievous impacts of racism from their political consciousness. In a wider analysis, Goldberg (2009) has traced the intimate articulation of this process with the evolution of neoliberal politics, and elsewhere argues that: 'institutionally, it is not that race has been made "absent" but that its presence has been rendered invisible and silenced (save to the sensitive eye and ear), purged of explicit terms of reference' (Goldberg, 2010, p 91; see also Lentin and Titley, 2011, Chapter 1; and Phillips, 2007). It is worth noting that under Blairism in Britain, New Labour continued the Thatcherite erasure of class from its prior salience within social analysis, replacing a concern with equality with the more malleable discourse of opportunity. (A transition all too powerfully echoed in the compliant forgetfulness of mainstream sociology, regarding their longstanding prioritisation of class as a key object of their work.)

Intermeshed with these processes Britain and Europe have, in the last decade, seen a remarkable retreat from a commitment to *multiculturalism* as an idea and working project, that aimed at developing systemic anti-discrimination laws, administrative processes and normative ways of fashioning equitable multiethnic coexistence (Back et al, 2002; McGhee, 2008). In recent years Angela Merkel and David Cameron, as heads of European states, have confidently asserted the failure of multiculturalism, as across Europe states have moved to a neonationalist assimilationism that marks a very significant retreat from the varieties of state pluralism developed between the 1970s and 1990s in countries such as Britain, the Netherlands and Denmark. A key element in this process has been the assertive expression of counter-narratives to multiculturalism (Hewitt, 2005; Husband, 2010) being routinely visible in national media. Cultural commentators and populist politicians have emotively rehearsed the assaults on the integrity and rights of the majority, that are the claimed result of a leftist fixation with defending the interests of minorities. Crying *political madness gone mad* has been a sufficient assertion to trump any attempt at rational debate around the racialised politics of urban life. And at the same time, following the cataclysmic events of 9/11 and the rioting in northern cities in Britain in 2001, the twin political agendas of social cohesion and security have substantially buried any sustained academic and political concern with current manifestations of racism (Husband and Alam, 2011).

The emergence of *homegrown bombers* in 2005 further amplified these trends, and the Muslim communities in Britain became the anvil on which opposition to multiculturalism was beaten out. The interwoven binary discourses of the *self-segregation of Muslim communities* and their perceived commitment to living in *parallel cultures* provided the creative weft and warp of a policy fixation with countering radicalisation, and the assimilation of minorities into the mainstream of an elusive *British way of life*. As Andrew Jacobowicz and Yunis Alam show (in Chapters Two and Three), in different ways, the research community is highly vulnerable to the impact of such political shifts.

These major framing political shifts in addressing the reality of ethnic diversity in Britain have themselves been underpinned by major structural changes in the social and economic formation of Britain. Britain, like other European countries, found itself from the late 1960s onwards to be increasingly vulnerable to the emerging transformation of the relation between capital and labour that we came to call 'globalisation'; the postwar policy of bringing labour to capital that shaped the immigration policies of this country became increasingly replaced by the transfer of capital to labour. Major industries in Britain could not compete against the cheaper labour costs in other countries, and by the 1970s, major employers, such as the textile industry, began to feel the harsh impact of international competition. With the radical neoliberalism of Thatcherism, this process of change rapidly accelerated, and the profile of the British labour market changed fundamentally. Major heavy industries such as coal mining, steel making and ship building became decimated, and the lifestyles and working-class cultures that had been their social accompaniment became detached from workplace values and routines that had given them legitimacy. (Sennett, 1998, has written eloquently about the social and cultural costs of such transformations.) Nor has it been only the working class that have felt decentred by fundamental disruptions to their life world. The middle class, too, have found that the quiet certainties of their commitment to home and career have been disrupted by the frailty of their pensions and jobs in the harsh world of financial leverage, economic collapse and international competition. There has been an unfortunate intersection of decades of neoliberal philosophy that has promoted individualism, with a period of economic and political turmoil that has made insecurity normative.

Seeking to sustain a life framed by consumption in the context of a *risk society* (Beck, 1992) provides the foundational conditions for the generation of those systemic anxieties that are the bedrock for the construction of feelings of realistic and symbolic threat (Stephan and Stephan, 1996: Stephan et al, 1999), the sense that 'others' are threatening the integrity of our wellbeing and of our culture. The structural and ideological conditions that have the potential for promoting the social psychology of intergroup competition and hostility have regrettably been scripted into the fabric of multiethnic British life (Dixon and Levine, 2012). As we have seen above, there are also those political forces at play that would intentionally, or unintentionally through their unscrupulous populism, give legitimacy and vitality to such sentiments. As Reicher (2012) has argued, we must look not only to identify the forms of racism, exclusion and oppression, but also for the means of their mobilisation. In the *opportunity society of* New Labour, and the contemporary consensual party political commitment to the 'stressed middle classes', the widening gap between the rich and the poor has been connived at by all the political parties. Using a cynical rhetoric that opposes the *strivers* against the *skivers*, the government has sought to bury the realities of structural inequality beneath a discourse that presents the moral inadequacy of an underclass as the reason for the failure of the poor and marginalised to thrive (see Levitas, 2005). The long trajectory of neoliberal ideology from Thatcher through New Labour (Back et al, 2002), to the current strident certitudes of Osborne and Cameron, has promoted the deconstruction of the supportive state, and the promotion of the profit motive as the sufficient engine for societal cohesion. In a collective exercise of magical thinking, government ministers incant such potent shibboleths of the neoliberal faith as *further efficiencies, resilience, and social cohesion*, while they oversee the construction of levels of inequality and acts of social philistinism not seen since the Victorian era. The real economic crisis that neoliberal, heavily deregulated economics created has provided a *politics of austerity* which, without irony, politicians and financiers invoke to explain why the continuation of the principle elements of their creed and practices must be continued. In this context, universities have become business enterprises within which the notion of knowledge as a public good has become an arcane and obsolescent belief sustained outside of the cadre of managers who implement the new realities of the commercialisation of knowledge (I discuss this in greater depth in Chapter One).

Neoliberal context

A key element of the argument here is that, while we may understand the production of academic research, and its relation to policy and practice through the lens of departmental and disciplinary networks, it is also apparent that we must simultaneously see the fit between these communicative and organisational networks and the dominant ideologies that frame and permeate this process. In this regard it is necessary in the current context to acknowledge the ubiquitous presence of neoliberalism and its many manifestations.

Neoliberalism has, over the last decades, emerged as the dominant ideology framing the practice, policy and understanding of the democratic process. As Tyfield (2012, p 155) has argued:

> Like classic liberalism, neoliberalism confers pre-eminent importance upon the market, but without taking markets as naturally emergent, rather they must be deliberately constructed (Lemke, 2011; Mirowski and Plehwe, 2009). Neoliberalism is thus not against the state but it is a political project that must itself be constructed through a state, which increasingly subjects itself to market discipline. Moreover markets are primarily valued as the optimal epistemic, not just allocative, mechanism, for both natural (technoscientific) and social (political) judgement.

In this regard, Estabrooks et al's (2008, p 1067) comment that the changing value of knowledge is 'increasingly regarded more as intellectual property and less as public good' is symptomatic of the permeation of neoliberalism into academic life.

Critically engaging with the internal dynamics of knowledge production and its external legitimation requires a willingness to stand outside of the immediate concerns of academe and interrogate the wider context within which the discussion of knowledge production, research and relevance takes place. Tyfield (2012) provides a robust critique of current models of science and technology policy studies, and suggests that we must first of all be able to understand the pervasive presence of neoliberalism as a determining politics and practice. We must then be able to reveal the mechanisms of its influence on both research and on the way in which we seek to understand the research–policy relevance dynamic. In essence he is warning us of using analytic tools that have inscribed into them key elements of neoliberal epistemology. He advocates the development of a *cultural political economy perspective*, which would, following Foucault (2008), necessarily employ a relational and dispersed conception of power. Thus this approach would not 'take as given contemporary understandings of politics, democracy, science, etc ... and their inter-relations' (Tyfield, 2012, p 163). It is in the dangerousness of assuming that analytic categories such as democratic accountability, or social relevance, have some self-evident meaning that the current logics of managerialism within universities, in advancing the *knowledge-based society*, have their power. Thus, for example, Jessop's (2010) intervention in proposing a cultural political economy provides at least one helpful vantage point for revealing the semiotic and institutional formation of current disciplinary and research fields. He specifically requires that there is a relational analysis of the 'role of discursively-selective "imaginaries"' and structurally selective institutions in the making of economic (for which read any domain of knowledge) practices, and *a fortiori*, economic policies (Jessop, 2010, p 344). Thus we should note that the economic crises created by neoliberalism have predominantly been addressed politically by discourses of neoliberalism immune to critique, and even by the celebration of crisis as opportunity (see, for example, Klein, 2007). And more widely, the crisis of deliberative democracy (Goodin, 2008) over the last decades has seen a 'deliberative turn' in theories of democracy which has proved entirely fruitful ground for a marketisation of the electorate as 'consumers' of research (see Dobson, 2014, for an insightful critique of contemporary conceptions of deliberative democracy).

Let me repeat the statement from Tyfield above: *Neoliberalism is thus not against the state but it is a political project that must itself be constructed through a state.* Neoliberalism is not some arcane economic theory; it is a philosophy of the relation of self and society that positions the market and consumption as the foundational basis for viable social relations. At the core of this vision is the commitment to the rolling back of the state, and its attendant acquired collective forms of democratic accountability and policy provision, with the expectation that this will be replaced by the logics of the marketplace and radical individualism. Hence, for example, collective mobilisation by labour, or by marginalised minority communities, necessarily represent a challenge to this status quo. Thus the very conception of democratic participation, and its modes of expression, are subject to the pervasive impact of neoliberal theory and politics. As Lentin and Titley (2011, p 168) have pointed out:

> … the state is not rendered redundant under neoliberalism.… Instead, it is engaged in "an intensification of some of its core features", in particular in intrusive and repressive functions of surveillance and control.

Presenting itself as a self-evidently reasonable commitment to economic expansion, and the removal of those archaic accretions of collective mobilisation that render social life 'so uncomfortable, inefficient and contested', neoliberalism has sort to present itself as almost above the factionalism of 'politics' in its promotion of benign democratic government (see, for example, Duggan, 2003). The radical individualism of this democratic order then, of course, finds great difficulties with those who persist in asserting their *collective* experience of marginality, whether they be, for example, minority ethnic communities, the poor or the poorly educated. Thus, for example, Lentin and Titley (2011, p 168), in their detailed analysis of the multiple intersection of neoliberalism with the formation of racialised modes of oppression and marginalisation, argue:

> In the individualizing logic of neoliberalism, history, politics and the state are increasingly written out of any analysis of disadvantage generally, and racialized disadvantage particularly. The focus on capital as a social corrector, rather than as a participant in the perpetuation of discrimination, inequality and poverty, is based on a denial of the reciprocal relationship between the state and liberal capital.

It is one of the perverse dynamics of neoliberal economic and social policy that the promotion of the market as the key dynamic of managing society results in successive social crises that require a strong state to provide the necessary remedial interventions. The multiple social upheavals of Thatcherism's experiment in neoliberalism created such civic unrest that draconian legislation and heavy state intervention through brutal policing became one of the leitmotifs of her regime (see Hillyard and Percy-Smith, 1988; Ewing and Gearty, 1990). State intervention, in shoring up the current Europe-wide financial crisis, would be another exemplary instance of this recurrent contradiction.

Thus in the argument to be developed throughout the chapters in this book, neoliberalism should not be seen as a discrete economic theory, with limited application in the economy, but must rather be seen as a dominant ideology with very far-reaching penetration into the explanatory discourses and practices of quite different areas of social life in the present era.

This concern with the role of hegemonic discourses within research communities, and their potential role in facilitating the formation and operation of *policy networks*, is entirely consistent with recent interest in the role of policy narratives in the policy process. As Shanahan et al (2011, p 536) have argued in developing their 'narrative policy framework', 'the socially constructed elements of public policy – those elements to which relevant actors ascribe meaning – are best captured through an empirical investigation of the stories coalitions strategically deploy. Stakeholders use words, images, and symbols to strategically craft policy narratives to resonate with the public, relevant stakeholders, and governmental decision makers, with the aim of producing a winning coalition.' And echoing Jessop's concern with the intersection of discourse and structures, so, too, in seeking to understand the dynamics in play between the researcher, funder and policymaker we should keep in mind Smith and Joyce's (2012, p 57) warning of the complexity of such institutional interfaces, and their evidence indicating 'the multiplicity of divisions informing knowledge translation' within such policy fora.

Practical realities of research input into policy

As the chapters that follow show, the operation of a creative synergy between university research, research funders, the third sector and government cannot be isolated from the social realities and politics sketched above. Changes in government commitments to anti-racism and to the management of ethnic diversity can have immediate and direct impacts on funding regimes for related research programmes through direct changes in government funding. But the shifts in the ways in which the government sets agendas and frames its conception of the policy issues clearly also informs the discourse and priorities of independent research funders who wish to remain visibly relevant to government policy and practice. This is by no means a non-negotiable fixed equation. But the interface between government and research funders is multilayered, and the shifting focus of government onto differing problem definitions may also involve the pragmatic political incorporation of new dominant theory and conceptions from academe to provide the authoritative discourse for the new policy regime. Thus in recent decades we saw the critical *power* and relevance of *institutional racism* wax and wane, and more recently we have seen the infusion of political relevance into the concept of *social capital*. Such shifts in the definition of *in vogue* terms are often difficult for research funders, and social scientists, to resist. As funds follow the new political framing of the world, so, too, researchers follow the funds. Tracking the recent growth of individual academic specialists and research groups in terrorism and radicalisation would, for example, provide one timely case study. Or, following Cantle's (2008) significant role in the government's commitment to *social cohesion* as the key conceptual basis for a whole tranche of initiatives following the riots of 2001, it would be illuminating to track the flow of funds into the former Institute of

Community Cohesion (iCoCo) which he founded in 2005, and which, in the words from his own website, *became the UK's leading authority on community cohesion and intercultural relations* (see www.tedcantle.co.uk). This work is now carried on by the iCoCo Foundation that promotes interculturalism and community cohesion.

This not to say that there was anything improper in either of these developments. On the contrary, it is the normality of these events that deserves our attention. However, such systematic studies into the flow of power and influence, from the definition of a policy agenda to the emergence of an accepted field of expertise, to the flow of research funds and the take-up of consultancies and the inception of new policy initiatives, would be a rare excursion into the study of the powerful rather than the marginalised. Such studies might reveal something of the complexity of policy networks, and the mechanisms of inclusion and exclusion of particular voices and epistemic positions, within specific policy fora (see, for example, Smith and Joyce, 2012).

The notion of a *race relations industry* is hardly new. We saw in the 1970s in the US, and in Britain, the proliferation of consultants offering their expertise in 'race awareness training' as local authorities, corporate enterprises and government sought to address their response to the growing challenge of civil rights and anti-discriminatory policies. The fact that this movement was predominantly theorised in relation to a body of theory that saw the problem as being essentially located in the troubled individual psyche did much to make it acceptable to large institutional bodies. It was preferable to an approach focused on institutional racism. Such markets in expertise provide a financial nexus between 'race relations' scholarship and research, the development of a consensus on problem definition and the emergence of funded research projects and practical policy interventions. The definition of expert in this scenario is often loosely determined, and not infrequently achieved, by self-election. In the heady flux of *timely intervention*, a planned, and meaningful, evaluation of the research/practical innovation is not necessarily a priority. See Turnpenny, et al, 2009, for a review of some of the forces at play in current policy appraisal.

The spiral of interlocked activity that emerges around the research–policy dynamic provides a critical mass of people and institutions, who, through their loosely concerted actions, provide short-term validation for both the framing theory and their individual practical engagement with *the issue*. It is noticeable that in these cycles of conjoined activity the individual actors enter into the research–policy nexus from very distinct institutional positions, with all the myopias and vested interests that that brings with it. This does not mean that all like some latter day Jeremiah should cry out, *There is no goodness in us!* But it does mean that we should assume that none enter into this arena in a state of innocence. This is particularly important to bear in mind when we note, as we must, that the one set of actors who are typically only marginally engaged in this process are the large swathes of people who are the claimed beneficiaries of this activity.

Epistemic communities and the creation of 'knowledge'

In responding to this brief descriptive account of some features of the contemporary 'race relations industry' we must recognise that we are not entirely without helpful conceptual tools. In particular, we know a good deal about the ways in which social networks of colleagues may operate in ways that are likely to create unintended limits on their creative processes and on their engagement with potential users of their research.

While we cannot adequately develop this issue here, we should note the existence of the considerable literature on epistemic communities, and the social networks, that shape both the production and dissemination of knowledge. The notion of *epistemic communities* points to the existence of a network of knowledge-based experts, typically professionals with all the legitimacy and normative culture that that may entail, who lay claim to competence within a specific area, and who profess a willingness and ability to apply this to policy issues. Epistemic communities may be constituted by a group of colleagues operating within a quite specific research group within a university. And it is not hard to think of such relatively stable research clusters that have a shared theoretical and methodological agenda, which they pursue *as theory*, and which they seek to legitimate by exporting its relevance to applied contexts. But even such concrete groups are likely to be a hub of an international communicative network, where distant colleagues actively engage in their shared endeavour.

As Knorr-Cetina (1999) pointed out, a key element within such epistemic communities is their *tacit* knowledge of their shared knowledge of professional routines, context and culture. Thus a key aspect of such epistemic communities is a common normative understanding of the distinctiveness of their knowledge, the appropriateness of their means of acquiring and disseminating this knowledge, and a taken for granted acceptance of the routines of recruitment and incorporation of others into their network. As Gore (2011, p 100) notes in his discussion of 'Epistemic communities in universities', the codified knowledge shared within epistemic communities can easily be communicated at a distance, but 'the tacit knowledge' is not so easily accessed.

This points to the concerns of the literature on *communities of practice*, which again seeks to underline the social dynamics of induction into a shared sphere of arcane practice, whether it be a sub-division of social science, competence in operating within a funding organisation, or developing policy within a non-governmental organisation (NGO) or government department (see, for example, Lave and Wenger, 1991; Wenger, 2007). In such contexts of institutional structures and interpersonal dynamics we become disciplined into a willing acceptance of not just a shared discursive practice that defines our arcane specialism, but also a practical consciousness of embodied practice that normalises our affective and behavioural repertoire. Thus part of the acculturated competence to operate within an epistemic community is an ability to negotiate our tacit knowledge with *insiders*, where, to echo Polyani (1983, p 4), 'we can know more than we can tell.' This, of course, constitutes the basis for a problematic interchange of knowledge and intent between members of different communities of practice.

Hence, a key element in the critique of the current status quo presented in this chapter, and this book, is the powerful construction of communities of practice, with a shared epistemic culture, who are, through *their practice*, reproducing distinct social networks and shared cultures of knowledge, and who consequently together generate knowledge and policy that is partial and reflective of particular interests.

Nor would it be accurate, or helpful, to see this process as located within specific research departments, particular funding bodies or specific government departments, as such epistemic communities are typically international in their routine networked communicative flows, and systemic professional organisational legitimation. They share international conferences, have common journals and professional organisational structures that even within national locations have shared international epistemic norms. At its worst the centripetal feedback loops of such epistemic communities, and their concrete institutionally based networks, can produce the sort of professional myopia that Matthew Flinders (2013, p 624), in writing of political sciences, referred to as 'methodological masturbation, theoretical fetishism, sub-disciplinary balkanisation and the development of esoteric discourses', that did little to demonstrate the relevance of the study of politics. Echoing Bellotti (2011), Flinders also points to the power of concrete networks within epistemic communities that provided a potent regulatory force in establishing and maintaining hierarchies of prestige and resource within the community.

In extending the relevance of this conceptual repertoire to our analysis here, we might usefully introduce the concept of Mode 1 and Mode 2 knowledge. Like all typologies, this distinction has the propensity to be transformed into a rigid opposition of distinct forms of knowledge production, which would be alien to the intentions of its founding authors (see Gibbons et al, 1994; Nowotny et al, 2001). In a revisiting of their argument, Nowotny et al (2003) have sought to make very clear that these modes of knowledge production are to be seen as interactive, and highly dependent on the wider social context in which these modes of activity are contextualised. But to lay out their initial position, we can do no better than cite this latter source. Nowotny et al argued that:

> (Mode 1) – characterised by the hegemony of theoretical or, at any rate, experimental science; by an internally-driven taxonomy of disciplines; and by the autonomy of scientists and their host institutions, the universities – was being superseded by a new paradigm of knowledge production (Mode 2), which was socially distributed, application-oriented, transdisciplinary, and subject to multiple accountabilities. (Nowotny et al, 2003, p 179)

Recognising something of the fluid and ambiguous nature of their initial introduction of this distinction, Nowotny et al (2003) have continued to try to refine both their definition of the core concept, and the ways in which they believe it could be appropriately employed, but for our purposes here, it may be useful to at least note some of the defining features of Mode 2 knowledge.

It is seen as being 'generated within a context of application'. This refers not just to the departmental locus of research mentioned above, but also more radically to the wider institutional and political context within which all research may be taking place. In other words, this differs from a linear trajectory that follows a route of 'research', 'knowledge transfer' and 'management', but rather points to a context in which the relevance of these processes are present *ab initio*.

This flux is echoed in the further assumption that Mode 2 research is 'transdisciplinary', not merely interdisciplinary. Again, this points to a further definitional feature of Mode 2 knowledge, which relates to 'the greater diversity of sites at which knowledge is produced'. The breakdown of professional barriers and the new capacity of social media informational systems are seen as facilitating a new set of social relations within research that breaks, or at least loosens, the hierarchical powers of disciplines, and expert versus applied knowledge. The concept of Mode 2 knowledge is thus both a typology of a different possibility of relationships between research and application, and *a description* of processes that are seen as being already initiated by changes beyond the world of academe. Nowotny et al (2003) note three such macro shifts:

- The 'steering of research priorities', where, for example, European Framework programmes at the international level and Foresight exercises by governments at the national level have focused research funds, and in the world of research funders, 'Much greater emphasis is now placed on thematic programmes' (Nowotny et al, 2003, p 182).
- The 'commercialisation of research' is seen as having had a major impact on knowledge production, and will be central to the argument presented in my chapter that follows. As Nowotny et al argue, 'With the emergence of a Knowledge Society, knowledge "products", many which are derived from university research, are increasingly valued, not in terms of their long-term potential, but in term of immediate market return' (Nowotny et al, 2003, p 182).
- Nowotny et al see the third shift in the wider environment for research as being 'the growing emphasis placed upon the management of research – and in particular, upon efforts to evaluate its effectiveness and assess its quality.' This, again, is not independent of the neoliberal concern with erasing independent sources of authority outside of the market, and of the reduction of 'value' to quantifiable marketised terms.

It is clear that the phenomenon of Mode 2 knowledge is not an expression of a spontaneous creative urge within the producers and consumers of Mode 1 knowledge, but is better seen as an emergent paradigm shift in the way in which research, and its relevance, is construed in contemporary society. It is the expression in academic and scientific life of detrimental changes in the trust invested in academics and scholars, and in the criterion by which their worth is assessed. Thus, not surprisingly, a fourth characteristic of Mode 2 knowledge is the introduction of 'novel forms of quality control'. The emergence of multiple performance indicators applied to academic knowledge producers is a reflection of the newly vibrant wider constituency of those who believe themselves to be both qualified and have a legitimate interest in assessing the output of researchers. One aspect of this is revealed in Turnpenny et al's (2009) review of the extensive nature of appraisal in relation to social policy, and of the multiple agendas being played out within it.

This leads me to the fifth of Nowotny et al's characteristics of Mode 2 knowledge, which I quote extensively here because of its immediate relevance to the arguments that follow in this book. It is identified as being *highly reflexive*:

> The research process can no longer be characterised as an "objective" investigation of the natural (or social world), as a cool and reductionist interrogation of arbitrarily defined "others". Instead it has become a dialogic process, an intense (and perhaps endless) "conversation" between research actors and research subjects – to such an extent that the basic vocabulary of research (who, whom, what, how) is in danger of losing its significance. As a result, traditional notions of "accountability" have had to be radically revised. The consequences (predictable and unintended) of new knowledge cannot be regarded as being "outside" the research process because problem-solving environments influence topic-choice and research-design as well as end-users. (Nowotny et al, 2003, p 187)

As an expression of the changed environment of accountability and of the recently emergent research infrastructures, the above statement is recognisably descriptive, in general terms, of shifts in the zeitgeist framing contemporary research. But it is gloriously over-stated. Within the social sciences one expression of the 'commitment to accountability' and 'reflexivity' has been the ubiquitous emergence of ethics committees that scrutinise all research proposals prior to submission and implementation. But this is, to a large extent, a classic instance of the new managerialism being passed off as accountability. The 'endless conversation' between researcher and research subject carried out by the members of such ethics committees is routinely drowned by the silence of the excluded voices. Academic colleagues, institutionally invested with ascribed ethical and empathetic competence, rehearse a symbolic ritual of 'acting for the other' as they exercise agency on behalf of those research subjects whose life experience, ontology and priorities they vicariously represent. The threat of legal recourse, rather than a fear of neocolonial hubris, is not infrequently the spectre in the room.

In a different context of potential 'reflexivity', on the occasions that I have been invited to join 'scoping' meetings about potential new research initiatives, it is other 'experts', including 'professionally accredited' members of the target ethnic communities, who speak for the absent targeted subjects. As Estabrooks et al (2008, p 1066) have argued, 'Major funding agencies are now urging researchers to integrate activities with policy- and decision-makers into their research projects in a newly emerging model of engaged knowledge translation.' There seems an awful likelihood that this is a process of widening the shared participative capacity of the major researcher–funder–policy actors, without in any way changing the marginalisation of those who may be the subjects and supposed beneficiaries of the research. I believe that class continues to be a major defining criterion of who you will meet in any such exercise in reflexivity and accountability. If you then wish to add to that the intersectional possibilities of ethnicity, faith, gender and age, then the optimistic assurance inherent in Nowotny et al's argument above seems more of a parody of the routine reality.

The concept of Mode 1 and Mode 2 knowledge can be seen as a meta-discourse that will allow us to track the flows of attempted influence over the current and future direction of the research policy interface. It is, at one level, a fruitful diagnostic tool that will open up for consideration our understanding of current research activity. At another level, it is an underdeveloped invitation to explore the hegemonic struggle over knowledge, and the flow of power associated with it, that is symptomatic of the neoliberal project. If we could assume that its key terms were stable, both in definition and usage, then it would provide a useful tool for interrogating in some detail the dynamics descriptively presented in the chapters that follow, as, for example, in the work of Estabrooks et al (2008, p 1075). In their study of the location of Mode 1 and Mode 2 knowledge production in healthcare studies they found that, 'the combination of discipline, faculty, and work setting combine to create the profile of Modes 1 and 2 knowledge production characteristic of a given group.' This suggests the possibility that personal disposition and personal politics may result in individuals actively seeking to place themselves in specific workplace environments, where their sense of commitment to healthcare practice may be perceived as having a more concrete expression. Equally, within the social sciences there may be those who find the more closed communicative environment of 'pure research' provides them with a greater sense of autonomy and agency among valued immediate peers than would be afforded by the 'dispersed' dynamics of Mode 2 knowledge production.

However, within the social sciences, it would be a grave error to assume that a clear boundary between Mode 1 and Mode 2 production can be easily maintained. The biographies of many social scientists who are regarded as major 'theorists' in their field would reveal that they were far removed from any closed circle of 'ivory tower' scholarship. Many have been, or are, actively engaged and deeply immersed in the social issues of their time, with social networks extending far beyond 'the shady groves of academe.' At the same time, those you would feel fully at home in a Mode 2 environment would be outraged to be characterised as being detached from theory development and application. Certainly, within sociology (widely defined), there is a demonstrable flow of theory into applied practice, as individuals committed to producing policy-relevant research very actively employ current theory. Indeed, it could be argued that this is a ritual of professional accreditation as researchers, ever sensitive to new vogues in theory, deploy these theoretical neologisms as a strategic ritual of epistemic belonging. However, individual and collective occupational locations along a Mode 1 to Mode 2 spectrum are not hard to find in most professions.

In the case materials and arguments presented in the chapters that follow, readers may find the conceptual language of Mode 1 and Mode 2 knowledge production a heuristic tool in developing their own understanding of the dynamics shaping the relation of research activity to policy development in contemporary ethnic relations. There has certainly been, as Nowotny et al have traced, a very significant shift in the political and institutional framing of research in this area. Mode 2 is at least inscribed into the dominant language of social research, even though its expression in the concrete relations of production may remain much more questionable. What remains to be actively revealed are the ways in which the political erasure of racisms, the commensurate counter-narratives to multiculturalism, and the logics of neoliberalism have become embedded in the particular discourses of research problem definition, thematic funding agendas and the highly selective interpretation of research analyses into operational social policy. It is the tacit knowledge of epistemic communities, and the framing ideologies that contextualise our specific endeavours, that are forged into banal routines in the institutional structures within which we work. It is in such contexts that we need to enquire not only into what it is that we do, but also just as importantly, what it is that we routinely fail to do. Often the meritorious professional discursive narratives that we have established as the legitimating carapace for our activities are heavily redolent of the wider ideologies and dominant social imaginaries of our time.

While the cognitive simplicity of construing policymaking as passing through a number of sequential stages may be comforting, the multilevel nature of policymaking, with the differently configured opportunities for different interests to make a significant input varying from locale to locale in this matrix, makes the imagined arena of policymaking a much more complex business (Asare et al, 2009). There is no shortage of theories of policy formulation and change, as a recent overview by Smith and Katikereddi (2013) succinctly demonstrates. Given the focus on specific institutional contexts, and their relation to research and policy formulation in the chapters that follow, it is perhaps appropriate to signal the potential insights offered by *historical institutionalism* (see, for example, Béland, 2005; Schmidt, 2010) and its emphasis on understanding the historical and institutional context in which decisions are made. This may be particularly potent in tracking the insidious routes of resistance to change, that is, policy inertia, but it also provides a critical lens through which to examine the key foci of power within institutions, and, in keeping with Jessop's (2010) suggestion, tracing the related flow of *selective discursive strategies* and their sites of legitimation. Additionally, the discussion about epistemic networks, offered above, would resonate with this approach, and would, within a narrower analytic frame, be consistent with some of the plethora of ideas offered within the *policy network literature* (Börzel, 1998). It is hoped that in reading the material presented in this volume readers will bring their experience, and their own analytic repertoire, to bear in evaluating and extending the arguments offered to them in these chapters.

Outline of the book

The authors of the chapters that follow have been selected because of their experience and expertise in relation to one element of the research–funder–policy equation. They present insights derived from their own professional experience of working on matters related to ethnic relations. They are not representative of all 'researchers', 'funders' or 'policy practitioners'. On the contrary, they have been invited to speak with a personal voice that reflects the concrete realities of their experience, and they do not have collective responsibility for the whole text. They have addressed the task of writing their chapter very much from within their own experience and perspective.

I write as a university-based researcher with a long involvement in seeking to apply social scientific theory and research to the development of anti-discriminatory practice within multiethnic societies. In the following chapter I seek to build on the opening account offered above, and offer a very personal account of what I see as critical flaws in the current research–funding–policymaking nexus. The argument is very much influenced by my own experiences, but I took heart in coming to write it from the frequent anguished recognition that my analysis attracted from colleagues around the world, when I spoke of my intention to pursue this theme here.

Andrew Jakubowicz, Yunis Alam and Muhammad G. Khan write as committed academics with quite different personal locations within academic research. Jakubowicz and Alam both note the impact of changing national conceptions of ethnic relations on the nature and relevance of research to policy. Jakubowicz notes the ways in which changing fundamental assumptions underlying what multiculturalism might mean become directly mapped onto the control of research communities. His account demonstrates how discursive and political shifts within different domains of policy may have degrees of independence from each other, in their origin and key modes of institutional expression, and yet cohere in having a cumulative impact. Thus, for example, the assault on social sciences and the preferential regard for 'the hard sciences and medicine' most certainly would have been played out with a range of actors, many of whom would have seen themselves as having little concern with multicultural policies. Yet, within a hardening right-wing neoliberal agenda, these moments of change played off each other very effectively. As he shows powerfully, in the Australian context, there have been sustained 'ideological and partisan arguments over the type, value and use of social science knowledge.' Australian social sciences have had no absence of the *public sociologists* now called for, and they have been routinely visible within the Australian politics of diversity. (Jakubowicz himself would stand as an outstanding exemplar of the species.) The mix of 'dangerous' social sciences and the access of vociferous public intellectuals to a highly politicised public sphere, where diversity has been a highly salient issue within Australian politics, has been a constituent element in what Jakubowicz describes as 'a volatile fluctuation in the closeness and impact of research, and the trust or mistrust by government of the academy.' His account of the facilitation and destruction of communities of knowledge around ethnic relations policy in Australia is a troubling insight into the fragile autonomy of Mode 2 networks committed to developing progressive equalitarian policies.

Alam roots his account of the challenges faced by an engaged researcher within a broad account of the development of race theory, and the mechanisms of racialising human relations. Such a concern with the potency of historicity in our understanding of the present is key to any attempt to understand the power of *social imaginaries* (Taylor, 2004), those deep cultural eddies of belief and feeling that infuse the enduring core of collective identities, and which become so potently energised by the nationalist discursive construction of 'self' and 'other'. It is such continuities of culturally embedded discursive and practical consciousness that have been so central to attempts to reveal the reproduction of 'whiteness' and of Orientalist and imperialist sensibilities into contemporary life. (This itself raises questions about who has the competence to execute such a reflexive task; see, for example, Young, 1990, for an early and telling critique of the 'history of history'.)

The issue of biography, identity and the negotiation of insider/outsider relationships with research subjects leads Alam to raise the problematic status of 'objectivity' in the social sciences, and while not routinely claiming such awesome powers, it is the case that most social scientists would wish to claim that in their choice of research method they at least provide an epistemic model that frames their work, and allows for an explicit shared discourse for contesting and evaluating the interpretation of their data. One of the key functions of the epistemic communities discussed above is to provide a stable working environment within which such consensual assumptions permit the suspension of crippling reflexive critique. Yet, in the area of 'race and ethnic studies', it is exactly this sort of sustained reflexivity that is required.

From early works, such as Ladner's (1973) *The death of white sociology*, there has been a continuous flow of critical analyses of the role of the individual researcher, and of the almost inherently compromised political ambivalence of research into race and ethnic relations. The recent (2013) special issue of *Ethnic and Racial Studies'* critical review of research on 'the relationship between race, politics and anti-racism' places this concern within current debates about public sociology (Burowoy, 2005), and echoes many of the concerns of Alexander's (2006) earlier special issue of the same journal, which specifically interrogated the challenge of employing an ethnographic methodology within this area of research and policy. While that issue specifically addressed ethnography as a specific methodological approach, the issues that it raised have a wide generic relevance to any consideration of the problematic of researching ethnicity and racisms. Alam, in exploring the challenges of being an 'insider' carrying out research within a community with whom he may identify himself, or where he may have membership attributed to him, places his account within this wider understanding of the politics of research in this area.

A point that is worth making explicit here is that in the area of concern of the contributors to this book, ignorance of the multiple epistemological and existential challenges of working in this area was not an available option. The politics of identity that so transformed collective political struggles throughout the 1960s and the following four decades through feminism, Black Power, post-colonialism, indigenous politics and the paradigmatic discursive shifts that came under the rubric of postmodernism, all contributed to a critical discourse within social sciences that at times was, and is, personal and abrasive.

This writer, as a white, male, now older, and now bourgeois *professor*, has had a permanent awareness that his 'political engagement' with critical research in this area has always carried profound contradictions. As someone whose career could be said to have been floated on the insidious concrete vitality of racisms and modes of exclusion, there is no comfortable evasion of the disparities of life story trajectory of myself and many of those who have been the focus, politically and substantively, of my research. As someone, who, over the past five years or more has been working with Sami colleagues in Sápmi, the critiques of the non-indigenous researcher (see, for example, Porsanger and Guttorm, 2011; Smith, 2012) persistently must be allowed to destabilise any sense of certainty about my role.

The question of 'positionality' in entering into an active role within the domain of research, research funding and policymaking is a non-negotiable ever-present itch that is well capable of becoming a debilitating sore. The accounts presented in this book provide some insight into how differing personal locations within specific institutional contexts frame this experience.

Given the extensive nature of the critical literature and the, at times, highly vociferous politicised discourses and movements, which have sought to challenge manifestations of gendered, racialised, class or other hegemonic modes of oppression permeated throughout academic research and policy formulation, it seems necessary to ask how it is that Muhammad Khan, in his chapter, should still be impelled to speak with such righteous anger about the routine abuses of identity and agency that he has experienced. As an academic at Ruskin College, Oxford, Khan's chapter derives from his long experience of being a youth worker who has actively sought to counter the marginalisation of Muslim youth in the British context, and who, more recently (Khan, 2013), has sought to provide an explicitly Muslim agenda for youth work. Echoing Alam's concern with the problematic dynamics of 'insider' status, he specifically addresses the emotional and existential violence of being used as a facilitator for others' access to Muslim research subjects. Khan, drawing on his experience of youth work and university research, provides a powerful statement of the use and abuse of the research subject, and of those intermediaries drawn into credentialising researchers who would document the experience of British Muslims.

The style of his writing will, for some readers, be too emotive and trenchant, and yet we must ask whether such a response is itself a reflection of the success of post-racial discourses of an equal opportunity society, within which anger at sustained assaults on identity and autonomy is viewed as inappropriately 'radical' and a denial of the achievements of British policies of inclusion. The robust critique of Canadian 'politics of recognition' and his defence of 'resentment', by First Nation scholar, Glen Coulthard (2007), makes a useful counter-point to Khan's response to the patrician neocolonial social contract he has been offered by those who would regard themselves as his allies in pursuing 'appropriate' diversity-sensitive policies. As Coulthard (2007, p 451) observes:

> Indeed, one need not expand much effort to elicit the countless ways in which the liberal discourse of recognition has been limited and constrained by the state, the courts, corporate interests, and policymakers so as to help preserve the colonial status quo.

The shocking element in Khan's chapter may then not be the vehemence of his argument as much as the realisation that at a time when British and European states pride themselves on their sensibility to diversity, the outrages experienced by Khan can still be so unselfconsciously perpetrated.

How is it that, despite all the literature and awareness evidenced above, this book must again engage with the concrete realities of racialised power expressed through the routine operation of institutional practice in research and policymaking? It seems inevitable that we must address the institutional and societal mechanisms that facilitate such strategic amnesia.

Both Emma Stone and Ioannis Dimitrakopoulos provide rich insights into the operation of organisations that both fund research and are intimately concerned with seeking to inform policy. The Joseph Rowntree Foundation (JRF) occupies a unique position within the British context, while the European Union (EU) Agency for Fundamental Rights (FRA) seeks to operate within a European context. The stresses experienced in seeking to provide objective and reliable data, while also providing a critical voice to inform state policy, are apparent in their texts.

As director of research at JRF, Stone provides a transparent and highly illuminating account of how JRF conceives, develops and funds its research. The account of the ways in which she and her colleagues seek to address the multiple challenges of working to develop research that will inform policy, and practice, provides the reader with concrete examples of institutional working that will serve as a valuable benchmark for comparative analysis of their own and other contexts. Of the many insights provided in this chapter, one of the most telling is, perhaps, the unsustainability of their open funding stream, which, in 2010, attracted nearly 900 applications for their possible resource base of 6-10 projects. (An international centre on whose board I sit has just received over 400 applications for fellowships, where in 2015 the possible success rate can only be in the region of 2.5 per cent.) The cost of rigorously assessing so many bids, and the cost of unsuccessfully submitting them, is one of the painful realities of the current research market. Thus in JRF's case the period between the call for programmes and the time for submission has been significantly shortened. This has the effect of meaning that only those research groups with established research capital in the area are likely to be able to submit a bid within the time frame. It means that here, as with other research funders, there is an active communicative space in which researchers seek, through a variety of means, to acquire advance notice of forthcoming bids prior to their public announcement. This process constitutes the creation of a privileged cadre who have a distinct advantage in pursuing funding, as the routes to accessing this privileged network are themselves shaped by criteria of institutional standing and individual reputation, which tends toward creating a centripetal vortex of *the usual suspects*, and which is hard to breach by policies of aspirational outreach.

Given the extensive experience of JRF as a very engaged Mode 2 creator of knowledge and promoter of policy change, it is surely telling that Stone reports that:

> ... we need to be mindful about balancing the (real, felt, or constructed) need for evidence on costs and savings, with the reality that the blocks to change are seldom – in truth – a lack of research or evidence.
>
> I am sometimes very sceptical of those within government, across any and all parties, who refer to the lack of evidence. There is always more we can know, but there is always more we know than is acted on.

This is a necessary challenge to the researcher's addiction to research, and perhaps requires some hard questions about the capacity, and willingness, of the researcher to pursue the necessary processes that would potentially facilitate the application of their analysis. It also asks questions about the institutional locations of researches and the extent, in reality, of their transdisciplinary networked capacity to penetrate into the policymaking fora where the power lies.

The account of an international research and policy relevant body, the FRA, within the political and organisational structure of the EU's internal human rights politics and practice provided by Dimitrakopoulos, provides a fruitful comparative account to that provided by Stone, writing on a national level. The FRA is mandated not only to 'provide objective, reliable and comparable data to assist EU institutions and member states in developing evidence-based policies on fundamental rights issues', but also, 'to establish networks of communication that will enable the results of its work to reach the attention of those who shape policies'. As Dimitrakopoulos indicates, the formal establishment of the FRA within the EU political system does, contrary to JRF's experience, provide it with at least a formal, if not exactly substantive, basis of influence within the EU policymaking system. But to those familiar with the misfit between the analyses provided by FRA and the highly selective interpretation and implementation of these by member states, we are again forced to note the brute role of hegemonic power, in its multiple forms, in framing the potential of research to shape policy.

Dimitrakopoulos' chapter provides a valuable concrete instance of one of the difficulties of international collaborative research when he points to the problem of data generated by partners in member states where the legal and conceptual language employed in defining key variables, and the modes of measurement of them, may differ from state to state. Thus, he argues that: 'The analysis of secondary data produced by the FRA is then *comparative*, describing, analysing and commenting on similarities and differences between member states, but the data on which the analysis is based are rarely *comparable*.'

We should perhaps note the ways in which innovation in theory, and the emergence of new conceptual tools, within social science can have a relatively rapid spread as they are taken up by epistemic communities that co-opt them into their existing repertoire. If we compare this with the frequent inertia in developing the implication of these ideas into policy, it perhaps tells us, against the grain of much of my argument here, that there is a greater relative autonomy within the academic sphere that is not easily matched in the domain of policymaking.

Although, as we have seen with the notion of community cohesion, when an academic concept has resonance with the particular political demands of the time, it can be rapidly and extensively translated into policy.

The account of the development of FRA's practice presented by Dimitrakopoulos provides a condensed account of how a policy-oriented agency may seek to develop its research repertoire, and its networked capacity, in order to seek to produce a closer linkage between defining research questions, formulating appropriate research, and monitoring its policy implementation.

Stan Kidd and Tony Reeves offer an insight into the challenge of seeking to service the needs of their diverse citizenry while simultaneously negotiating draconian cuts in their budget. Their need for intelligence with *instrumental utility* strongly underscores the particular expectations of local government in their dealings with the research community. Their account of the marked difference between nation states in the degree of exercise of control the central state has over regional and local government is invaluable in highlighting the need for specificity when examining the nexus of institutions, and the location of power, when considering the development and implementation of policy. The description of the grievous constraints under which a local government in England currently operates should ameliorate the hubris of committed researchers who feel underappreciated, or frustrated, in their attempts to work as partners with local government in revealing social realities and generating analyses with *instrumental utility*. This is, perhaps, all the more crucial given the quite evident cross-over of values between local authority personnel committed to 'serving the needs and protecting the interests of our communities' and the aspirations of researchers informed by a variety of conceptions of public engagement. Describing their role, Kidd and Reeves assert that:

> On the one hand, we need high-quality, timely information that describes and codifies the deep characteristics of place, people and socioeconomic dynamics in order to frame and inform effective policy and decision-making, service delivery and other policy tools. On the other, we need a fundamental understanding of the impact of our own policy interventions and the impact of other exogenous phenomena on the people, place and domains of socioeconomic existence. These particular and reflexive drivers of intelligence and research, along with our fundamental duty to make value-creating, practical

difference to the wellbeing of a dynamic, complex and multiply challenged district, differentiates our research milieu and motivation from those of academia and policy think tanks.

As a researcher, this is a description of an institutional site of policy and practice with multiple opportunities for co-working and shared endeavour. However, what may be strikingly different are the different experiences of accountability between the sphere of academic production and that described in this chapter. While my following chapter seeks to address quite explicitly the current constraints within the domain of academic research, it must be recognised that the directness of the excise of political control at the level of the local state is very particular. In my chapter, one of my purposes is to assert the indirect, as much as the direct, political pressures within current academia, but the political pressures operative within local government are often direct and have the mandate of electoral legitimacy. A change in local government may have draconian effects on specific areas of local policy, and, as Kidd and Reeves indicate in their chapter, successive changes in the transfers of powers from the local to the central state has made local autonomy highly constrained and subject to the reactive policy whims of central government (see Husband and Alam, 2011).

In contrast to the aspirational language of Mode 2 knowledge production and utilisation, Kidd and Reeves provide a grounded account of the multilayered, and perhaps finely nuanced, relations between the actors engaged in the research–funding–policy nexus. Linking with the account of Stone, they argue that:

> Even when academic or policy institute research is more directly aligned to evaluating practical public policy concerns, it is not necessarily directed to specific local contexts, unless it has been commissioned by either local public bodies directly, or by agencies such as the Joseph Rowntree Foundation which undertakes place-based micro-research. In the latter case, the utility of such research to local authorities can be influenced by such factors as a consensus on the assumptions and data underpinning the research brief, a mutual commitment to the salience of the hypotheses under investigation, and an effective relationship between the researcher and the authority, as well as with other stakeholders in the research exercise. All of these factors need to be carefully managed while at the same

time not compromising the efficacy and independence of the research. This involves a delicate balancing of the interests of researcher and stakeholders and a keen focus on effective design, governance and the accommodation of a common purpose.

This grounded insight into the politics of research and policymaking at the local level provides an invaluable corrective to the optimistic attractions of the theoretical visions of *transdisciplinary*-engaged policy-relevant research. In particular, their distressing accounts of the prescriptive, top-down nature of so much policy innovation underlines the persistent need for a critical political economy framing of any understanding of the relation of research to policy.

For all three of these contributors it is apparent that the best available evidence from research lies at the heart of policymaking, and yet a recurrent theme running through this text is the problematic nature of research income generation. These contributions cumulatively present a troubling picture of the current dynamics that are tying together the research community, research funders and policy formulation in relation to British ethnic relations.

This book arises from an international symposium organised by the Centre for Applied Social Research at the University of Bradford, where, under the Chatham House rule of confidentiality, the participants robustly addressed the theme of this book. The concerns shared in that meeting provided the confidence to assert that this book is a necessary intervention into the current research–policy dynamic.

ONE

Constraint and compromise: university researchers, their relation to funders and to policymaking for a multiethnic Britain

Charles Husband

Introduction

As already indicated in the Introduction to this volume, the stimulus to this book was essentially a personal biographic concern with the developments in the relation between academics, research funders and the policy milieu. This concern was heightened by the quite concrete changes in the British university sector as the wider neoliberal ideology of the government came to permeate throughout the structures and values of the management of British academe. The retreat from knowledge as a public good, the rapid commercialisation of higher education, and the micro-management of individual academics within this regime all conspired to elevate my degree of anxiety that all was not well in this triangular relationship.

The aim of this chapter is quite modest. It is merely to raise in simple terms the problematic nature of the current relationships between research and policy. This does not aim for high theory or extensive empirical evidence, but aspires to point to the impact of the radical changes in the institutional environment on university-based researchers' capacity to engage wholeheartedly in policy-related research. Given its personal biographic origin, this chapter is necessarily written very much from the perspective of a university-based researcher with an established commitment to developing social scientific research that will inform politics and policy around diversity, equality and multiethnic coexistence. Noting the very major ideological shifts in the political environment that frames both academe and ethnic relations in Britain, the argument developed here seeks to provoke a wider, and more honest, public debate about the capacity of social scientific research to contribute to the development of policies aimed at challenging racism and promoting equity in multiethnic Britain.

Most academics operate not only with immediate colleagues in their home department, but also within *a community of practice* (Lave and Wenger, 1991), where they share common core values and modes of practice with a cohort of fellow professionals. These include not only immediate colleagues with common disciplinary, and possibly applied, concerns, but also a transnational web of contacts who form a supportive network of dialogue and collaboration (a dispersed, but possibly highly significant, epistemic community). Within such a community of practice there are mechanisms of support, and discipline, which consolidate shared convictions about the merit of their shared theoretical repertoire. One outcome of this professional environment is the very real possibility, and probability, of sub-disciplinary myopia, resulting in a closed circle of self-definition, and professional affirmation, tied to participation within an artificial proscription of appropriate method and seminal theory (depicted in extreme form in Flinders' 2013 account of elements of political theory).

There are particular conferences where academics foregather to reaffirm their in-group identity and to test out the boundaries of obsolescence and innovation in their theory and method. Typically there are subdivisions of specialisms at such meetings where *specialist* identities may be refined within the framework of their broader disciplinary affinity. And within these structures there are hierarchies of status and influence that may provide the basis for mentorship, career facilitation and personal support against the rude blasts of university life. Such conferences are also theatres of performative display where not only professional colleagues, but also publishers and members of the research funding and policy milieus, may identify current high fliers.

Each academic, like myself, stands at the hub of a nexus of contacts and pressures that define their professional identity and shape their professional practice. While they may have made individual choices about the academic identity they have sought for themselves, they may have varying insight into the constraints on their agency that their routine practice within the current research environment imposes.

Background

In the period 2008-10 I was involved in data collection for the Joseph Rowntree Foundation (JRF)/AWYA (Association of West Yorkshire Authorities) project that resulted in Husband and Alam's (2011) *Social cohesion and counter-terrorism: A policy contradiction?* A serendipitous side effect of this data collection was that I became aware of the plethora of projects that were implemented in the name of 'community cohesion' or the 'Prevent' agenda. Without having the opportunity to pursue this in any meaningful way, I became deeply concerned at the *institutional pragmatic necessity* that framed the rapid development of some of these interventions. This was particularly so under the Pathfinder scheme, which was in itself a case study in crass governmental imperatives overriding measured policy innovation. These partial insights coalesced into a growing concern about the use and abuse of social scientific theory in the framing and *legitimation* of such projects. Thus, for example, the theoretical notion of *the contact hypothesis* seemed to enjoy a wide familiarity among local authority staff, and it 'appeared' to be comfortably invoked to legitimate a range of short-term interventions that were doubtfully linked to a cautious interpretation of the practical application of this body of literature (see Pettigrew and Tropp, 2005). I was not able to pursue my concern, nor was I able to validate the assertions made above, but the sense of unease remained strong as an industry in community cohesion interventions developed in Britain. I had a strong sense of the use and abuse of social science in a policy context where a governmentally created market in community intervention was being matched by a plethora of individuals who were either employed by independent agencies, or were local authority staff impelled by the local application of central government directives *to act and to take up the premise and language of community cohesion.*

These concerns were also inflamed by my role as a scientific adviser to the UNESCO programme – the European Coalition of Cities Against Racism (ECCAR) – a coalition of over a hundred European cities committed to implementing a 10-point plan of action to eradicate racism in their cities. Here there was again an opportunity to have 'glimpses' of what constituted best practice in different cities, and the variety was extensive. Sometimes the concern here was more to do with the glaring absence of insights from contemporary social science, and sometimes it was again a concern about what might be being done in the name of social science. (I resigned in 2011.)

At the same time, as a 'senior' member of staff with responsibility for providing a research lead in my university, through a newly established research centre, I was aware of the pressures on colleagues as they sought to be 'research active' within a university regime that subjected them to conflicting demands, in an institutional context where I was part of the managerial process.

Thus this chapter is not presented as a theoretical exegesis of the correct modelling of social scientific research in relation to the development of policies for the management of multiethnic Britain. It is, rather, a cry of alarm in the face of a research environment that radically needs to be critiqued and repositioned. It reflects a non-negotiable anxiety about the state of play in the relationship between academic research, research funders and the contribution of social science to informing attempts to improve interethnic relations. It asserts that there is currently *a collusive denial of concern* that is shared among the participants in this network of involvement, where the successful players have a shared interest in not exposing the internal flaws in their mutual dependencies.

The observations here are based on the British university system, although in my fellowship at the Helsinki Collegium for Advanced Studies (2008-11) I noted the regrettable transformation of its working culture as the university responded to the governmental change of the universities' legal framework, and conversations with colleagues in Europe and elsewhere have demonstrated their own familiarity with many of the issues raised here.

Universities as a locus for research

Changing workplace culture

British universities have in essence become large commercial enterprises in which their survival is based primarily on income generation. In this context, the recent government changes in the funding of teaching in the humanities and social sciences (namely, the withdrawal of core funding), has exacerbated the situation for humanities and social sciences within the larger university sector.

Universities have a long history and varied development across the world. But it would be a truism to say that they have been in a perpetual state of evolution. In the 'Western European world', that evolution has taken a very particular path over recent years. It is a trajectory marked by the incursion of neoliberal economic models and a distinct commercialisation of academe. Readings' (1996) *The university in ruins* was an early robust analysis of this development. More recently, Ginsberg (2011), in his *The fall of faculty: The rise of the all-administrative university*, has produced a tirade against the diminution of the control of academic affairs by the academics themselves, and their increasing subjugation to the dominance of administrators whose business models perversely distort the values and concerns of the academic staff. In the UK, Collini's (2012) *What are universities for?* has eloquently argued the case of the problematic existence of the humanities in a higher education system driven by performance indicators and a funding regime that are alien to the concerns of the humanities. His arguments equally well apply to the social sciences that have found their block grant for teaching removed and their endeavours shaped by a skewing of research funding, and 'impact' assessments that have distorted their role in the universities and society.

The shifting location of social sciences within academe and social policy that is framed by analyses such as these is not only a shift in the funding regime of higher education; it is also marked by a profound ideological shift in the understanding of the role of higher education in society. This has seen a marked shift toward demanding an explicit and *immediate* pay-off to society for the investment in higher education, and a marked erosion of the idea of knowledge as a generic public good. It seems brutally indicative of this situation that government responsibility for higher education is vested in the Department for Business, Innovation and Skills. More recently still, McGettigan (2013), in *The great university gamble: Money, markets and the future of higher education*, in an analysis that focuses on the political economy of higher education, has provided a detailed account of these processes. In particular, he demonstrates how the opening up of the university system to private providers will distort the traditional values and role of universities as the government seeks to promote '"value for money" rather than standard quality' (McGettigan, 2013, p 5). As McGettigan notes, the rapid thrust to put in place these radical changes was pursued without primary legislation and with limited parliamentary scrutiny. And as he further notes, the ideological shift beneath this process was made explicit by the Campaign for the Public University's (2011) 'Defence of public higher education', an external critique of the market-led vision of university activity, which asserted that:

> These changes will encourage students to think of themselves as consumers, investing only in their own personal human capital with a view to reaping high financial rewards, and discourage graduates to think their university education as anything other than something purchased at a high price for private benefit. (cited in McGettigan, 2013, p 25)

The same document noted that the Browne report on the future of higher education (2010), *Securing a sustainable future for higher education*, 'made no mention of the public value of higher education' (McGettigan, 2013, p 64). This conclusion was anticipated in Collini's comment on the Browne report, namely, that 'This report displays no real interest in universities as places of education; they are conceived of simply as engines of economic prosperity and as agencies for equipping future employees to earn high salaries' (2012, p 187).

All research in British higher education is now framed by this resolute marketisation of their activity within a regime that is marked by micro-management of researchers' activities. Ginsberg's account of the situation in the US is not unfamiliar in the UK as universities have created an expanded cadre of administrators whose function is to generate and monitor performance indicators of academic staff activity. This is not confined to the intrusive processes of the national REF (Research Evaluation Framework), with its concerns with output, 'esteem' and 'impact', but is also echoed in the individual tracking processes of universities that monitor each individual's teaching performance, administrative activities, number of research applications (how many successful/how many rejected) per annum, amount of money generated through research grants, and through Research Knowledge Transfer (RKT) (that is, charging for disseminating information you have already been paid to generate).

Thus it is reasonable to argue that for academics seeking to carry out social scientific research within the current regime of British universities, they are likely to find themselves in a very constrained context, with multiple cross-pressures making them increasingly subject to strategies of individual survival and career advancement. In this context, where your professional life may be broken down into work points, with each element of your practice being allotted a weighted value, it is easy to slip into a neurotic concern about optimising your survivability within your working environment. Walk into any university and note the number of staff working from home when they are not lecturing, in order to minimise the *interference* they may experience from colleagues and students. Individual productivity, rather than collegiate endeavour, is the logical workplace rationale within this managerial regime. The collegiate environment of collaborative practice has proved highly vulnerable to the individualised evaluation and exploitation of members of staff within a regime that has commercialised academic life.

The centrality of research is crucial to the viability of universities, directly through income generation, and also through the feedback loop of the prestige that is associated with a university having an extensive repertoire of high-quality research. This is increasingly so where the government research evaluation exercises (Research Assessment Exercise, RAE/REF) have quite deliberately sought to promote a much more steeply ranked hierarchy of universities, with a small core of Ivy

League like institutions of international excellence at the top (currently self-defined as the Russell Group). When one of the criteria for the evaluation of research activity in a university is 'research culture', then the availability of substantial research overheads from research grants to be top-sliced to facilitate the consolidation of research centres and university initiatives is critical. Outstanding institutions in a nationally well-resourced university sector are entirely admirable and a critical stimulus to the whole. But when, as at the present, this policy is being pursued within a national zero sum financial structure, the expansion of richesse for the few is being achieved on the basis of the impoverishment of the many. It follows that the better resourced, and more prestigious, universities will be attractive to academics seeking career progression. In this sense, the self-fuelling logics of research excellence are justified. But it also distorts national academic research communities by rendering active and successful research groups in lesser-ranked institutions merely nurturant environments for young colleagues, who will then leave when their CVs are appropriately enhanced so that they can enter into institutions that provide more resources, and career advancement.

As Alam notes, citing Burawoy (2007, p 38) in Chapter Three, the flexibility to permit sociologists to adopt a more flexible relationship between career, research and policy is too often a privilege of those who 'have or had comfortable positions in top-ranked sociology departments, where conditions of work permit multiple locations.' While academic mobility has often been seen as the *sine qua non* of individual academic status, it is also the case that there is a merit in academics becoming established within particular locales where, particularly for social scientists, their grounded knowledge of the local communities and political environment can enrich both their understanding and potential policy contribution, thus facilitating the realisation of Mode 2 research practice. Despite the routine embedding of 'community engagement', 'widening participation' and 'impact' in the agendas of university administrations, in the current context, the stressed workloads of most academics in British universities are not congenial to their making major personal commitments to community involvement in their surrounding locale. The cumulative sedimentation of networks and local knowledge is a highly desirable outcome of stable academic employment that is far from optimally facilitated within the current regime.

The REF exercise of 2013 will have generated outputs that will explicitly rank individual departments, and cumulatively, individual universities in its forthcoming report of December 2014. The subsequent market in prestige will have very concrete effects on individual universities, departments and researchers. Where universities are currently charging £9,000 a year (for undergraduate degree programmes), there is a keen market in the prestige of departments and between universities for student numbers per se, and for students with high A-level grades, since this is another performance indicator that feeds into the ranking of university departments nationally. Additionally, with the pressure on universities to increase their RKT income, university departments are under pressure to maximise their prestige through research since this is directly related to the marketability of the research staff, and to the income they may be able to elicit through Knowledge Transfer Partnerships.

Research, then, is centrally riveted into the *commodification of knowledge* that is a lamentable and obvious feature of the contemporary university system in Britain.

Within this context it would not be surprising to find individuals driven by the internal logics of personal professional career progression. Flinders (2013, p 628), for example, in his trenchant assault on the internal dynamics of academic political science, argues that:

> The incentives and sanction system within political science has therefore traditionally placed little emphasis on the professional responsibilities of scholars to the public; the strategy for those who want to progress swiftly through the academic ranks remains one of cultivating a niche (that is, hyper-specialisation), writing specialist books and papers that very few people will ever read....

And in their study of academic activity in the area of health research, Estabrooks et al (2008, p 1068) note that while such academics may work within an area increasingly permeated by Mode 2 philosophy, they still routinely find themselves having their career progression determined by Mode 1 performance criteria. The individual, and collective, experience of many professions at present is that they are encountering a radical destabilisation of their working environment, in which workplace routines, levels of staffing and managerial ideologies are in rapid flux. The contradictions inherent in this process may at one time have generated collective resistance, but the zeitgeist of the current era is more typically anxious compliance with imposed change, and a defensive investment in professional identities.

A key element of the argument developed throughout this book is the permeability of the boundaries between such professional identities and the ideologies, and economic force, of wider society. As Jessop (2010) suggests, we cannot complacently interrogate the role of professions from within the logic and routines of their own practice and boundaries – the wider transformations of power, and their modes of expression in national, international and local contexts must be factored into our analysis.

Why should this be an issue? Implications for research practice

The pursuit of funding is now not only driven by the insistent curiosity of academics; it is an activity demanded of university staff as an explicit feature of their job description. To be regarded as *research active* is now both a necessary element of the self-definition of the majority of academics, *and* a structural requirement of employment within the university system. The drive to develop a research bid is now externally driven, with research centres and university departments setting benchmark performance indicators of the number of bids that must be submitted per person per year.

This means that the gestation time for thinking through a bid may be radically foreshortened. If an individual scholar is working within a regime where they are required to submit a specific number of research bids within a particular time frame, then it may be this *performance indicator* that impels their creative activity rather than a well-considered and personally meaningful research question. It may mean a number of colleagues join in literally fabricating a research bid in which only a minority of people are fully invested, despite the increasing internal reviewing of bids before their transmission to the research funder. Additionally, in a British and European academic system, where many staff do not have tenure but move from research project to research project as a floating population of research fellows, the continuity of their career employment and their capacity to feed their families requires that they maintain a forward-looking programme of research bid preparation. Where potential success rates may vary between 25–30 and 2.5 per cent, a provident person would have more than one bid in a cyclical process of development.

This external pressure to generate new research bids may mean that individuals may be operating inefficiently because they do not have the time to fully reflect on the data from their current research project, and to optimise the output through considered analysis and consultation before they must engage with their next project. The transdisciplinary connectedness assumed in the model of Mode 2 knowledge production suggests that the first wave of data analysis and published output from a project might best be viewed as merely the early fruits of this research activity. Further *sustained* dialogues with other interested parties in their dispersed community might create a second, and contextually embedded, extension of this material as it is filtered through the expertise, priorities and audiences of other actors. It is argued here that the current situation of university-based researchers too often mitigates against this possibility.

Additionally, the situation is currently such that individual academics pursue funds, but do not necessarily define research agendas. The role of the research funder in defining research themes has become central, and one consequence is that individuals may warp their personal interest and stretch their professional competence in order to *follow the money.*

Research centres within the university structure

As a key element in profiling the research activity of a university, research centres play a critical role. They are important institutional spaces in which a specific collegiate research culture may be built, that stimulate and support individual research, and collectively build a research marque, a distinctive theoretically informed research style that becomes widely identified with this cohort of scholars. Such research centres can be valuably understood as communities of practice (Lave and Wenger, 1991) in which institutional structures and ideologies intersect with the individuals' attempts to make sense of their own professional identity in this context.

Research centres and professional identities

Researchers in this context may all be social scientists, but within this institutional setting they become self-defined through their specialist role, and perhaps through their commitment to developing a specific theoretical model. Thus I would assert that we can speculate that there are two types of research academic:

- The first type, *open/pragmatic*, gets up in the morning and says: 'What can these theories do for my research today?'
- The other, *focused/committed*, gets up and says: 'What can I do for my theory today?'

We can ask 'Why does this matter?' The answer is that because, when in the context of seeking research funding the focused/committed researcher wins a grant, they are likely to start by asking 'What can this research topic do for my theory?', rather than asking 'What range of theoretical perspectives do I need to make sense of this issue?'

This becomes particularly significant when the individual researcher is embedded in a research group that has an established commitment to a particular theoretical position. In this context all the centripetal forces of collective group dynamics are likely to promote a professional myopia that exaggerates the validity of applying this perspective, and simultaneously effectively marginalises other potentially relevant theoretical or methodological approaches to the same problem. In the political economy of academic production it is worth noting that publishers have, in recent decades, been happy to expand their publications lists and journal catalogue in order to feed exactly this degree of specialism, yet again closing the circle of peer review within an arbitrary demarcation of scholarly practice. Key figures within specialist fields become primary definers of the theoretical and methodological repertoire of their area, and through journal editorial policy provide a niche market for its valorisation and dissemination. In such an academic milieu individual scholars may happily ensure that they are not confounded by being required to engage with theoretical agendas outside of their own specialism, which they may then celebrate in dedicated conferences with their confreres. Such routine networking may be particularly relevant in an era when the time lapse between the call for research bids and their submission has progressively narrowed. Insider information about forthcoming bids consequently becomes increasingly significant. Being networked with significant colleagues, and with research funders, becomes increasingly relevant to the preparation and submission of a successful bid. The capacity of university research centres to build the capacity to create, and effectively exploit, networked information flows around forthcoming research bids, and preparatory team building, is part of their *raison d'être*. And it becomes part of the feedback loop that consolidates their viability over time.

Whether tensions such as these are apparent to the funding body through the application is questionable. In some instances it will be precisely the reputation of the individual and their specific competence in this field that gives them a positive edge. In other instances it may be that the funder has a rather more optimistic aspiration about the academic range of insights that may be brought to bear in addressing the research question.

If it is the case, of actively selecting the prestigious *open/pragmatic researcher*, then we may ask what sort of political-organisational perspective has allowed the funder to regard this specific model as appropriate to underpin the research. Is there a synergy between the funder who has no prescriptive expectations of specific outcomes, and is hoping that the research will reveal potentially unanticipated findings, and the researcher who is prepared to employ a range of tools?

If it is the case where the *focused/committed* researcher is committed to a particular perspective, then we may ask, will the researcher's commitment to their own theoretical agenda skew the research findings inappropriately? It may, of course, be the case that the chosen research teams represent a known *safe pair of hands* whose approach can be relied on to produce an analysis within an anticipated narrow frame of reference that is congenial to the funders' interests. As we found in a study that included examining the allocation of government funds through the 'Prevent' agenda, it was apparent that being risk-averse may be a persistent institutional response to the selection of projects in contentious areas (Husband and Alam, 2011), a position that can only be expected to increase with the increased competition for research funds and the prevailing ideology of science serving the customer.

In sum, we should note the power of professional identities and the normative pressure of research communities committed to a specific theoretical agenda and its associated methodology. Such research communities are often nurtured through their concentration in specific research centres, where the interpersonal dynamics reinforce the professional specialist identity. We can ask in every instance of funded research what ideological baggage is associated with the theoretical perspective underlying the research proposal. We can also seek to be sensitive to the swings of fashion for particular methodologies and specific theories. We have seen, for example, an international vogue for *social cohesion* despite the fraught nature of the concept (Husband and Alam, 2011), and Wright and Baray (2012) have, for example, persuasively warned of the way in which prejudice reduction models of social intervention focus on the advantaged group as both the problem and the agent of change. In highlighting the internal ideological assumptions of social cohesion and much prejudice reduction research, they assert the legitimacy of an alternative *collective action* perspective, arguing that: 'A collective action perspective concerns itself with equality across groups, not harmony, and focuses on social justice, not social cohesion' (Wright and Baray, 2012, p, 227). It needs no great imagination to see why such a perspective finds little favour in governmental research funding.

Research centres as organisational entities

Institutionally (if not academically) *the key role of a research centre is survival.* This means that the senior management of such centres have priorities that are fundamentally managerial. In the highly competitive world of contemporary research, one core task is to retain the best performers (a task given a particular edge in the market created by the REF in the UK). Thus we see once more that the pursuit of research funds is likely to have an institutionally instrumental dimension. It is the research director's role to nurture the activities of colleagues in such a way that they have a continuous stream of grants coming through the centre that will enable individual researchers to have career stability, and that will enable the research centre to maintain its core competences and external reputation. Directors are therefore likely to be *complicit in the selling of research excellence to potential funders.*

In doing this are they likely to honestly make transparent and public the competing pressures placed on research active staff who, depending on the institution, will have teaching and administrative obligations, and will be expected to engage in RKT activity, activities that may have an adverse impact on their ability to fulsomely meet their obligations to the research funder.

This also raises the question of the autonomous powers of research directors, who again, depending on their institution, may find that they have very limited capacity to protect their research staff from the super exploitation of individuals that has become endemic in British universities. The current range of performance indicators that universities may, and do, place on individual members of staff (research grants submitted, research income generated, RKT income generated, number of doctoral students supervised [and completed on time], engagement in community outreach, esteem, impact, courses taught, administrative responsibility...) effectively ensures that only the very fortunate can engage with externally funded research from a position of routine control of their working life.

The same institutions that have prioritised research as a key element of their financial viability and international prestige have seldom meaningfully addressed the working stresses of their employees. Early stage researchers are routinely required to embrace self-exploitation if they are to compete within the current research milieu, and their research directors may find themselves virtually powerless to intervene in defence of these individuals, and of the integrity of their research, in an institutional context where the researchers are marginal in an organisation that has become a commercial enterprise driven by external performance indicators that bear little relevance to the ethos of the pursuit of knowledge and the facilitation of scholarship. Research directors may have very limited control over the funds their colleagues bring into the university, where 'senior management' and finance directors may have differing priorities for research-generated overheads. They may also have no managerial control over the teaching and administrative loads placed on their research colleagues by structures of line management that produce parallel, but not equal, distributions of authority and control.

In sum: the academic as compromised research partner

This context sketched above is a central element in the collusive denial of the *reality* that frames the contemporary research environment. Many academics in Britain and elsewhere will recognise the workplace culture and institutional environment outlined above. They will be able to contribute their own telling anecdotes to the many I have not placed in this text. The university institutional context for academic social scientific research has become profoundly corrupted by the changes in the ideologies framing university life, and by the consequent radical changes in the ways in which individual researchers may relate to their research funders, and to the aspirations they may have for the policy relevance of their work. There is a collusive strategy of university senior management to assert that all is well, and that they can get their staff to run faster, jump higher and fit 'their offer', in terms of taught courses and research competences, to the demands of the commercialised environment in which they find themselves. The necessary pursuit of funding has made university staff increasingly the weak partners in the dialogue with research funders.

The definers of research agendas and guarantors of research quality

There are many issues that could be raised here about the intersecting relationships between university researchers and their funders, but in the space available here, we will raise only a few.

Emergence of research themes

One significant and foundational issue relates to the question of who determines the research agendas that result in the funders putting out a specific call for research bids. There is, for example, a dynamic and sometimes less than transparent relationship between research funders and the academic community. It can be the case that a specific innovation in research may open up a new area for enquiry that relatively rapidly shapes a research agenda. The take-up of Putnam's *Bowling alone* (2000) would be such an example of the fortuitous intersection of academic research and contemporary political sensitivities (Field, 2003). The extensive uptake of the concepts of social capital and social cohesion in the UK and in Europe, despite their conceptual ambiguity and political baggage, is a splendid exemplar of the complex definition and policy take-up of research themes. This example also illustrates the potential of extra-national influences in shaping policy vogues, and the capacity of such vogues to replace considered evaluation of relevance with a desire to be *in the frame.*

Thus in our enquiry into the current situation, one of the questions we may want to address is how it is that specific research agendas come into being. Funding bodies have their own means of establishing advisory boards and other means of reflecting on what should be the research priorities for defining the expenditure of their resources. (Emma Stone, in Chapter Five, this volume, provides a valuable account of such an internal process that invites questions about what may be the reality, even when intended transparency and reflexivity is undoubtedly in place.) We might ask, 'How are they recruited, and with whose voice do they speak?' Government departments are major funders of research, and in this regard we might expect the funded research to have a more direct route to influencing policy. (Although in an era of austerity, some of the departments that in the past might have funded social scientific research have experienced draconian cuts in their budget, and have consequently radically withdrawn from this activity.) This may have coincided with the government becoming more interventionist in seeking to control other research budgets in which they have an interest. For example, the Economic and Social Research Council (ESRC) has seemingly developed a linkage to government agendas that has been reflected in their recent funding activity (for example, re-radicalisation and security). Independent research funders such as the Joseph Rowntree Foundation (JRF) and the Leverhulme Foundation, in this context, therefore have a critical role in their ability to adopt a committed position in regard to policy issues.

Expectation of impact

If we were to seek honest replies to what university researchers would see as an ideal relationship with research funders, the response would probably be something like: *they fund us adequately, trust us to carry out the research with a minimum of interference, and then support us extensively in disseminating our findings.* Perhaps 40 years ago there was a time when the first two elements of this wish list were relatively attainable. But the expectations for dissemination were very much regarded as something that the researchers would carry out through their own routines. And that, very often, was the publication of a book and some articles, and the presentation of papers at appropriate conferences. The emphasis on impact was, by today's standards, highly underdeveloped. In the 1960s and 1970s, when disciplines such as sociology, cultural studies, mass communication and social psychology were rapidly developing as established disciplinary areas, there was, perhaps, an incestuous excitement in the revelation of new research insights and theoretical developments. This does not mean that there was no aspiration to social relevance. On the contrary, that was a strong feature of much research at the time. The difference between then and now was the expectation of what the researcher should do to ensure this impact. The ESRC, which would be seen by many as the benchmark standard for social scientific research in the UK, has no such ambiguity. Under the heading 'What the ESRC expects', it asserts that: 'ESRC requires the researchers we fund to consider the potential scientific, societal and economic impact of their research', and then proceeds to provide an extensive 'Impact toolkit' (see www.esrc.uk/funding-and-guidance/impact-toolkit/what-how-and-why). An insight into elements of the rationale for this emphasis is to be found in the same subsection in a report/'brochure' entitled *Partnering with business: How business-academic collaboration can drive innovation and growth*, in which the chief executive officer (CEO) of the ESRC, Professor Paul Boyle, states:

> Supporting economic performance and sustainable growth, and developing collaborative partnerships with business and policy are key priorities for the ESRC. The ESRC's knowledge and experience makes the ESRC ideal partners for business and by working together we can directly benefit business and inform policy development. (www.esrc.ac.uk/_images/KE_brochure_web_tcm8-23749.pdf)

A reader who is unfamiliar with the current context of social scientific research in Britain might want to browse through this website, and its many embedded sub-sections, in order to begin to get some appreciation of what dissemination of research findings is now likely to mean for a funded researcher. It certainly means a very significant change in the range of activities associated with being a recipient of a grant than would have been the case in the past. The aspiration to make academic researchers more accountable for the dissemination of their research is, in most cases, entirely laudable, but the question that immediately arises is whether in the context described above they are enabled to fulsomely engage with this responsibility by their employing institution.

In addition, we should note that the tool for assessing impact in the current (2014) REF process, for example, offers a very limited space in which to provide an adequate evidential basis for the claims of impact that are being made. External 'experts' have been operating as consultants advising universities on how to maximise their *self-reporting* in this process. Yet again, we are led to ask whether the rhetoric of impact is matched by a seriousness of purpose that would give real leverage to the supposed beneficiaries of the research. As an exercise in confident exposure to the evaluation of claims of relevance, the current REF exercise is an invitation to creative self-aggrandisement within a review system devoid of real accountability.

Some academics, it has to be said, might reasonably be described as being constitutionally unsuited to some of the processes of dissemination. Whether by temperament, or underdeveloped social skills, some excellent social scientists may not be best suited to disseminating their findings. They can, of course, hope to rely on the aid of their university's communications department that assiduously seeks to promote their institutions' brand and RKT. However, the professional skills, and apparently necessarily assertive claims making, of these colleagues, can lead to researchers being positioned across a scale, from gratifyingly amazed to horrified, when they see the proposed representation of the findings and personal expertise by communication experts attuned to the community of practice of public relations (PR) practices. But equally, university communications departments, too, find themselves stressed with the demands of academics seeking to pursue their own impact and esteem.

Research funders are very adept at providing guidance on dissemination and impact, but typically do not have the resources, or intent, to actively engage in meaningfully promoting particular projects. Thus it is that the universally acclaimed aspiration that academics should be accountable for the impact of their research adds to the pressures on individual researchers, with unidentified long-term consequences – for them and for the credibility of the current model.

There is great emphasis on impact in the current evaluation of research, and yet we might question whether research bodies are themselves in the business of promoting follow-up to the research that they have funded, since their performance may be assessed in relation to the range of initiatives they have funded rather than in terms of sustained follow-through on emergent insights. It could reasonably be argued that there is a frequent collusion over the claimed degree of engagement of the researchers and the funders with the communities that they seek to serve through research, since both are routinely not accountable to these communities, but are more intimately engaged in a dialogue between themselves, permeated by barely suppressed struggles over relative control of the research field. This collusive tension is then typically swathed in a sincere, but barely credible, mutual discourse of *engagement* with target audiences, where a few 'representative' individuals and organisations stand in as proxy for sustained in-depth engagement.

Accountability, admin and funding

The researchers' daydream of being well funded and left alone to pursue their research, suggested above, has become more problematic over the last decades. As research funders sought to manage the regrettable reality that not all funded research produced substantive quality outcomes, then so, too, has the degree of routine monitoring of the research process become a more intrusive element of the research process itself. The principle investigator responsible for a grant now finds that they are being required to manage a substantial programme of regular reporting on the financial management and execution of the research. Far from being left alone, the main relationship between a research team and their funder is now shaped by processes of routine reporting within relatively short time frames. This has not only produced a new workload on researchers, but has also placed a great deal of emphasis on research management skills. Again, this is not unreasonable, but it does have consequences. Thus, for example, one of the logics of research centres that feeds into the practice of research funders is located in the consequences of the *effective creation of reputation*. Funders, whether governmental or independent, are accountable for the expenditure of their funds, and this has a tendency to make them risk-averse. There is a logic here where established experience in successfully managing research projects within a university context can build an administrative infrastructure, within successful research groupings, that does facilitate their efficient reporting processes, and builds their reputation with funders. Consequently there is a centripetal tendency to *favour the usual suspects.* These forces are likely to limit the range of people who can reasonably be expected to find funding.

Additionally, as more and more academics are required to pursue research funds, and as research funding in certain areas has become more limited, competition for funding has increased. Universities have aggressively sought to extract *full economic costs*, or even costs plus, and consequently the unit cost of research projects has increased, and the number of grants issued must be at risk of diminishing in the current economic climate. At the same time, *some* non-governmental research funders are clearly aware of the pressure on academics to bring in research grants, and are seeking to barter with applicants to accept contracts that would result in the project being inadequately funded, or ineptly executed, or both. Myself and colleagues in recent years found ourselves in a very positive dialogue with an international non-governmental funder, where there was explicit agreement that they wished to fund a specific research project that we had proposed, but they then proceeded to a process of forcing down the available funds, seemingly on the assumption that we would be unable to resist and fudge our way around the unviable costings. They were wrong, but it was a very educative experience.

The multiple pressures shaping the relationship between researchers and research funders are not trivial in their consequences, for researchers and research fund managers as individuals, and for the health of policy relevant research more generally. There is a great need for a more honest and robust dialogue.

Researchers and communities of interest and non-governmental organisations

Research funders and university-based researchers frequently share an explicit claim that they are engaged in the pursuit of valid data and analyses that will inform policy decisions at the level of the national or local state, and in civil society. Typically such policy-relevant research has one or more communities of interest that are the intended beneficiaries of this shared intervention on their behalf. Given the long history of critiques of academic research, and the cumulative impact of the development of autonomous voices that can speak on behalf of researched communities of interest, it has become normative that such research can demonstrate its *connectedness* to such target communities, and is central to the assumptions of Mode 2 knowledge generation. This demonstrable engagement with target audiences is often a necessity in facilitating access to an appropriate sample, and to providing a smooth route for dissemination, and both of these are key to legitimating the political relevance of the research. This scenario raises a number of awkward questions.

Perhaps the most obvious issue arising from the argument above is to ask whether the protestations of connectedness, reflected in the promises of post-research commitment of the researchers to the community they accessed, are really delivered. It is intrinsic to the argument presented here that despite the increased formal attention to accountability and impact, the structural conditions under which research is carried out has moved little in terms of ensuring a meaningful sustained engagement with the intended beneficiaries of research.

Of course, where the intention of the research is to expose the ideological nature of current government policy, and its malign impact on sections of the British population, then expecting the published analysis to be taken up positively by the relevant government department is naïve, and academics are familiar with the eloquent silence that greets unwelcome research. Often, in such circumstances, the researchers in question have seen themselves as preparing ammunition that others are better equipped to fire. But this, too, assumes an effective liaison between the research team and the active players in non-governmental organisations (NGOs), the third sector and the media. This inevitably returns us to the concerns expressed above, about the real resources of time and energy that any researcher may have for this sustained commitment to the dissemination of their research. It raises questions about the networked social and political capital of specific partner NGOs, who may themselves have only limited access to the machinery of policy formation. Stone, in Chapter Five, pointedly notes that ignorance of the facts is seldom the problem in relation to inertia in policy development. Social science research on the powerful and the privileged remains a rarity as the condition of the marginalised provides a preferred focus of research. But more information about the nature of deprivation and exclusion requires complimentary information on the hegemonic practices of self-interest of the privileged. The levers for change in the contemporary neoliberal political regime do not present a nurturant environment for the effective operation of a dialogic public sphere.

The currently discredited mechanisms of deliberative democracy have produced an environment where populist assertion is more potent than reasoned argument underpinned by carefully presented data. The emotive politics of UKIP (UK Independence Party), or the Tea Party in the US, are driven by the epistemology of *Alice in Wonderland*: 'What I say three times is true.' Thus the discursive style and preferred modes of political influence employed by academics and linked partners may be particularly inopportune in the current environment. There is a haunting possibility that some proportion of research is destined to be a politically tolerable level of expressive critique of the status quo, whose de facto function is to sustain the aspirations, and belief, of researchers, funders and activists that democratic deliberation is still a viable means of challenging inequity in society.

Positioned against the emotive and declamatory discursive style of populist politics, it is also possible that the 'professional' modes of acceptable discursive style may sit uneasily with the explicitly political accounts of the relevance of research that might be employed by the voice of the researched, rather than the correctly modulated terms of the researcher. For example, does the robust voice of Khan, in Chapter Four of this volume, sit comfortably with your expectations of his *academic* status? It is always worth asking: does the research liberate the autonomous voice of the researched, or does it only find expression through the expertise of the researcher? The resistance of the powerful to attend to the unmodulated voice of the powerless always invites the academic researcher to willingly, or unwillingly, occupy a mediating role in presenting policy relevant arguments, and why would they do so?

Waisbord's (2013) critique of the role of claims of *professionalism* in journalism, with its attendant claims of expertise, authority and social responsibility, could equally be applied to the 'professional' partners in the construction of the research–funding–policy nexus. At an individual level, each player is enveloped within an institutional environment that accords them legitimate claims to exercise power, underpinned by a shared epistemic framework and behavioural routine that is capable of anaesthetising any serious engagement with reflexive doubt about their competencies and political roles. If, in addition, we add to this context Friedson's (2001) views about the normative status of professionalism as having a 'third logic', that through technical competencies provide services that are socially relevant and beneficial, then we can see the people framed by our analysis here may additionally perceive themselves as being not only 'expert' but also virtuous. As Waisbord (2013, p 126) paraphrases this perspective:

> ... professions cultivate a different logic from the market and state bureaucracy. They aim to represent public interests expressed in the pursuit of health, justice, and safety, goals that are above the narrow considerations of markets and bureaucracies.

This normative claim to virtue and independence can reasonably be seen to be expressed within the mission statements of social science professional bodies, public sector professions, NGOs and university charters. Part of the tacit knowledge of epistemic communities relates not only to their possession of arcane knowledge, but also to the reasons why they should be trusted in the exercise of it – for *the public good*. This carapace of collective virtue may be critical in giving moral weight to the reassurance provided by routine practice within a community of practice, and effectively disarm academics and other engaged professionals from reflexively critiquing their being positioned as mediating the voices of those whose interests they claim to serve.

Thus the issue of voice and claims to 'legitimate' experientially based grounded insight serves to ask harsh questions of the researchers, research fund executives, and those who would speak on behalf of interest groups. As a white male of ambiguous years, it is palpably the case that my career has benefited through my *commitment* to anti-discriminatory/anti-racist politics. I have become a professor with all the privileges that go with that. I have, of course, developed a variety of defensive arguments for this perverse situation, but it nonetheless leaves the organic intellectual BME (black and minority ethnic) person who possesses profound insight into the operation of racisms with a sound basis for questioning my integrity. At the same time, it is not apparent that the recruitment of more BME academics and executives would, of itself, resolve the challenge, since the experience of the BBC, for example, has illustrated how changing the ethnic profile of the workforce may not effectively change the workplace culture. That is a long-term process (Campion, 2005). (Yunis Alam, Chapter Three, this volume, addresses the complex problematic of being a member of a minority ethnic community within the research community.) Who speaks on behalf of whom is, of course, also a well-rehearsed problem in relation to choosing third sector partners for developing policy-relevant research. As already noted above, a tendency to be risk-averse and to choose a safe pair of hands may distort the potential range of players in such partnerships (Alam and Husband, 2011), and this does not address the vexed issue of essentialism in giving legitimacy to specific ethnic identities through working with and through groups who claim to represent them (Anthias and Yuval-Davis, 1993).

University researchers and research fund executives have no easy solution to the challenges they face in addressing the relevance and legitimacy of their research ambitions by embracing a hopefully 'authentic' world of policy and practice outside of their own milieu.

Conclusion

This chapter has not sought to provide an inclusive scholarly review of the academic literature that has explored the tensions between research and its aspirations to have policy relevance. Nor has it attempted an overview of the current state of the contested politics of multiethnic coexistence in contemporary Britain. And the reader doubtless will agree that in that at least it has been remarkably successful. This chapter has sought to echo the experientially based nature of all the contributions to this book. It has attempted to present an account of a deeply felt and honest concern with the current context of research claiming to inform ethnic relations policy in Britain. In fact, the argument has predominantly addressed the generic flaws in the current relationships between research, research funders and the policy milieu, since it is these fundamental disparities between rhetoric and practice that define the bedrock problematic, which is then further skewed by the racialised politics and institutional practices that particularly frame ethnic relations in Britain.

The concerns expressed above, and to be developed further in the chapters that follow, address the claims currently made by university researchers, in terms of their now highly developed institutional rhetoric of relevance and impact, and the contradictory pressures built into the current research environment. The radical changes in the managerial ideology framing university life and the multiple pressures on research funding necessitate a forced period of reflection on the triangular trade in knowledge, funds and influence that is seeking to inform contemporary ethnic relations.

TWO

'Hating to know': government and social policy research in multicultural Australia

Andrew Jakubowicz

Research and community: the academy and the state

A few days before the national election that swept the Australian Labor Party (ALP) from office in September 2013, the conservative opposition parties (known as the 'coalition' because of the Liberal and National Party collaboration agreement) announced that one of their first acts would be to transfer funding from the humanities and social sciences research to 'the hard sciences and medicine' (Briggs, 2013). They proposed that taxpayers should only support useful research, such as treating diabetes. Philosophy, social anthropology, and a raft of other already poorly supported fields would, in future, it was implied, find their funding cut even further. The coalition pledged that climate change, a particular hate-object, would be removed from the list of national research priorities should it win office.

The Australian newspaper (a News Ltd broadsheet that had thrown its weight behind Rupert Murdoch's crusade to end the Labor government) Higher Education section then sought comment, a baited hook to which this author rose (Lane, 2013). I pointed to the contradiction between the incoming government's declaration of support for freedom of speech no matter how offensive, and its desire to constrain what research could be published from grants it would fund. In response, a raft of comments pilloried the social sciences, demanding that taxpayer-supported academics should be shunted off into the real world to make a living. Such antagonism to the social science research community is not new: the first signs of conservative containment of unpopular or confronting social science research outcomes dates back to another change of government in 1976, where a leading sociologist, Jean Martin, had her work on Vietnamese refugees defunded by the incoming Fraser coalition government (Shaver, 2014; see also Encel, 1981).

The return of the Hawke ALP government in 1983 redirected public attention once more towards the potential value of social science research in the creation and evaluation of public policy, although not necessarily in positive ways. The ALP commissioned a review, and then closed down the Australian Institute for Multicultural Affairs (AIMA) (Council of the AIMA, 1983, 1986, pp 7-13, 28-9), a Fraser-era institution under the direction of Petro Georgiou, just previously senior advisor to the Prime Minister, and later to be a Liberal MP. It had been criticised by ALP influentials in the academy and civil society for having a political agenda allied to the more progressive wing of the Liberal Party, an antipathy to anyone with Labor links, and an aggressive mode of interaction manifested most clearly in its director's personal style. Facing rising criticism of inaction over its replacement, the Hawke government then created a Bureau of Immigration Research (later to become the Bureau of Immigration Multicultural and Population Research, BIMPR). In turn, the BIMPR was closed down by the incoming coalition government (BIMPR, 1996) under John Howard in 1996, but this time there was to be no institutional replacement, only a small very policy-focused research group in the Immigration and Ethnic Affairs/Citizenship Department. The Rudd and Gillard Labor governments (coming to national power in 2007 and 2010) left this situation unchanged, with the only sign of their awareness of the issues being a raft of inquiries and advisory bodies advocating for some national research framework around settlement and community relations (Australian Government, 2011; Access and Equity Panel, Australia, 2012; Vamvakinou, 2013a). Yet at the defeat of the second Rudd government in 2013, nothing had been put in place, nor did the incoming government do anything in its first year in office.

Despite its perceived bias, AIMA had done one crucial thing: it had instigated a process of interaction and communication among and between its diverse stakeholder groups – from government, through academe, large not-for-profit organisations, and the emergent ethnic sector. While there had been a small social science research community generated by the imperatives of the Department of Immigration's recruitment and settlement programme, it was really with the advent of the first modern Labor government after 1972 that the relation between the academy and the state seriously expanded, soon to be caught up in ideological and partisan arguments over the type, value and use of social science knowledge. The five decades of relationships that have followed the initial recognition of cultural diversity as a feature of public life in Australia have been marked by a volatile fluctuation in the closeness and impact of research, and the trust or mistrust by government of the academy.

Ground rules

While there had been a small but important group of researchers concerned with immigration and settlement from the advent of the postwar immigration programme (demographers, sociologists, psychologists and social anthropologists; see Borrie, 1975), the first sustained government research into the social and political impact of the 'migrant presence', as it became known, was initiated by Liberal Immigration Minister Billie Snedden in the dying days of the White Australia policy. Snedden's Department of Immigration, well known as a bastion of conservative and assimilationist ideology, was required by the Minister to report on the number, extent and operation of 'national groups'. Jim Houston, a bi-lingual francophone ex-teacher, was assigned to the task in 1968, and began to tour Australia tracking down, documenting and writing up the governance and activities of over a thousand of what would today be described as ethnic community organisations. While Houston's report was finished some years before publication (National Groups Unit, Department of Labor and Immigration, 1974), it created in the mind of the bureaucracy and among politicians aware of its existence an increasing realisation of the size and potential influence of the migrant groups. In 1973 Houston was approached by recently appointed ALP Immigration Minister Al Grassby, to prepare a working paper on settlement issues and policy; reporting directly to Grassby and by-passing the Department, Houston produced a game-changing paper, the first to foreground the idea of Australia as a multicultural society (Grassby, 1973). Grassby as a political figure would become inextricably tied to this concept, and its explicit goal of recognising and including ethnic communities in the ongoing conversation about the Australian nation.

The first main social policy research report that *inter alia* considered 'migrants' produced for an Australian government, the Commission of Inquiry into Poverty, was chaired by a Melbourne economics professor, Ronald Henderson, and initiated in the dying days of the long duree coalition government (1949-72). These studies were not ultimately published until the end of the Whitlam government period in 1975 (Henderson, 1975), although they encapsulated the welfare reform agenda that had driven the establishment of the Inquiry in its full form.

Henderson (1975) found that when the cost of housing was taken into account, recently arrived migrant household units had a one in eight likelihood of falling below the poverty line. For an immigration programme that had long been lauded as a fool-proof means of introducing fairly low-cost labour into the economy, such revelations supported emerging arguments about the role of migration in facilitating a dual labour market, one characterised by ethnic background and English language skills (see Collins, 1988). Henderson referred to the pattern of systematic exclusion and endless self-exploitation of parents and children that typified the life experiences of poorer non-English-speaking background immigrants. Thus, by 1975, the government was aware of the role that research could play in uncovering social issues that might well lie below the everyday concerns of the public service, even though such research could present the political leaders with challenges that would appear difficult to address, let alone resolve. The value lay in the role of research as an early alert mechanism, allowing time to develop and implement policies that might otherwise be overwhelmed by suddenly emerging crises. However, despite such potential benefits, such research and the research communities around its production were often viewed by both the bureaucracy and the politicians as too risky and uncontrollable.

Jean Martin, the migrant presence, and the first Vietnamese refugees

A useful example of the dynamics that emerged as a more sophisticated perspective on immigrant settlement was unearthed through the lens of social science research that came through the work of Dr Jean Martin. Martin had been researching into immigrant settlement since the 1950s, and was well established as a key figure by the mid-1970s. Her research work for the Henderson inquiry on the question of immigrant poverty was used to frame the report's findings and recommendations, while her main monograph in the field, *The migrant presence* (1978), remaining after nearly four decades a ground-breaking and germinal work in the field, drew on her research for the Australian Population and Immigration Council (Borrie, 1975). Dr Sheila Shaver has used archival records to explore exactly how one of the most important pieces of Martin's research, on the first Vietnamese refugees to arrive in Australia in mid-1975, came 'unstuck' (Shaver, 2014: forthcoming). Martin was invited by the Prime Minister, through the head of the Immigration Department, Dr Peter Wilenski, to carry out the work as an independent piece of sociological research. However, even though the work began and some funds were provided, the crisis that led to the dismissal of the Whitlam government swamped any attempt to regularise and embed the research in an acceptable format. The Fraser coalition government was elected in December 1975, and as one of its first acts, Martin's research funding was terminated by Cabinet in February 1976. While some of this work on the Vietnamese refugees was published in reports of government inquiries, her death in 1979 closed things off, and she was the last scholar to work under the aegis of the postwar immigration project of the Australian Social Science Research Council (now the Academy for Social Sciences in Australia). Her project was picked up by one of her students, Frank Lewins, who produced *The first wave* (1985, with J. Ly). The close relationships of an inner circle of researchers working with the public service changed dramatically with the Fraser government, and a level of suspicion began to grow affecting both sides of the relationship. As Shaver has argued, in terminating Martin's research, the government closed itself off from a key capacity to foresee and intervene in social problems that would escalate over the coming years. It was not that they didn't want to know; it's more, it seems, that they didn't want a relationship where the researcher had autonomy over the research outcome. The control over publication of research would, from that point on, be one of the most significant contested and conflictual parameters of the research relationship between government and the academy.

Researching social change: an author's personal perspective

While 'public sociology' has recently found a central stage in debates about scholarship and politics, driven by Michael Burawoy's presidency of the American Sociological Association (Burawoy, 2006), I have been a minor advocate of an engaged social science since writing my PhD about urban change, ethnic and class subcultures, and social movement in Sydney during the 1970s, applying methodologies then that included participant observation, action research, policy engagement and social organising. My first policy-oriented research was for the Poverty and Law division of the Poverty Inquiry, producing the first Australian study of migrants and the law (Jakubowicz and Buckley, 1975). The Poverty Inquiry ignited a community of scholars around real issues of social knowledge and social justice, providing resources, information and data, and generating an imperative that we engage with each other, and with the communities and agencies about whom we were researching. It was during that period that my PhD research fed my involvement in two government advisory bodies, the Migrant Task Force (Migrant Task Force Committee, NSW, 1973), which was Grassby's attempt to re-orient migration settlement policy and programmes away from its assimilationist and White Australia recent history, and the National Drug Advisory Council, where Attorney General Lionel Murphy was looking for alternatives to the punitive pursuit of marijuana smokers and the gaoling of heroin users. The Migrant Task Force provided the basic ideas for what would become the policy of multiculturalism under the succeeding government, especially through the Federal Government's Inquiry into Post-arrival Services for Migrants and their Families, chaired by Melbourne barrister Frank Galbally, and often referred to as the Galbally Report (1978).

During the mid to late 1970s I was employed by Professor Hilary Rose at Bradford University in England, a place I had washed up in after following the then 'hippie road' from Australia through Asia and Europe. She planned to set up a city/university agency, a social action centre, where the students and scholars from Applied Social Studies could work with the communities of one of the most culturally diverse and disadvantaged cities in the UK. While the fraught urban politics of Bradford at the time made the exercise somewhat explosive, the organisation was established and continued for many years. One of my most valuable experiences was the research undertaken by the Leeds Political Economy Group, especially the action research on industrial change driven by Dr Ron Wiener that underpinned the creation of the Trade Union Research and Information Centre in Leeds (TUCRIC) (Wiener, 2002).

I was privileged to work with Wiener and a group of industrial shop stewards who were part of a University of Leeds adult education class. The task was to track changes in work arrangements, changes in technology and industrial struggles, as a way of predicting likely changes by management in the operation of plants, thus providing forewarning of potential industrial closedowns and redundancies. We were to operationalise theories of labour process transformations into the real world, and through this, empower employees to gain greater purchase over their workplaces and help them bargain more effectively with employers. This experience helped me to understand how systematic research was critical to improving the opportunities for more marginalised and vulnerable social groups, not only by giving them 'arguments' to muster against authority ('speaking truth to power'), but also by increasing their own sense of how important their everyday experience was as the basis for knowledge.

Back in Australia in 1979, my job was to develop the Centre for Multicultural Studies (CMS) at the University of Wollongong. Wollongong is an industrial steel town about 50 miles south of Sydney, with a large working-class migrant population, and a very limited and diminishing set of job opportunities for women. The city was facing a series of significant transformations brought on by the acceleration of globalisation. Women's traditional employment in clothing and textiles, no longer protected by tariffs, was moving offshore; the residual clothing industry was based on domestically produced piecework, known as 'outwork' (elsewhere as 'piecework'). The industry was poorly paid, badly regulated, dangerous and highly exploitative. Some women had tried unsuccessfully initially, to get work as 'steel workers' at the steel works, leading to an ultimately successful 'Jobs for Women Campaign' (SBS Television, 1984, 1994).

Meanwhile the steel works was undergoing major changes in technologies of production, creating significant job losses exacerbated by product dumping by importers and international low-wage competition. These class and gender dimension of change were further complicated by a sudden 'racialisation' of the city generated by the inflow of Vietnamese workers produced by the end of 'White Australia' and the refugee intake in the wake of the end of the Vietnam War. Racist groups were flourishing, and existing European immigrant groups were not necessarily as comfortable with Asian migration as they had been with each other. The university centre would play a leading role in the creation of the community-based Illawarra Migrant Resource Centre (IMRC), an agency funded under a Commonwealth programme recommended by the Galbally Report.

Research projects included one on outwork in conjunction with the IMRC, which had identified the crisis in women's employment as a first priority. The project tracked the workflow associated with outwork, from the source (usually a major clothing brand in Sydney) through the middlemen to the outworker. At the time, outworkers were judged as 'self-employed', and were harassed by trade unions, and abandoned by health and safety officials. However, in a move 'outside the square', the IMRC, with the CMS, came across an injured outworker suffering from overuse injuries, brought on by very stressed working conditions, and poor ergonomics. A case was taken to the Workers' Compensation tribunal; the evidence demonstrated that this outworker met all the conditions of being an employee, only that she worked at home. She had no control over the labour process, the price she was paid, or the conditions of employment. The Court found that she was effectively employed by the middleman on behalf of the brand company, and they had responsibility for her safety and injuries. Within a year or so the trade unions had changed their position on outworkers, and began to recruit them as members and argue for improving their conditions of work.

This series of experiences reinforced my sense that collaborative research with communities would produce higher-quality knowledge than research that was distanced from the people on whom it was focused. Through the 1980s I worked on a number of projects that sought to use social science methodologies to bring social 'realities' to the awareness of policymakers. One of these, 'Equal Disappointment Opportunity' (Meekosha and Jakubowicz, 1987), provoked a considerable reaction from the Department of Community Services, even though the minister at the time, Senator Don Grimes, was most supportive. The tension focused on a complete disagreement over the nature of the research problem: the Department was under pressure to adapt to the cultural diversity of Australia's ethnic communities, by this time very much more influenced by the tens of thousands of Indo-Chinese who had arrived under the orderly departure programmes of the previous six or seven years. The Department had developed a raft of programmes covering everything from children's services to aged care, and felt that the programmes were fine, but the ethnic communities either did not understand them or were not willing to use them, that is, there was a 'migrant problem' that lay in their cultures and required cultural change among the potential clients. Our research, on the other hand, pointed to the distance between what was provided, and the needs as articulated to us by our community research partners. Furthermore, there was evidence of structural racism, where procedures that awarded access to services were biased in favour of majority culture clients. The situation was not improved by an atmosphere of funding crisis where the government, in its 1986 Budget, forced departments to reduce expenditure, such that across the board the major service departments all sacrificed their programmes for minority ethnic groups as their first action. The report's title came from an interview with a senior public servant, who proclaimed the best that could be hoped for between majority and minority community people seeking access would be 'equal disappointment opportunity'. As part of our research contract required the Department to agree that the report could be distributed to everyone who participated in the research, public pressure from community organisations finally forced its release. The Department refused to endorse the report or act on its findings. The impact of the research was difficult to assess; many of the evidence-based arguments we made did trickle through the system, and they had purchase for some years over practice.

Within a short time any corporate memory of the report, its context and its implications faded, especially as Department structures changed. Within two years (when commissioned for another project on assisted accommodation) we were unable to find any officer within the assisted accommodation area of the Department who had any awareness of the report, despite its detailed documentation of accommodation assistance priorities for ethnic communities (Chesterman, 1988). Moreover, many of the issues that we raised were still unresolved nearly 30 years later, remaining on the agenda of lobby groups seeking to advance services for cultural minorities (Milgiorino, 2013).

Facilitation and destruction of communities of knowledge

The early investment in research under the Whitlam government, especially through the Poverty Inquiry, produced a base line of data about the relationships between various parameters of inequality, including social class, gender, disability and ethnicity, and the challenges for social policy of these often-hidden dimensions. Such insights also fed the growth of a more engaged social policy environment, one that sought to empower communities through recognition of both the shared and the specific dimensions of need. The Australian Assistance Plan (1974) and a new Cities programme (1975) brought together many of these dimensions with a geographical awareness of the concentrated and overlapping effects of disadvantage in specific localities. In this they reflected Australian versions of the initiatives developed under targeted urban programmes in the US and Canada, and in the Community Development Project in the UK. The interaction of government, the academy, and civil society organisations with local communities produced some of the first modern community organisations. Thus, in New South Wales (NSW), the Western Sydney Regional Council for Social Development, an agency sponsored under the Australian Assistance Plan of the Whitlam government, would be one of the first to espouse the importance of community development and leadership facilitation among ethnic groups, feeding the process that created the Ethnic Communities' Council of NSW in 1975, and then the state government's own Ethnic Affairs Commission in 1976 (to be relabelled after 2000 as the Community Relations Commission for a Multicultural NSW).

While conservative governments seem to have the greater suspicion of social science research (as exhibited by each incoming conservative government in Australia in 1975, 1996 and 2013), the Labor Party has had its own tussles with the field. Social science (apart from economics and demography) as a set of research practices seems to require a quite high-level 'product champion' in order to gain a place at the policy table. Shaver (2014) demonstrates the key role of Prime Minister Whitlam's ex-adviser Dr Peter Wilenski as Head of the Immigration Department in securing Dr Jean Martin's place; as soon as Wilenski was removed, Martin's support in the bureaucracy died.

Under the Fraser government (1975-83) which had sent Martin packing, Fraser's adviser, Petro Georgiou, a political scientist, drove the agenda for the Galbally Committee, and was then appointed to head AIMA. Fraser's defeat in 1983, by Bob Hawke, was followed by Georgiou's departure from AIMA, a review of the Institute in 1983 by a team of ALP appointees (including social scientists) (Committee of Review of AIMA, 1983) and its closure in a scorched earth ethno-cleansing during the 1986 'horror' Budget. The Fraser/Georgiou/Galbally trio had been particularly innovative in the field of ethnic and multicultural affairs. Labor, on the other hand, while not antagonistic to multiculturalism, had no significant product champions, although the Shadow Minister Mick Young and his adviser Ursula Doyle would play key roles in sustaining the bi-partisan milieu during the early period of the Hawke government.

However, faced with a demand from their Prime Minister to cut back expenditure, every minister turned to their newly instituted ethnic priorities as a source of savings. This context saw AIMA closed, the Special Broadcasting Service (SBS) almost amalgamated into the Australian Broadcasting Corporation (ABC), and swingeing cuts in welfare and education. The widespread negative reaction to the 1986 Budget debacle forced the government to reconsider its direction on research, producing two new agencies – a Bureau of Immigration (1989), Multicultural (1994) and Population Research (1995) in Immigration (BIMPR, 1996) and an Office for Multicultural Affairs (OMA) (1989) within the Department of Prime Minister and Cabinet. The Bureau would hold regular conferences, initiate its own research, and contract researchers to produce a broad range of policy-related and wider social research. OMA would in parallel also contract specific policy research associated with government priorities. At the time this did not seem to be confusing, as the types of work tended to be rather different. For instance, the Bureau was more concerned with population and immigration issues (multiculturalism was a later addition to its brief), while OMA explored attitudes and values associated with multiculturalism, and how key agencies of the multicultural project were performing (for example, SBS or the media more widely).

Besides providing new resources to support academic research, and generating a wide range of publicly accessible data and studies, both the agencies contributed to a flourishing of knowledge, debate and argument around issues associated with immigration, settlement and diversity. If we take the growth in the community of policy-responsive social science in relation to cultural diversity, to begin in the early 1970s and fluctuate though build through the period until 1996, the election of the Howard government in that year marked a serious braking of the momentum.

In the name of financial prudence, but in fact as the sharp end of an ideological attack on multiculturalism, the 1996 coalition government began to terminate a number of Hawke and Keating era initiatives. Office of Multicultural Affairs was closed, and the very limited (and now ideologically suspect) multicultural affairs area moved back *in toto* to Immigration, with its research role also truncated. The Bureau was also closed, and its remaining acceptable research transferred back to the departmental structure of Immigration. The impact of this latter move can be deduced from two key documents, one being the last list of Bureau publications, the other being the slightly defensive tone of the following year's annual report from the Department.

The final BIMPR projects and publications list appeared in its last Bulletin (August 1996). Key 'new projects' included a study of how poverty had changed in Australia from 1975 to 1996, led by the recently departed director of BIMPR, Dr John Nieuwenhuysen, in his new role as chief executive officer of the Committee for the Economic Development of Australia. There would also be studies of the impact of immigration on Australian cities, the initial labour market experiences of immigrants and other projects drawing on the first wave of the Longitudinal Survey of Immigrants to Australia (LSIA), the only real BIMPR initiative to long survive the agency's demise. The Bureau also supported the first study of black African settlement, signalling the arrival in Australia of humanitarian settlers from the Sudan, and an assessment of 20 years of the Galbally reforms to migrant welfare on civil society.

Projects that were well underway when the Bureau was closed included a 1996 census atlas, a second encyclopaedia of the Australian people, a survey of population issues, a century of photographs of immigration, and an exploration of citizenship and national identity. Work was being supported on Muslim women, homelessness among Indochinese youth, the ethnicity of immigrants, and the first major study on religion and immigration. There were dozens of other research projects in the field, illustrating the efflorescence of intellectual curiosity and the energetic engagement with a multiplicity of dimensions of social change, and the vigorous excitement of a multicultural society two decades in from its first acknowledgement as such. One major contribution supported by the Bureau was the publication in the pre-internet era of a series of commissioned bibliographies, ensuring the widest possible circulation of research that addressed social issues. Central to the concerns of the Bureau were the position and experience of immigrant women – in terms of health, employment and participation. In all, some 21 pages of projects are reported, and hundreds of publications had been supported, as listed on the 'Making Multicultural Australia' site. The tap, however, was turned off very quickly.

The 1996-97 Annual Report of the Department of Immigration and Multicultural Affairs, under its sub-programme on Research and Statistics, noted the demise of the BIMPR:

> Most activity focused on managing and producing research reports commissioned by the former Bureau of Immigration, Multicultural and Population Research (the Branch continues much of the core work formerly undertaken by the Bureau, whose Melbourne office formally closed on 15 November 1996); ongoing management of the Longitudinal Survey of Immigrants to Australia (LSIA) and the release of associated information; production of a range of statistical publications and services; provision of library services; and the development of a Business Plan to produce a more focused strategy for better meeting portfolio research and statistics needs. (DIMA, 1997)

There was no definition of what might be core, and what 'non-core', although the Department went on to note, under the heading '(i) Needs of the Minister and the Portfolio', that:

> The LSIA remained the central research activity of the Portfolio. It is designed to provide reliable data for Commonwealth and other agencies to monitor and evaluate immigration and settlement policies, programs and services, and to provide a basis for the development of future policies....

It is the most comprehensive survey of immigrants undertaken and, because of its longitudinal methodology, it avoids many of the pitfalls and potential allegations of speculative or unsubstantiated research findings that haunt many research endeavours....

While no new research was commissioned, the number of research reports published surpassed by 20 per cent the number published during BIMPR's final year of operation. This increase was achieved through a combination of the special efforts of staff and the adoption of in-house editing and advanced digital publishing technology. This has also resulted in necessary cost savings.

The sub-programme finalised and published 42 research reports and initiated a new internal bidding round for research proposals for 1997-98. It also sought to enter into research partnerships with several external agencies to access other research funds that may be available from non-portfolio sources.

The closure of BIMPR resulted in a rationalisation of the Department's library services and a refocusing of its core activities to meet the portfolio's information needs...

The Business Plan has better positioned the sub-programme both to conduct a more targeted research programme in 1997-98 and to provide relevant, accurate and timely statistical data and other information to meet client needs.

The main impact of the closure was to significantly constrain the range of research and the types of issues. While there was a last spurt of material released from the end of the Labor period, thereafter the research function of the Department (its name would drop the Multicultural component in 2006 to be replaced by Citizenship) would contract and lose its overarching concern for the social justice questions that had driven a key dimension of the Bureau era. The research population in the academy would also decline significantly over the following years, its communal networks fragmented, and research funding withdrawn. The government would also restrict the flow of information, and tie research ever more closely to the priorities of the Department in meeting the coalition's agenda. Social justice was not part of the coalition lexicon, although concern about social cohesion definitely was.

Theorising harmony

At the 1996 election that returned the coalition, one of the issues was the rising rhetoric about national identity, the racial make-up of Australia, and the question of racism. Added impetus for this debate had been contributed by Pauline Hanson, a pre-selected Liberal candidate in Queensland, whom Howard had to dis-endorse after she made some significant comments that were widely seen as racist. Hanson went on to win her seat as an independent, and enter the Federal Parliament. She then established her own political party, One Nation, which was successful in the 1998 Queensland state election to the degree that the coalition lost power there, and the ALP was returned on One Nation preferences.[1]

Prior to the election, the Commonwealth Senate (in an alliance between libertarian and coalition forces) had rejected government attempts to criminalise race hate speech, with the coalition committing itself to a pathway of 'education'. Following its victory, the coalition commissioned a market research firm to survey Australian attitudes to cultural diversity, and to propose strategies as to how issues of racism might be addressed. The research was completed in 1997, and on the back of its findings and recommendations the government announced the Living in Harmony programme, with the key component being Harmony Day (elsewhere in the world known as the International Day for the Elimination of All Forms of Racial Discrimination). Unlike other research commissioned by the Commonwealth in the past, and published for public access, the research reports were locked away under orders of the Prime Minister, under rules of Cabinet secrecy.

Why was this research, on which a programme that would last for over 15 years would be based, apparently so dangerous? For 13 years I tried to find out, requesting from minister after minister and parliamentary secretary after parliamentary secretary access to the data. At the time, those of us interested surmised that the research would reveal rather too high a level of support for the perspective advanced by Hanson, against whom Howard was running a wrecking campaign steered by one of his then junior ministers Tony Abbott, who, by late 2013, would be Prime Minister of Australia. Despite approaches and Freedom of Information (FOI) requests from journalists, the reports

---

[1]   Unlike the UK, where each MP is elected 'first past the post', many Australian jurisdictions allow some form of preferential voting, which sees the lower supported candidates having their votes redistributed until one candidate receives 50 per cent +1 of the formal votes cast. Preferences prove crucial to most election outcomes.

were never released. Then, in 2011, the Labor Attorney General Robert McClelland arranged for the normal government strategy on information (keep it locked up unless it has to be released) to be reversed (make it available unless it has to be kept confidential) (OAIC, 2013). Soon afterwards, a Department official indicated that I might like to try again with a FOI request: this time it worked. I received the research reports, minus the research brief and the survey schedule, then, after a further FOI, the implementation strategy and documents associated with the launch of the Living in Harmony programme, including a slightly weird 1998 launch video which sought to encapsulate the research findings (DIAC, 1998/2012).

Announcing the commencement of the research in 1996, the new Immigration Minister Phillip Ruddock said "Australia has been fortunate to be comparatively free of the more virulent forms of racism ... we cannot afford to be complacent.... Increasing community awareness through community education is our best viable long-term approach" (20 August 1996). With that statement Ruddock pre-empted the findings of the research, and guaranteed that whatever anti-racism strategy might emerge would not step outside the confines of his 'education' template. The findings of the research are important for two reasons – first, to identify why a conservative government might find them so threatening that they would need to be locked away prospectively for 30 years, and second, to identify how governments might want to limit the dissemination of information about society as part of their strategy of political control. Essentially the coalition leadership had a number of problems: its lack of firm action at that point on Hanson's more outrageous statements was increasingly painting it with a similar brush, especially in international media reporting; it was anxious to invalidate any allegations by its political opponents that racism lay deep in the heart of Australian conservatism; and it did not want to legitimise more extreme right-wing claims that Hanson's attitudes were 'mainstream'. At the same time, they were appropriating some of her policies to try to win back conservative voters who had drifted further to the right.

Eureka Research, the research company used by the government, found in its qualitative focus groups and quantitative survey work (Jakubowicz, 2011) that the majority of their respondents were at the very least mildly racist or prejudiced, with a significant minority strongly so. Indeed, the company reported that it had great difficulty in forming enough focus groups of people who were not prejudiced to balance the overwhelming numbers who were. The broad aim of the research was 'to explore and understand the subtleties and nature of racism in the Australia of the late 1990s with a view to mounting an effective mass media and/or education anti-racism campaign.' The campaign would have to fit in with the coalition's vision of Australia 'as a country whose people are united by the common cause of commitment to Australia'. The first student of this vision, Hanson, quickly dubbed her movement 'One Nation'. The research would seek to discover whether there were indeed core common Australian values that could serve as the 'central unifying message' promoting tolerance and diminishing racist attitudes and behaviour. However, what it found apparently so shocked the government of the day that the report was declared too dangerous for release to the Australian people whose attitudes it had investigated and who had paid for its surveys and conclusions.

The research sought to identify what values Australians actually shared, what they knew and understood about these values, and their awareness of the benefits of shared values. It also examined what people thought might be the personal and social costs of racism, what people thought racism was, and how it was manifested. Specifically, what should such a campaign be called? What definition of racism would work for different people? The qualitative research undertaken through some 30 focus groups would determine the likely causes of contemporary racism, its focus, and how effective different messages might potentially be in reducing racist sentiments, and thereby racist behaviour (or the reverse – reducing the behaviour and thus modifying the sentiments). The focus groups comprised about one-third 'positive' ('short social distance' from other groups), and the remainder 'negatives' ('long social distance'), and were designed to place like with like to elicit the confident expression of 'socially undesirable attitudes'.

The first qualitative report concluded that there was 'a clear need for an anti-racism campaign' (Jakubowicz, 2011, p 59). Moreover, the research uncovered a crisis in what it meant to be 'an Australian'. The consultants argued that the crisis, stirred and debated in the context of Hansonism, actually provided a rare opportunity to reaffirm Australian core values through defining them: that is, through asserting that being Australian meant accepting diversity, and that such values were in fact widely held by Australians, whatever their national origin. (The Australian Citizenship Council was then commissioned to carry out national consultations to determine what these core values might be.)

The study had determined that many Australians were deeply insecure about what was happening to the country, and it was this anxiety that rendered the questions of values and identity so salient and intense for so many people. If Australians in general could be assured both that core values of acceptance existed, and that they were widely shared, the insecurity (which was widespread in Anglo and non-Anglo groups, and often reflected concerns they had about each other) might be ameliorated, and a stronger sense of Australia as a non-racist and diverse community 'of which we can all be proud' might be fashioned, 'to the benefit of harmonious community relations for decades to come'. Thus the underlying issue became, how do we strategise to reduce anxiety about difference?

Ultimately none of the data nor the findings and recommendations was released for wider public scrutiny, nor was its methodology or analysis tested in any scientific literature. Nevertheless, the key finding of the research, which was advice not to mention racism and to stress Harmony, did become the core logic of community relations strategies from that moment on. Thus the government policy that followed avoided issues of racial discrimination, denied that Australia was a 'racist society', ignored issues of minority rights, and concentrated on building harmonious and tolerant relations between groups. This approach survived the anti-terrorism panic after 11 September 2001, the bombings of Australian tourists and others in Bali in 2002, the London transport bombings of 2005, and the summer riot in Cronulla in Sydney in 2005.

However, the general focus on wider community relations began to tighten in the face of these global events, towards a specific concern with the behaviour of Muslims. By 2006 the Howard government moved most of research funding associated with the Harmony project to focus on Australia's Muslim communities, under the so-called National Action Plan. Through the 11 years of the coalition rule the level of public knowledge about diversity, which had been so remarkably expanded through the work of the BIMPR, was reduced to dependence on a small trickle of uncontroversial research reports, many of which were only released (if at all) after they had been cleansed of any elements that might elicit adverse public comment.

Social inclusion and social research[2]

The long years of conservative control of information about diversity has really only been relieved through the work of a small group of socially committed scholars. The suppression of the Eureka reports had been one trigger for the focus by a Sydney social geographer, Kevin Dunn, on quantifying racism in Australia. He had received

---

[2] For a more extended discussion of social inclusion during the Rudd period, see Boese and Phillips (2011). For a recent summary of research on minority youth and social inclusion see Jakubowicz et al (2014).

some support for his work on Islamophobia and local government from the tail-end resource of the BIMPR; however, he was to depend on Australian Research Council support for his major studies, with another geographer, Jim Forrest, of the extent and location of racism, and its socioeconomic and attitudinal correlates. They managed to bring together critical social theory about racism with systematic surveys based on matching census profiles. By the return of the Labor Party to government in 2007, the Forrest and Dunn studies (2006a, 2006b) were effectively the only large-scale survey-based empirical work in the public realm. One of the key areas of concern for the new government was the problem of social exclusion, and its implicit response in policy, 'social inclusion'. The social inclusion discourse was imported from North America and the New Labour period in the UK. A Social Inclusion Board was asked to develop criteria for social inclusion, and to report on the extent and nature of social exclusion.

The first Board report of 2008[3] made no mention of issues of ethnicity or racism, understandably as it drew on existing government statistics and research, none of which had explored this territory for over a decade. The next report (Australian Social Inclusion Board, 2012) responded to widespread criticism of this failure by drawing on Forrest and Dunn's work, but was able to make little policy sense of the data and findings. The Board, and indeed much of the government's research infrastructure, had been stripped of any capacity to consider questions of ethnicity, culture, migration and refugee status, or experiences of racism, as issues requiring some considered and collective response.

The former government's Multicultural Advisory Council had lapsed in 2006, and was not re-invigorated by the new government until 2008. The Labor Minister gave the Council a brief to prepare a report on multicultural issues and suggest directions for development. The report, *The people of Australia*, recommended that a research capacity be re-established (Australia, Government of, 2011). It was not until early 2011 that the government, now dependent on the Greens for parliamentary support, released its response, and accepted that something would need to be done on the research question, flicking it to the now re-named Australian Multicultural Council (AMC) (created in August 2011) to define. The AMC had done nothing on this issue (for which it was given no resources) by the re-election of the coalition in September 2013.

---

[3]   The closing of the Board has removed its reports from easy access, but see Australian Social Inclusion Board (2009).

Meanwhile two other review reports surfaced, one following on from *The people of Australia,* on access and equity in government services (Access and Equity Inquiry Panel, 2012), the other a joint parliamentary report, *Inquiry into migration and multiculturalism in Australia* (Vamvakinou, 2013a). Access and equity had been introduced as a policy framework and government institutional set of practices in 1984 by the then ALP Immigration Minister Chris Hurford, to refocus policy on the disadvantage experienced by immigrants seeking employment in and services from the national government; it had waxed and waned in effectiveness over the decades. By 2010 it had become routinised and secured little purchase on the activities of government departments. The Access and Equity Review recommended that:

> 19. That the Australian Government consider adequacy of current provision for research, including national research priorities, on the practical outcomes of the migration program. This assessment should particularly include research on interactions between the Australian Government and Access and Equity target groups and interactions with temporary entrants. (Access and Equity Panel, Australia, 2012)

The government response to the review produced in March 2013 reflected an increasing awareness of the wider issues for social science research that could underpin robust policy. It supported the review recommendation, and added:

> Australian government departments are considering key challenges in incorporating social science research and evidence into policy development and the government's future research priorities for policy. The Australian Government is considering a National Research Investment Plan which provides a strategic framework and a set of principles to guide the government's investment in research. The Plan aims to ensure Australia has the capacity to conduct research in areas of national priority and provides advice on the future role of the national research priorities. In addition, the Department of Immigration and Citizenship has an annual program of research into the practical outcomes of the migration program. It is set each year to address priority issues, data, research, evaluation and analytical gaps to inform the work of the department. All

relevant research produced by agencies is to be referred to in Agency Multicultural Plans. (Australian Government, 2013)

Meanwhile, the parliamentary report argued a stronger line about the effects of the failure of policy to adequately support and communicate research that might help the migration settlement process to be more successful. In summary it concluded,

> The reduction in national research capacity has had a significant impact on the ability of agencies to deliver, monitor and evaluate their efforts. The absence of qualitative research also hampered the work of the Committee. As such, rebuilding research capacity is a priority to ensure policy and programs are well informed, tailored and effective. (Vamvakinou, 2013a, p 10)

One of the Committee's chapters focused on research and multiculturalism, opening with the reflection that:

> The Committee heard from a number of sources about the challenge of accessing useful data across a whole range of issues. Advocates of research included academics of world standing, state government bodies, and even the Prime Minister's office, which complained that its Social Inclusion policy couldn't function effectively because data was so poor. (Vamvakinou, 2013a)[4]

Submissions expressed concern about the decline in research capacity, especially qualitative research relating to immigration, cultural diversity, and settlement participation in employment outcomes (Chapter 7).

The Committee then reported to the director of the Community Development Division of the Department of Prime Minister and Cabinet, and to the director of the Australian Population and Migration Research Centre, both expressing concern about the lack of research capacity and findings, and the latter noting an undermining of research since the closure of BIMPR. The Committee supported the Access and Equity Review recommendation, and included some additional ideas:

---

[4]   Hundreds of detailed submissions (some of them racist and anti-immigrant) are at Vamvakinou (2013a) Appendices A and B.

Recommendation 14 at 7.31: The Committee recommends increased collection, by the Australian Government, of accurate and up-to-date disaggregated data in order to identify trends in migration and multiculturalism, and to measure and address CALD [culturally and linguistically diverse] related disadvantage.

Recommendation 15 at 7.32: The Committee recommends the establishment of a government funded, independent collaborative institute for excellence in research into multicultural affairs with functions similar to that of the former Bureau of Immigration, Multicultural and Population Research.

The institute should have a statutory framework articulating key principles of multiculturalism, functions in research and advice to government, and a cross sectoral independent board.

This institute should actively engage with local communities, private business and non-government organisations and provide data for better informed policy.

The qualitative and quantitative research capabilities of the institute must enable up-to-date and easily accessible data and research analysis on social and multicultural trends.

More dedicated research into long-term migration trends occurring within Australia and the social effects of migration – such as the local impacts of migration on cultural diversity and social inclusion within Australian society – should be supported.

The Committee particularly recommends an increased emphasis on qualitative data collection.

Recommendation 16 at 7.33: The Committee recommends the Department of Immigration and Citizenship collect data to support research to collect data on secondary migration in order to better drive services to where needs exist. (Vamvakinou, 2013a, pp129-30)

Recommendation 17 at 8.40: The Committee recommends that the Australian Government undertake greater qualitative and quantitative research on Australian expatriates, and diaspora communities settled in Australia to better inform Government policy. The Committee recommends that such research should be carried out by an independent research institute in collaboration with business councils, chambers of commerce and community groups. This research could be undertaken by the previously proposed independent collaborative institute for research into multicultural affairs. (Vamvakinou, 2013a, pp140)

The Committee's final report was released in March 2013 to an already heated pre-election context, where the financial profligacy of the Labor government was a major target of the Opposition's campaign. So while the Opposition members and senators on the Committee supported all these recommendations, they did so with this proviso:

> Coalition Members and Senators support ... these recommendations in principle, but are mindful that the recommendations would involve the expenditure of new funds. Coalition Members and Senators consider that these recommendations ought only to be implemented if it can be undertaken within existing budgetary parameters. (Vamvakinou, 2013a, p 249)

The re-election of the coalition in September 2013 brought with it the expected but uncompromising negative attitudes to social policy and research. Its Wastewatch Committee targeted social science and humanities grants by the Australian Research Council (ARC) as 'not a good spend of Australia taxpayer money' (ABC News, 2013). It was reported that the ARC was set to lose AU$103 million over four years, mostly from the humanities and social sciences, with money redirected to medical research. It is worth considering the implications of such a move. The projected spend for new projects funded by the ARC for 2013 in 2012 provides some idea of the likely impact. In the Social Behavioural and Economic Sciences panel, some AU$43 million had been committed over three years, in Humanities and Creative Arts about AU$32 million. On a rough basis that is about AU$25 million pa; the proclaimed cuts would break down to about AU$25 million pa. That would mean, should the cuts eventuate after the rhetorical impact had lessened, there would be no support for any new humanities or social science research. Given the comments in the reports above on the dire state of research within and sponsored by government, and the current dependence of scholars on the ARC for any research that addresses cultural diversity and social justice, the consequences would be serious.

While people working in universities may find this an extreme expression of conservative ideology, there are wider social consequences.

A society without knowledge about itself is likely to discover all too late the impact of social inequalities and conflicts that could well have been anticipated and averted, were there the knowledge available to do so. Yet to ensure that ignorance would be its preferred pathway to bliss, one of the first decisions of the incoming government was to close down the Social Inclusion Board; with its closure disappeared its difficulty in defining the cultural diversity dimensions of disadvantage. No other institutions of government would be interested to do so.

Conclusion

Australia, a colonial settler society with a significant and unresolved set of tensions between immigrants and their descendants on the one hand, and indigenous peoples and their descendants on the other, has demonstrated two trajectories of understanding the role of research in the operation of its multicultural democracy. They reflect the two contending master narratives that underpin the unresolved tensions over Australia's colonial and post-colonial history. The dominant narrative casts the development of Australia as the triumph of civilisation over nature, of European and especially that fortuitous amalgam of Christian and British genius over primitivism, and of technology and capitalism over self-absorbed and archaic tribalism. The counter-narrative explores the specific colonial and racialised history of Australia, foregrounding the role of the British Empire and its particular forms of colonial exploitation, its development of categories of acceptable and unacceptable subjects, and the role of the Australian national state after 1901 in constructing its own new imperial project. These competing narratives have become intertwined in what have been described variously as the culture[5] or history wars, which play out in how the national state addresses its authorisation of knowledge about the past and the present.

Research about diversity thus plays a critical role in how diversity is imagined, interpreted and 'managed' by the state. Given the colonial history of Australia and the critical role that racism played as a mobilising and justifying ideology for the dominant power, racism remains a continuing irritant to the operation of Australian governments. The return of a neoliberal economic/conservative social policy Abbott coalition government to power in 2013 thus reignited still strongly smouldering public dilemmas about race and racism. The Howard coalition government of 1996 to 2007 to a significant

---

[5]   From 'the Left', see Sparrow (2013); from 'the Right', see Paterson (2011).

degree represented a re-assertion of White power and Anglo-Christian moralities and ethical hierarchies in the face of an increasingly multiracial, multicultural and multifaith society, sharpened by rising paranoia about the spread of militant Islam and home-brewed terrorism. The Labor governments of 2007 to 2013 wavered once more towards some form of adaptation to the real social diversity intensified, as it had been by the more population-growing immigration policies of the later Howard period. In addition, Labor's asylum-seeker policies had led to an increase in unlawful arrivals, mostly from the violence-wracked societies of Iraq, Afghanistan, Iran, Burma and Sri Lanka. Under Labor the discussion of what to do about racism, which had been essentially abandoned and banned by the 1998 Howard decision to suppress the Eureka report, and replace anti-racism with the language of harmony, was resurrected. While Rudd essentially followed the Howard line on playing down racism as an issue, Australia faced significant critique at the United Nations (UN) Human Rights Council (HRC) over its policies. Just prior to presenting at the 2011 meeting of the Committee in Geneva, the government of Julia Gillard (who had replaced Rudd in a coup in mid-2010) announced a re-affirmation of multiculturalism, the appointment of a full-time race discrimination commissioner, and the initiation of a national four-year anti-racism campaign.

Abbott's Attorney General George Brandis campaigned before the election and announced after the victory that he would legislate to remove racial vilification provisions from the Race Discrimination Act. Under the influence of the neoliberal think tank the Institute for Public Affairs (IPA), which had campaigned against racial vilification laws since one of their major public spokespeople, Murdoch press commentator Andrew Bolt was found in 2011 to have breached the provision and been censured for it, Brandis appointed Tim Wilson an IPA activist as human rights commissioner. Wilson's comment on his role included the memorable phrases:

> ... public policy is not driven by evidence, it is informed by evidence. Public policy is driven by the political values of those elected to govern. Those values determine what issues the government believes needs to be tackled, how they then approach it, how they weigh evidence, and the policy solutions ultimately proposed. An "evidence-based approach" amounts to discarding the choice of democracy for government by technocratic bureaucracy, particularly

when much of the evidence is financed by government to justify their decisions. (Wilson, 2013)[6]

Rarely has there been such a clear statement of the role that ideology plays in trumping research. For the next parliamentary period the field of research on race and cultural difference would be a designated space for a resumption of the culture wars.

---

[6]   Wilson (2013); but see his IPA colleague's rather different view at Staley (2008).

THREE

In-group identity and the challenges of ethnographic research

Yunis Alam

Introduction: racialising reality

In this chapter I explore tensions and synergies within ethnographic research that has social policy resonance and reach. Specifically, I argue that where research fields and their researchers share an arc of politics and identity, impacts on the researcher may be varied and potent. Before this, however, I provide some context for the way in which writing around race and ethnicity has been of a political nature, and can be traced back to the West's earliest contacts with the 'colonial other' (Loomba, 1998, p 72). Establishing this foundational premise around the nature of writing and representation frames the ensuing discussion in which I explore how insider/emic status can have an impact on traditional professional boundaries and identity more generally.

Political endeavour can be seen through the development of action, partisan, activist and critical forms of social research (Hammersley, 2000; Letherby, 2003; Gomm, 2004), and through the production of literature, including fiction, more generally (Orwell, 1946/1984). Research which has political orientations, for example, feminist, anti-racist and activist, may seek to remedy forms and bases of inequality, injustice and discrimination (Ali et al, 2004; Bloor, 2004; Gomm, 2004). This is particularly, although not exclusively, the case with 'race' research and writings, including texts that were produced *before* early academic 'race and ethnic studies' literature. William Foote Whyte's (1943) *Street corner society*, St Clair Drake and Horace Cayton's (1945/1962) *Black metropolis* and Jacques Barzun's (1938) *Race: A study in modern superstition* are all highly significant in their own right, but they are also emblematic of the academy's broadening scope of inquiry during the first part of the 20th century. Furthermore, the emergence of interest in this subject matter demonstrated race to be a construction tightly linked with the practice and legacy of Western colonialism and, in the case of Whyte's work, for example, America's multiethnic identity. However, race and ethnic studies research is located within, and as a consequence of, the context in which the concept of race was being formed. Indeed, race as a rationally defined concept came into common usage in the period from the mid to late 18th century. This period is commonly seen as the high point of the Enlightenment, yet it is during this era that doctrines about race came to be articulated in a consistent manner (Solomos and Back, 1996, p 32).

Early writing around 'race' was often geared toward categorising human populations according to physical/phenotypical features, and tended to correlate these differences within a hierarchy of ability, intellect, disposition or other markers through which distinctiveness could be perceived, explained and then refracted back into wider social consciousness as common sense, rational or even scientifically grounded knowledge. Moreover, organising the world in this manner helped maintain any attendant inequities, even if the inequities predated the invention and utility of race as a concept. For example, race and racism did not lead to the Atlantic slave trade, but the division of humans into discernible species certainly helped maintain slavery as an unproblematic, and rational, ideological lynchpin which ran in tandem with the evolving system of capitalism. Indeed, as Williams noted, 'A racial twist has thereby been given to what is basically an economic phenomenon. Slavery was not born of racism: rather, racism was the consequence of slavery' (Williams, 1944/1994, p 7).

During the 18th and 19th centuries, the impact of scientific writing, and Darwinism especially, further reinforced racial typologies and corresponding behaviours, traits and what were deemed to be innate abilities among diverse populations. With increasing globalisation running alongside the spread of Western imperialism, race became a peculiarly broad topic of interest, and came to form an important element of identity-making through feeding into definitions of citizenship, nation and more generally, 'otherness' (Goldberg, 2001). Thus, while neither 'academic' nor 'policy-focused', the literature promoting race as a valid concept can be framed as part of a broader political venture validating intertwining racist, and economic, agendas. Edward Long's *The history of Jamaica* (1774/2002), for example, argued that Europeans and blacks were different species of the human genus, and furthermore, that the Atlantic slave trade was a rational cull of genetically inferior races.[1] Similarly, Marriott (1999) discusses a range of authors, including Kingsley[2] (1860), who constructed robust and recognisably racist representations, while Knox's work perpetuated representations of the Irish 'other' in which behaviour, culture and disposition coalesced and conflated with nation, religion and 'race':

> ... in the ordinary affairs of life, they despise order, economy, cleanliness; of to-morrow they take no thought; regular labour – unremitting, steady, uniform, productive labour – they hold in absolute horror and contempt. (Knox, 1862, p 320)

Such examples, and the wider representations of the Irish and other ethnic groups through news media and magazines (including *Punch*, for example) defined and sustained the ideologically grounded construction and practice of racisms. For this to work, a model of racialisation, supported through the economic system, had to be maintained and developed to such an extent that race and racialised thinking became common sense, 'normative' and habitual thinking (Downing and Husband, 2005). While Downing and Husband focus on race and representation within contemporary mass media, 'race thinking' during the 19th century was aided through a much smaller variety, and quantity, of newsprint, theatre and even literature. Ideas about race, then, were transmitted to particular audiences, through particular means and often overlapping contexts whereby they were accepted, developed, reinforced and embedded. Kipling's poetic and politically inspired comment (1899) on the prospective American invasion of/intervention in the Philippines (*The white man's burden*) had interpretations dependent on the readers' vantage points (see Murphy, 2010), but the poem also elicited critical responses. Hubert H. Harrison, a black socialist, preacher, activist and educator, critiqued the pro-imperialist stance that many interpreted within Kipling's

---

[1]   For Long, blacks were lazy, liars, promiscuous, cowardly, savage and debased (see Long, 1774/2002, pp 351-83).

[2]   On his travels in Ireland, Kingsley noted, for example: 'I am haunted by the human chimpanzees I saw along that hundred miles of horrible country. I don't believe they are our fault. I believe ... that they are happier, better, more comfortably fed and lodged under our rule than they ever were. But to see white chimpanzees is dreadful; if they were black, one would not feel it so much, but their skins, except where tanned by exposure, are as white as ours' (Kingsley, 1860, quoted in Schwarze, 2002, p 75).

poem through his *The black man's burden: A reply to Rudyard Kipling* (1920). For Harrison, Kipling's poem had a sharp resonance with the pattern and practice of American imperialism – including its motives – and was conflated with the experience, subjugation and suffering of blacks within a highly racialised, unequal and unjust America. Harrison's retort aimed to undermine Kipling's sentiments, and by extension, attack the normative and unquestioning ideological matrix of empire, race and capital that bred a myriad of systemic and sporadic inequities. Clearly, Harrison's work was political and positioned, but its very creation was dependent on an existing position it countered. Similarly, the literary/autobiographical writing of Equiano (1789/1999) indirectly undermined prevalent understandings and perceptions of non-whites, and in so doing, gave greater credence to the Abolitionist Movement in Britain. This tradition – of narrative making/unmaking or argument/counter-argument – is common to a range of disciplines, and is an integral aspect of knowledge production inside and outside the academy. Indeed, social science depends on this practice in order to evolve and reach into new realms of interest and their explanations.

Social science interventions into critiquing race and racism

In the US, the Chicago School of Sociology, in particular, Robert Ezra Park, explored diversity[3] and helped situate the field of race and ethnic studies within the academy. Perhaps more significantly, W.E.B. Du Bois' *The souls of black folks* (1903/2007) profoundly introduced a black perspective into the sociological framing of race. It is striking, especially today, to consider the enduring vitality and richness of Du Bois' work and its linkage with his own identity. Here, for the first time, was a black sociologist exploring hyphenated identities in various ways, including the introduction of the concept of 'double consciousness', and throughout the breadth of his writing (which included literary and overtly political works) validated black culture in the way that Hoggart (1957) and Williams (1958) sought to validate British working-class culture some five decades later. Du Bois can be defined as one of the first insider sociologists who located his own identity within his research fields as an acutely political endeavour linked with his insider status rather than establishing or exploiting subjectivity for epistemological and methodological ends (see Monteiro, 2008).

---

[3]   This included migration and the 'race problem', for example (see also Deegan, 2001).

In the British context, it was with the advent of 20th-century mass migrations from former colonies to the 'mother country' that a desire and capacity within social science to undermine normative, institutional and structural racism eventually grew more robust. Although in the 1960s a range of established black and minority ethnic (BME) community groups gained strength and support through solidarity, they were often narrow in terms of their composition: the Indian Workers' Association (first formed in 1938), the Pakistani Workers' Association (1964) to be followed by Bangladeshi and Kashmiri Workers' Associations (see Ramamurthy, 2006). At this point, sociological writing around ethnic diversity was couched within an exploratory frame which aimed to describe the differences of relatively newly arrived 'others' as well as focusing on the difficulties they encountered (see, for example, Banton, 1955; Griffith et al, 1960; Desai, 1963; Patterson, 1963; Uberoi, 1964; Dahya, 1965; Lelohe, 1966). As these immigrants became settlers, and communities, the research focused more on the experience of racism along with inequality, citizenship, the nature and impact of immigration policy, criminality, policing strategy, education, and social policy more broadly (see, for example, Foot, 1965; Rex and Moore, 1967; Deakin et al, 1970; Humphry and John, 1971; Walvin, 1971; Watson, 1977; Hall et al, 1978; Anwar, 1979).

The diverse range of 'race' academics during the 1960s and 1970s were not of the same ideological bent. Indeed, Foot, Hall, Humphry and John, for example, were oriented toward a politically anti-racist front in which race was the most salient and structural determinant of social position, discrimination and oppression. Others, such as Anwar, Deakin and Walvin, approached diversity from the vantage point of liberal egalitarianism which, although not *anti*-anti-racist, was certainly at odds with the more radical and often neo-Marxist analytic frame which gained cache in a range of sociological sub-disciplines at the time. The development of a body of responses to and critiques of racism lacked a singular political perspective.

Coupled with this top-down interest, whether from an academic or policy vantage point, there emerged a cohort of BME researchers, anti-racist activists, pressure groups and organisations such as the Campaign Against Racial Discrimination, the United Coloured People's Association and the Institute of Race Relations. Of particular note, the Asian Youth Movement/s, organised at local levels by young, male South Asian activists, had more radical approaches to challenging racism (Ramamurthy, 2006, 2013).

If the 1950s and 1960s were characterised as moments through which 'race' became present and often problematic, then the following decades carried over and amplified this perception. The 'Winter of Discontent' epitomised the decline in British industry, and a series of race moments, including the palpable rise of the far right in some inner cities as well as the 'race' riots (Notting Hill Carnival, 1976; Brixton, Toxteth, Manchester, Birmingham, Leeds, 1981) served to further conflate disorder and unrest within second and third generation, British-born South Asians and African Caribbeans. *The Scarman report* (1981) contextualised the riots against a backdrop of deprivation and the heavy handedness of the police, but denied any widespread presence and impact of racism (especially institutional racism) within the police. Essentially, the police did a difficult job, and occasionally, one or two 'rotten apples' might have pushed the wrong buttons or allowed their passions, and biases, to get the better of their integrity-rich professional identities. Conversely, Scarman did point to the alleged failings of the African Caribbean family and its culture (see Scarman, 1981, para 2.23; Gilroy, 1987, pp 129-40; Husband and Alam, 2011, pp 23-5). Gilroy, echoing Hall et al (1978), in particular, asserts that the conclusions made by Scarman are themselves built on the deterministic characteristics of what are essentially, and through coded language, posited to be culturally inferior and problematic races:

> It is only "race" which marks those who detonated the riots as different from their more passive white neighbours. The distinctive cultural patterns, both expressive and familial, which emerge from the report, almost by default, become the key to understanding the cause and character of the conflicts. (Gilroy, 1987, pp 135-6)

It wasn't until the 1980s, however, with the Honeyford (Solomos, 2003, pp 104-5) and Rushdie Affairs (Asad, 1990; Ruthven, 1991; Fhlathuin, 1995), that the framing of ethnic relations shifted balance and developed a new perspective. Both events demonstrated the emergence of an up to then unseen, assertive Muslim identity which challenged the prevailing political, and often homegenising, idea that all BMEs were in the same existential boat. Furthermore, British Muslims were not passive, accepting and tolerant of discriminations, as the first generation settlers were perceived to have been; given that second and third generations had been through the British educational system and socialised within a Western environment, they had a capacity to own the language and system of rights-based citizenship. In turn, it should have been no surprise that their responses to racism were, in some senses, very British: political activism, and indeed, riot and civil activism, go back to the 'Bawdy House Riots' of the 17th century (Harris, 1990, p 82), added to which revolutionary and political movements of the 19th century (Anti-Corn Law League, the Chartist movement, the trade union movement) certainly fed into the repertoire of British democratic practice (Briggs, 1984; O'Brien, 1998).

By the 1990s, the politics and practice of ethnic relations became supplanted by the acceptance and celebration of a more benign form of multiculturalism and recognition of diversity – local councils and service providers offered 'race awareness' training, members of the Royal family ate samosas, a black presence could be registered within media and, after a hiatus of over five decades, non-white MPs won seats in the 1980s.[4] Against this backdrop, in which second and third generation British-born Muslims were now having children of their own, the experience of racism continued: in education, housing, employment and on the street. In 1997, The Runnymede Trust published *Islamophobia: A challenge for us all*, which in clear and unambiguous terms outlined the nature, extent and impact of anti-Muslim media representation, racial violence and a range of discriminations around gender, education and criminal justice (The Runnymede Trust, 1997). In the same year, Lord Macpherson of Cluny completed his inquiry into the murder of Stephen Lawrence, finding that institutional racism had been a factor in the police investigation of his death (Macpherson, 1999). Throughout the preceding 18 years of Conservative rule, there was little ideological space for multiculturalism. This was demonstrated through restrictive immigration legislation, removal of educational provision for non-English speakers, and more broadly, an over-arching Orientalist, arguably racist, perspective.

In combination with the growing concern around global Islamic terrorism, a further seismic shift in ethnic relations emerged through explanations for the 2001 riots/'northern disturbances' in Oldham (26 May), Burnley (25 June) and Bradford (8-9 July) (see Bagguley and Hussain, 2008). With echoes of Scarman 20 years earlier, the relatively complex phenomenon of riot was explained through the assertion that the riotous communities were all similar in that their ethnic and religious heritage led to a lack of community cohesion, a situation of their own making as they were culturally predisposed to self-segregate and thus live insular and parallel lives. In effect, it was argued, these communities were divorced from wider, whiter society

---

[4]   Shapurji Dorabji Saklatvala was MP for Battersea North from 1924-29, but it wasn't until the 1980s that Jonathon Sayeed, Dianne Abbott, Paul Boateng, Bernie Grant and Keith Vaz were elected to the House of Commons.

because that was what they wanted. A range of reports written before and after the riots further reinforced this culturally deterministic logic, often discounting or diminishing the impact of white flight, social stratification or even racism (Cantle, 2001; Clarke, 2001; Denham, 2001; Ouseley, 2001; Ritchie, 2001). As usual, and rightly so, academic interest fed into the mix with a spectrum of writers offering their more nuanced interpretations and analyses (Kundnani, 2002; Phillips, 2002; Bagguley and Hussain, 2006, 2008; Finney and Simpson, 2009). As I explore below, this most recent framing of ethnic relations has had a heavy impact on the academy, and demonstrates the pressure of funding, politics and identity within the system, with different perspectives finding funding from different sources.

Not surprisingly, but certainly not accidentally, social and community cohesion came to dominate academic, policy and public spheres during the 2000s. While a not universally accepted paradigm of managing ethnic diversity, the discourse of community cohesion firmly, but wrongly, placed some 'ethnic' problems at the door of some 'inward-looking' and 'insular' communities: Muslims (Phillips, 2002; Simpson, 2004; Husband and Alam, 2011). In many ways, this was a political and policy retreat, and also appeared to be something of an intellectual regression to the thinking in the 1970s where the variety of British South Asians were labelled as 'Asian', and British blacks as 'West Indians'. Equally, and although the word 'assimilation' was rarely used, 'citizenship', 'belonging', 'loyalty' and 'Britishness' were conceptually applied in relation to British Muslims specifically. Perhaps ironically, the shifting of British politics to the right, with its frequently fear-fuelled fixations around immigration, suggests that, if anything, insularity and a desire to be segregated from others has become a defining feature of what is purported to be mainstream British identity.

Within the broader narrative, there has been noticeable movement from one philosophically underpinned paradigm of ethnic relations to the next. Assimilation gave way to integration; integration fed into calls for race equality and anti-racism; multiculturalism superseded race equality until a revised form of integration and social cohesion, also bound up with de-radicalisation, became the dominant framing devices. A banal, everyday and unproblematic British Muslim presence may be the norm (Alam, 2006; Phillips, 2009), but forced marriage, the control of women's bodies (and their clothes), jihadi terrorism, educational under-achievement, crime, sexual grooming, the existence of 'no go' zones, parallel lives and the motivated, intentional practice of self-segregation within some multiethnic areas[5] are still focal points. These are all smaller aspects of the larger shape that constitutes Islam in Britain. My reading of this is not intended to suggest that these issues are either irrelevant or, indeed, mythic, but rather, they have come to frame particular groups with particular traits and form a meaning system akin to the processes of racialisation that took place decades ago. It has marked a distinctive retreat from the nascent recognition of intersectionality and diversity that was becoming expressed in social policy from the Race Relations Act 1976 onwards, and now offered an assertive, essentialist conception of majority and minority identities framed within what Fekete (2001, 2009) has called 'xeno-racism'.

Ethnographic research and the deconstruction of racisms and lived inequalities

The partial, and selective, context sketched out above seeks to locate current research practice within a continuum that operates alongside representation and identity politics. Ethnographic research, especially that which depends on the biographical repertoire of skill set, research interest and personal politics of those with insider credentials and status, does not necessarily have to be political in orientation, purpose or even outcomes. However, while accepting that objectivity is a mythic aspiration of social scientific research, the 'engaged' ethnographic researcher can lend an 'edge' to their research. Although the significance of autobiography and the situatedness of the ethnographer within the field is key (Hastrup and Hervik, 1994), the construction of a field itself 'is about controlling the thought processes of the ethnographer, not the behaviours or thoughts of the participant group' (Madden, 2010, p 39). Nevertheless, as an approach that in many respects depends on the subjectivity and identity of the researcher, ethnography has built within it means to exploit the researcher's varied self – not only at the point of 'writing up', but especially when it comes to selecting/constructing the field, getting access and then going about the business of generating data. The vantage point of the insider ethnographer, therefore, may require little repositioning, or at worst, minimal adaptation to the field and its population.

Constructed from the vantage point of a Western gaze on a non-Western field, early anthropologies and ethnographies held within them a driving curiosity. Parts of Chagnon's *Yanomamo: The fierce people*

---

[5]   In regard to this latter point, see, for example, Carling (2008); for a rebuttal, see Simpson et al (2009).

(1968/1997), Malinowski's *Argonauts of the Western Pacific* (1922/2009), and Firth's *We, the Tikopia* (1936/1957), may read like adventure novels, but they did seek to survey and explain societies/cultures that had developed usually outside of Western modernity. Often, these were previously hidden sites, invariably characterised as 'primitive', savage and, while not always expressed explicitly, born of inferior, older and pre-modern civilisation. In some cases, interpretations were later questioned and critiqued[6] as being excessively subjective and even exaggerated. What remains significant is that anthropology and ethnography have woven within them the centrality of the researcher that remains a distinctive and core feature of contemporary practice. Research exploring ethnic relations – with its apparent attendant but distinctive correlates of tradition, belief and practice – has a similar tendency to map, explain and in some cases remedy that which sits at odds with Western society and culture. Britain's BME communities, and other minorities, have not been couched as primitive, but their apparent distinctiveness has been a significant element of rationale for their study.

Although Bradford, for example, is not a remote, uncharted and unsurveyed island, parts of it have been painted as being isolated, exotic, problematic, and thus made all the more distinctive. In research contexts, there is a bottom line: they are different and therefore, at least in part, they are worth investigating, their cultures and belief systems worthy of explanation. Why else would the likes of Lewis (2007), Khan (1977) and Bolognani (2007, 2009), to name only three, actually bother to draw lines of intersectionality between their chosen ethnic groups of interest with gender, education, 'integration' or any other focus of investigation? There remains a fascination with the cultural and racial 'other', but this is balanced with an overarching belief that some research 'good' may be done which would then feed into wider understanding, appreciation and acceptance of those being researched. Of course, it would be remiss of me not to mention that having any research specialism can have a positive impact on an academic's career trajectory. Researching race has in various ways become a highly beneficial aspect of academic identity and authority in that claims

---

[6]   In particular, Chagnon's work created controversy around how the Yanomamo/i were represented/constructed as violent, that Chagnon did not depict naturally occurring behaviour but rather staged some of the scenes (which were filmed), and furthermore, Chagnon was complicit in creating tension and violence through his distribution of goods. For more details, and examination of other issues at the heart of this controversy, see, for example, Borofsky (2005) and Tierney (2000).

making, knowledge production and 'expertise' are essential in the construction, and impact, of professional identity.

Academic research probably doesn't have to be complex, but it usually is. This might seem like an obvious, arguably simplistic, assertion, but there is little doubt that researchers operating within the social sciences and linking their work with social policy have to negotiate pressures at various levels. Research might aim to influence government policy, but also seek to further or undermine a particular ideological position. Similarly, research can be relevant to stakeholders and interest groups, but simultaneously help develop a research area agenda, approach, culture and even refine the parameters and scope of one or more disciplines. Furthermore, the mainstream industry of social research often works through top-down funding models which, with the coupling of state-led imperatives, has a further impact on the professional and political identities of researchers: from inception to beyond completion. In addition, there is the capacity for academic research to be explicitly political in terms of which questions it addresses and how it addresses them; and although this may not always be driven by a 'researcher as activist' mode, the social sciences have a long tradition within 'race' and ethnic studies wherein partisanship and the politics of representation are integral and can unfold in various, overlapping ways. There are cycles of publication and counter-publication in which positions are secured, undermined or given further legitimacy (through state appropriation, for example), as in the case of a broad and arguably tokenistic (rather than substantive) commitment to forms of multiculturalism which was only to be later reversed and reread as problematic (Hewitt, 2005; Back, 2007; McGhee, 2008; Husband and Alam, 2011; Alexander, 2013; Modood, 2013).

This is not to say that the researcher's capacity to negotiate the often competing needs of the funder, the university, the government, the academic community, the communities being researched and of course, any audiences (Gunaratnam, 2003; Kalra, 2006; Becker, 2007) is necessarily a consistently available skill when doing research. However, when 'race' research intersects with insider status – and this can be felt through ethnography – the researcher's identity may be bound closely to the research rationale, process and outcomes. This becomes especially clear in relation to how the researcher is perceived/read/negotiated/constructed by research participants, and furthermore, the extent to which identity is a key a component that influences the decisions made and the routes taken (de Andrade, 2000; Lee and Simon-Maeda, 2006; Nayak, 2006; Brannick and Coghlan 2007).

The practical processes and intellectual justifications around how ethnographies are originated, researched, developed and finally produced can be emblematic, indeed, deeply illustrative, of the capacity within sociology and its texts to become an explicitly *public* endeavour (Burawoy, 2005, 2007). And here I share Burawoy's argument around a public sociology which, among other things, enables change through a feedback loop of knowledge production and political praxis (civic or otherwise). In his broader discussion around the nature, role and place of sociology, Burawoy explores the ways and places in which sociologists become, or choose to become, located, as either policy-oriented, critically or professionally grounded, or having a public, perhaps civic, commitment. There may be movement between and within these realms of location during a sociologist's career trajectory, but it is also possible for overlap between these zones of sociological identity. As Burawoy states,

> James Coleman, for example, simultaneously worked in both professional and policy worlds while being hostile to critical and public sociologies. Christopher Jencks … is unusual in combining critical and public moments with professional and policy commitments. Arlie Hochschild's sociology of emotions is strung out between professional and critical sociology, whereas her research on work and family combines public and policy sociology. (Burawoy, 2007, p 38)

The capacity to change, adapt and innovate allows social science to grow and reflect the nature of a changing world. In this context, there are some especially useful interventions from Becker (2007), Back (2007), Gane and Back (2012) and Back and Puwar (2013). Gane and Back in particular explore the continuing significance of the intertwined political, moral, professional and 'craft' dimensions of C. Wright Mills' approach to sociology. Key to their discussion is the view that sociology need not be bound and limited by methodological myopia, and indeed, can go further and become more effective and relevant if energised through political commitment and a desire to be accessible, public and with reach beyond academic and specialist audiences.

While we may celebrate and become inspired by approaches which allow us to innovate and to invest our political, moral and intellectual identities within research and writing that we deem important, relevant and necessary, the likelihood of living up to this ambition is relatively small. For the most part, the funding structure, its streams and priorities dictate who can afford to research, and can even determine *which* research area, and approach, is likely to generate research income. As discussed above, there has been a remarkable ideological shift in focus from discrimination, economic and educational under-achievement to an agenda with a palpable focus on (de)radicalisation, social/community cohesion and calls for research which seek to undo, or at least respond to, the alleged failings of multiculturalism rather than acknowledging, let alone exploring, seemingly banal, unspectacular and everyday multiculture (Back, 2007, p 148; Alam, 2006, 2011) that is more evident but less potent than a broader and unrelenting race narrative constructed through fear, threat and dangerous difference.

Despite the expansion of scholarship around 'race', the presence and impact of *racism* within the discourses of policy fora, political rhetoric and broader public consciousness has conversely diminished. Like class, popular and policy discourses present racism as a term that is archaic and reflective of a warped ideology in those who employ it. At the same time, the existential impact of racism remains a tangible determinant of an individual's life experience. The writing out of race is epitomised by claims of a 'post-racial society' that continues to be strongly contested from a range of disciplinary vantage points[7] (Wise, 2010; Chin, 2012; Lentin, 2012; Ikuenobe, 2013). What is more, regardless of our own politics, and no matter how active or grounded we believe ourselves to be, our research agendas are rarely our own: our research has to somehow, by the very nature of the academy, tie in with policy agendas set by the government of the day as transmitted through various research councils and other funding organisations. Of course, the politically grounded researcher can conduct research without funding, or without even academic support. Indeed, in the sphere of literary production, most subsidise their writing through ordinary 'day' jobs: Orwell, Nabakov, Larkin, Stoker and Kafka being some well known authors whose 'creative writing'[8] did not pay the

---

[7]   See also Yuen and Ray (2009) for an enlightening review of the TV series 'Lost' and 'Heroes' with specific reference to the ways in which non-white characters are utilised in very specific ways according to their what their ethnicities continue to connote within what can be termed a broader typological scheme of the racial/ethnic/non-white 'other'.

[8]   I have chosen to envelop this term in quotation marks because, at a fundamental level, all writing is, to some extent, creative. However, the term is usually made in reference to writing that is more comfortably couched as literary and artistic endeavour, as opposed to writing that has more 'factual' or fictional dimensions.

bills. However, within the university context, one expectation of the academic role is research endeavour. Academics have to resolve the pressures of 'professional' development and advancement within the university system, and while not all researchers are driven by a desire to climb the ranks, recognition of increasing skill, expertise and experience is valuable to the individual and the institution. Furthermore, each step climbed on the ladder of promotion (lecturer to senior lecturer to reader to professor) usually falls within at least the aspirational model of academic, intellectual and professional development, possibly reassuring or enhancing professional identity and wellbeing.

But research endeavour, or even 'being research active', is a multifaceted element of the academic role. Being research active means more than simply doing research, and indeed, can also include reference to a range of performance indicators including the submission of funding proposals, engaging in the business of 'knowledge transfer', as well as an expectation that findings will be published, disseminated, have impact, gain esteem and influence policy. Many of these indicators are also central to the ways in which academic researchers are measured and evaluated within the scope of the Research Excellence Framework (REF) (formerly, the Research Assessment Exercise, RAE), which in itself constitutes another dimension of professional identity by asking if your research is good enough to be submitted. The pressure to be a part of the research funding system is itself, therefore, systemic. If you are research active, then you demonstrate this through bidding for and acquiring funds, executing the research, delivering reports, publishing and disseminating findings in the forms of articles, books and conference/policy papers.[9] In this model, funding is central. Indeed, acquiring research funding gives substance to professional identity, integrity and competence: the more funded projects you are awarded, the stronger your academic credentials, and the greater your credentials, the more esteem you are afforded, and this can lead to further promotions, expectations and obligations.

In this context, Bhattacharyya and Murji's (2013) argument is compelling. Public sociology cannot, and indeed should not, be necessarily translated into commercial equations in which knowledge transfer, research income and other markers of esteem, impact and

---

[9]   Each of these activities has further dimensions: writing a funding bid also means engaging with administrative, logistical and financial aspects; when it comes to publication of a book, the researcher usually has some degree of involvement, ranging from jacket design to dissemination strategy as well, for example, the processes of editing and peer review.

influence may well disrupt, or even corrupt, research intentions, processes and outcomes. That is, activist, partisan, critical and other forms of what might be called 'public' sociology, and the research which underpins and feeds off it, is and of itself intrinsic to the idea of the academy: knowledge and its production is an inherently intellectual and hopeful, but by no means elitist, endeavour. In order to serve our publics, however, we must ensure that our research is meaningful, innovative and liberating without being 'dumbed down', marketised or commodified.

The reach of the rarely spotted independent scholar notwithstanding, academic research within the social sciences is today more dependent on external funding than ever before, but that pool is itself diminishing, thus decreasing the chances of getting funding in the first place. While this does not necessarily mean funders are the most powerful actors within the domain of research and knowledge creation/dissemination, it does suggest, however, that researchers will have to continue to become more innovative, and in some cases, may well have to compromise their politics as well as their research ambitions in order to make their bids more viable. This is not necessarily a bad thing, but the impact it can have on the discourse in which the research matter sits can become skewed with findings and data oriented toward a funder's needs and expectations, rather than those of the researched and the researcher. I explore in due course two examples in which similar issues arose and were negotiated. Before that, some discussion of researcher identity within the sphere of research around ethnic relations is required.

Identity and research practice

The role of the BME insider as researcher in pursuing, carrying out and disseminating policy-related research within the current British political context figures as a significant point of this discussion, in which it is necessary to explore how the self-perception of the researcher as a hybrid, policy-sensitive and community-embedded academic can itself become a site of tension and conflict. Specifically, engaging with one's own 'communities' can have an impact on the nature and rationale underpinning research decisions, but can also invoke the possibility of community expectations and sanctions. Conversely, perceived research success can further fuel rising expectations of the researcher's 'power' and credibility. While this chapter is by no means meant to be a call for sympathy for the plight of the poor insider researcher, the detail and questions asked within the research journey are relevant as a means of situating the researcher within a more comprehensive but intersecting context where the cross-currents of personal/political identity form confluence and contradiction with the needs of the academy, funders, research audiences and participants.

The ability to make connections, form relationships and foster trust with anyone, let alone research participants, is one of those facets of humanity that can be taken for granted and is often ignored or marginalised during the write-up phase of any, especially qualitative, social research. To some extent, our job is to dig and mine data from our sample. Of course, this is a crude way of looking at the practice of social research, and there are many examples of researchers who go much further than merely seeing their sample as 'data' (see, for example, Griffin, 1960; Liebow, 1967, pp 232-56; Khan, 1977). I make this observation – biased and to some extent made all the more cynical as I've chosen not to interrogate it in any depth for several years – now, because it is a relevant component of the broader argument I am shaping. Research, as an idea and practice, is inherently political (Liebling, 2001; Knowles, 2006; Lee and Simon-Maeda, 2006; and especially Oakley, 1981, pp 30-61). Who does the research, how, why and *with* whom it is done, are questions that elicit responses suggesting research has close connections with various forms and locations of power. Here, I am referring to everything from (political/state) agenda-setting in research to the smallest and largest manifestations of power imbalance between researcher and research subject during their formal and informal interactions[10] (Ali, 2006).

Today, insider research is a valuable element within the panoply of sociological inquiry. Research around 'race' seems to yield cohorts of researchers who may be politically, philosophically and 'ethnically' connected with the subject matter: aspects of identity are invested and located within chosen research subjects, and as such, the endeavour is conducted from a position far from objectivity and impartiality. As Ali (2006) notes, however:

> There is an implied criticism of "subjectivity" which is wearingly familiar and one that obscures the complex relationship between subjects, epistemology, politics and research. Being "too subjective" or "over-identified" with

---

[10] Ali's discussion of concerns around ethnographic research connected with 'race', for example, is complemented with frank reflections linked with how data are generated, interpreted, selected and presented. These imbalances and pressures can end up creating further exploitations, and indeed, reinforcing power hierarchies within research processes and beyond.

> the research and respondents results in "bad research" and
> self-indulgent texts. (Ali, 2006, p 476)

Within ethnography, the integration of subjectivity, partisanship and reflexivity is not necessarily problematic in terms of the impact it may have on the quality of the data. For that matter, such integration does not disrupt or adversely offend ethnographic principles or methodological rubric. However, ethnographic holism, coupled with personal and political ownership of and investment in a research area, asks more of the researcher. Insider researchers conducting ethnography have a different and arguably more embedded range of compromises, benefits and costs to encounter than researchers who, for example, can view their subject matter from a position of relative detachment. How this plays out in practice depends on the personal and psychological attributes of each researcher. If your funder chooses to ignore, or render moot a finding that you deem valuable, noteworthy or otherwise significant, how do you respond? Equally, if you believe the source of funding to be 'tainted', and given the pressures of the research system, disruptive forces may be carried into your research. In regard to this latter question, you may simply refuse and walk away, but if you do that, another researcher may end up undertaking the research in a manner that you regard as poorly conceptualised, imaginatively shallow, and at odds with your politics.

Politics and practice of ethnography: some reflections

After the relative success of a small, but reasonably long-term ethnographically oriented research project which aimed to represent the voices of young, British-born, Pakistani Muslim men, Professor Charles Husband and myself were given the opportunity to carry out similar but larger-scale research with a more diverse population. The project was funded through a panel of funders, each contributing a share to the overall cost. However, part of the funding originated for the then New Labour government's 'Preventing Extremism and Terrorism' (PET) funds which were distributed to various local councils which, having large Muslim populations, were perceived as being the potential locus of future terrorist threat. One purpose of the PET funding, it seemed to us, was to conduct work in which *social cohesion* could be enhanced and *radicalisation* decreased. Both were terms in contemporary political discourse that we regarded as highly ideological in their construction and application. Our immediate reaction was to refuse the funds on the grounds that our political and professional integrity would be compromised: we didn't ideologically, or theoretically, buy into the broader overlapping premise. Not only that, we were keen to ensure any research we carried out came from our aspirations, not the mindset of what we deemed to be a government which was revisiting, rehearsing and making normative a racialised discourse around ethnicity, identity and faith.

The research went ahead in 2007, but without the element of PET funding (our funders secured the resources from other streams), and we ended up inadvertently subverting the cohesion/de-radicalisation agenda by empirically demonstrating that while social cohesion and the 'Big Society' were, despite assertions to the contrary, already manifestly present (Alam, 2011), the coupling of social cohesion with counter-terrorism had a net negative impact. For many, especially those whose task was to roll out both policies at local government level, there was a clear and deep contradiction between the two (Husband and Alam, 2011).

On a more a mundane level, there were experiences in the field that also illustrated this kind of contradiction and the invidious position that we, as researchers, found ourselves in. There were instances in which the research motives were interrogated by potential participants: the idea of yet more research in which they (British Muslims) figured as an object of scrutiny was part of the wider, self-fulfilling and problematic cycle of representation. This was not the first time I had encountered this as a researcher. In 2000, while employed as a field researcher conducting focus group interviews around forced marriage, anger and frustration was directed at myself. But this was understandable, for in this context, I was not a researcher but a representative of the state pushing a particular agenda to be given further legitimacy with research data. In addition, I was perceived as someone who was practically attacking, undermining and selling out my own community.[11] While this was somewhat upsetting, my own analysis came to a similar conclusion. In a sense, such fears were justified because there were elements and themes within the data that the final report ('influenced' by the funder) marginalised or ignored: the funder was not interested

---

[11] Although I have not encountered regular, intense and explicit condemnation about my research around a particular issue in which ethnic identity is central, there have been examples wherein my literary work has been critiqued as being dangerous and demonising 'my community'. Literary and ethnographic production have a range of similarities (from field selection to narrative skill), and indeed, the concept of representation (Julien and Mercer, 1996; Hall, 1997) is common and especially significant to both when produced from the vantage point of marginality.

in that data because, I reasoned, that data upset the narrative it wanted to finesse. The difficulty is one that especially early researchers may face: refusing work makes it difficult to develop your career within academia. Granted, this might be a shallow interpretation, but again, being employed has its benefits, and part of you does believe it's better to be in a position to instigate change from within. If you refuse, then the opportunity ends.

At the same time, such experiences often have a flip side. It's usually quite a humbling moment when participants profess a pride, and on occasion surprise, in the fact that you work in what remains, relatively speaking, a fairly respectable, comfortable and what can still be perceived to be a middle-class, and generally white profession. And while this often reinforces my view that research is a political, and power-laden, arena, I understand the source of the compliments and sense of pride. Even studying at university, never mind working in one, certainly in my childhood and into my twenties, was a venture I believed beyond my reach; the forces of social structure, *habitus* (Bourdieu, 1979/1984), and the existential labour that came with being of working-class and Asian/Pakistani/Muslim heritage culminated in expectations outwith academia. At school, there was an expectation that kids like me – where we lived, how others thought we lived and what they thought we could and *should* achieve in our lives – all had an impact on self-perception. As such, it's possible and even usual for a disruption in the perception of others when they encounter something, or someone, that sits outside of their normative field of expectations. Seeing a young black man behind the wheel of an expensive sports car may cause surprise, but often it is followed by a series of sense-making processes: he is either up to no good, or the car is not his. When it comes to making sense of encountering a working-class, Yorkshire-accented, Pakistani Muslim male academic, then I'm not sure what people think, but the combination of ethnicity, class and profession may produce some benign confusion which then may or may not lead to other reactions. I should note that this reflection is not intended to somehow celebrate or aggrandise my academic identity, but rather as a way of illustrating the extent to which the reading of identity is open and dependent on context.

The sense of pride that I believe I recognise is in essence about community: he's a university lecturer, but he's one of *us*. While this can be all very reassuring, and even rewarding, it can lead to the more problematic bind of being 'claimed', or having the capacity to speak for the groups to which you belong. This may echo the idea that BME academics appear to be more predisposed to 'being seen as "responsible for race matters'" *within* university contexts (Bhattacharyya and Murji, 2013, p 1362), but it is essentially an aspect of academic identity that is implicit and, of course, negotiated according to our moral, political and personal make-up. Here, then, lies another dimension of the insider researcher: not only an academic 'expert', but possibly being known as a representative and even role model. With this representative facet comes another level of credentialisation and authority, what Khan calls 'ethnic informers'[12] when referring to BME writers of English literature (2006, p 186).

Similarly, the notion of 'responsibility' can become significant in terms of research integrity as well as personal and community politics. For example, what do you do with data that somehow feed into and support arguments contrary to your own, or worse still, reinforce policies that you interpret to be ideologically dangerous? If you ignore or exclude the data, you may feel you have compromised your research, rendering it tainted, incomplete and biased, even though you believe that qualitative research in particular is especially constructed to begin with. That doesn't matter: you know you may exclude a voice, a quotation, an utterance that was real and that dilemma should be somehow dealt with ... ethically. In the course of the interview or whatever other method that generated the data, you have no problem engaging with the speaker and challenging their viewpoint: again, you are immersed and you are an insider. Moreover, your ethnographic approach – as you have developed it over the years – gives you license to get in deep in order to be 'real', natural and at close hand with those with whom you co-construct the world. But it's still not that simple. If one of your sample sounds off about an issue that you fear will be picked up on, taken out of context, skewing the balance of your findings and thereby becoming emblematic of your research, you have to make a decision. Does your responsibility lie with the data, or its impact?

---

[12] In Khan's discussion, she explores the extent to which such 'ethnic informers' can, in effect, perpetuate (mis)representations of the groups which figure in their literatures as they have the capacity to relocate the hegemonic struggle (of representation, colonialism, etc) from 'the frontier' to the internal realm of the group in question. Furthermore, in relation to representations of Muslims and Islam, she argues that they have 'internalised the racist and orientalist readings of Islam that colour the dominant discourse ... as the "insider" echoing the hegemonic constructions of the "outsider", such an individual reinforces the allied processes of pathologisation and of depoliticisation by providing an authentic note of endorsement to prevailing relations of power' (Khan, 2006, p 186).

I acknowledge such issues are not peculiar to the ethnographer alone, but they conflate with and add to the body of cost to the insider researcher. Of course, the likelihood of risk is built into the broader research philosophy that we choose to adopt and develop. Community response, whether sanction or support, may not be at the fore of our research endeavour because certain principles tend to override what are often couched as 'ethical' issues: the data speak for themselves, the funder (as an outsider) may not be concerned with any impacts (present or future) on the reputation of the researcher, and, of course, the researcher has to balance the competing needs of career development, community position and self-perception. In addition, you may feel the research issue needs to be interrogated, despite its sensitive, political, and in some cases, 'taboo' nature. Pressures, risks and constraints do not necessarily have to be grand or due to externalities to ourselves as researchers. Our own mindset, disposition and body of work that constitutes our identity is central to our practice. After research encounters, some of us may think about what actually happens when we are out there, in the research field, doing what we think constitutes research. The diary entry below around ongoing research on car culture unintentionally illustrates how a potential research participant is 'recruited', and although recruitment can be a relatively simple endeavour, it can give rise to arguably neurotic complications and questions.

> I wait in the queue to pay, and the driver of the GTO stands behind me. I keep stealing a look at his car, and keep thinking about turning around and speaking to him, getting a foot in, introducing myself and asking him about his car. But I've been doing a lot of that, lately, and it kind of gets wearing after a while. But ... these cars, they don't come along every day, so eventually I do the usual introduction, and he seems genuinely interested in what I'm saying.

Some phrases in that segment give me pause for thought. First, 'getting a foot in' is sales talk. The fact that I appear to be a little unsettled by my recruiting zeal seems to reflect some degree of anxiety, perhaps guilt about exploiting unwitting candidates. I do my 'usual introduction', establishing rapport with the driver, thus securing the likelihood of an interview somewhere down the line. I close the sale. And every time this happens, it feels like a sale. It reminds me of a scene in the film 'Glengarry Glen Ross' in which the character Blake, played by Alec Baldwin, arrives to motivate real estate salesmen. His ensuing highly charged motivational speech[13] makes reference to selling being a 'man's game' within which there is the fundamental need to 'close' the intended mark through use of well established sales mantras such as ABC (Always Be Closing) and AIDA (Attention, Interest, Decision, Action). Granted, potential research recruits are not 'marks' in the way that potential buyers of real estate are in the film, but I do 'offer' a proposition all the same. As such, I aim to secure *attention*, provoke *interest* in my research; the capacity for a *decision* to be made followed by *action* is woven into my patter. It is not unethical, immoral, and while there may be some relatively innocuous exploitation of another human being, it isn't damaging or harmful.[14] Within the process, I choose to exploit my relative power and authority as a way of gaining access (*I work at the university, I'm a researcher, and I am asking you to inform my research*) and tempt the candidate with the chance to talk about their car/car history. Often, I perform as an insider, but this is not projection fixed in the confines of one marker of identity: ethnicity, class and gender are stitched together with the twin threads of biography and presentation of self. In the context of a repair workshop, I adopt the necessary argot, not just in terms of speaking about injectors or flanges, but by following conversational styles to include expletives, slang and accent. When I encounter an academic who happens to be driving a beautiful vintage Jaguar, our conversation is more refined, but again, our masculinities and class markers allow us to talk about horsepower, cylinders and synchromesh. Being an insider holds more than one facet of identity, and in some ways can be exploited further through adopting the characteristics of a chameleon, certainly when *getting a foot in the door*.

Sanghera and Thapar-Bjorkert's (2008) discussion around issues linked with accessing data implicitly highlights the utility of being (rather than going) 'native', of already being an insider and the inbuilt advantages of ethnography.[15] An ethnographically naturalistic approach can be helpful in recruiting participants, establishing trust and the generation of 'honest', valid and textured data. In turn, the researcher

---

[13]   See https://www.youtube.com/watch?v=v9XW6P0tiVc for the scene from the film.

[14]   Indeed, in this, as in other projects, there is concrete evidence that research subjects actively enjoy the opportunity to talk about issues that are important to them.

[15]   While there is nothing wrong with using gatekeepers (indeed, within ethnography, this is fairly common practice), engaging with an array of participants through natural, organic and freewheeling encounters has its own benefits, and can indeed have an impact on the generation of data itself.

can more fully understand and relate to data because a more fulsome relationship with participants may already be in place. They also explore the extent to which gatekeepers can help or hinder access to samples/sites which are, in whatever ways, politicised or home to groups and communities that may be 'reluctant and wary about speaking with strangers due to the climate of fear and suspicion' (Sanghera and Thapar-Bjorkert, 2008, p 558). In the context of research around car culture more generally, participants seem to enjoy the conversations, questions, interviews, moments of participation, and in general, the opportunity to do 'car talk' (Featherstone, 2004) as they may have an extant interest in car culture. At the same time, talk around the car also feeds into the manifestations of race on the road. While this is not intended to suggest race is everything, it certainly suggests its impact remains pervasive.

Despite the nature of the fieldwork notes and reflections I produce, I like to think I am merely being myself when in the field, but even this is an assertion with connections to social identity, self-perception and the presentation of multiple and fluid selves, facets of which slip and slide beneath and through each other all the time (Goffman, 1959/1971; Argyle, 1967/1994). Drawing on Goffman's dramaturgical metaphor, the nature of the 'front' I perform, which gives context and defines the situation to others, is closely related to all the other roles I perform. The only issue to be negotiated and to some extent overcome is ensuring my researcher role does not override my insider status. In short, what I aim to communicate is that while I am a researcher, my insider status predates and possibly trumps my professional role. *I might be a researcher working at a university, but I am like you*: ethnicity, class, gender, taste and – in the context of cars, like you, I have a (growing) knowledge and appreciation of car culture. To reiterate, my insiderness is not just about those broad markers of identity noted above, but about attachment, belonging and awareness of a particular scene and its moments.

The research around car culture, as opposed to work that has specifically focused on ethnicity, suggests insider status rests on a rounded, yet fluctuating and varied identity practice in which an array of qualities, markers and dispositions can intersect and overlap, vanish and materialise; different elements of memory, experience, viewpoint and positionality form the basis of identity as it plays out in each unique situation. The car, given its presence and impact, appears to mean something to everyone who, in one way or another, has encountered it. In order to engage with this range of humanity in any ethnographic depth, it has to be necessary to develop a capacity for affective empathetic identification that may inform mutual comprehension. More particularly, however, reaching distinctive samples (car modifiers, for example) also requires such a capacity to be honed and made all the more keen.

Conclusion

Of course, much of the discussion above may suggest my own practice is characterised by an overly reflective, guilt and anxiety-ridden neurotic pedantry. I confess, perhaps based on a sustained experience of the cross-pressures in academic life, this may hold some validity. However, my response is more pragmatic. While these questions and issues are all relevant, they simply need to be dealt with through either compromise, innovation and a degree of focus which, in essence, comes all the way back – for me at least – to a matter of personal politics. As a 'minority ethnic' researcher I permanently experience the ethnic and racial framing of myself and my work. How my work is read cannot naively be dissassociated from the possible readings others will make of the linkage between my identity and my analysis. In being explicit in relation to my insider status, I am acknowledging the experiential sensibilities that are brought into my research. In self-consciously sustaining an awareness of that identity through my research practice, I acknowledge the responsibilities that come with owning and claiming that ethnic identity. I take responsibility, for example, for anticipating the potential utilisation of my research findings by the far right, and take on board the additional commitment to owning the research beyond its publication. Academics cannot be responsible for the perverse hijacking of their research, but they are able to take responsibility for the careful attention to the manner in which they generate and frame their data.

Some may be disappointed at how I've framed the discussion that seeks to develop, make sense of, and perhaps justify, my practice. The arguably crude metaphor around recruiting may even seem unprofessional, bringing social science into disrepute and insulting the nature of the relationship between the researched and researcher. However, what I've aimed to demonstrate is that whatever methods or approaches ethnographers use to 'get in', there are consequences on self and external perception. There may be research areas that are less politicised, but nevertheless ideologically framed, where ethical and philosophical dilemmas may have less resonance, but where there are defended subjects, or research which takes place in sites which have already been extensively mined (or written about in the absence of research), then questions about practice might be raised and reflected on.

To conclude, research from the engaged, insider researcher, while complex and at times demanding, has benefits and costs which are built on and consequential to the status of the researcher. Integrity of data may be enhanced due to already being part of the group or community under the research spotlight, but this affiliation and belonging does not guarantee amnesty from sanctions, or indeed, decrease the chances of being claimed as a speaker, or representative. Within the broader narrative of research around ethnic relations, the role and impact of the insider as researcher may well continue to develop and add levels of complexity, nuance and insight that would otherwise be absent. Central to the ideas I've discussed, however, is the continuing and often lived experience of race: as a marker of personal and community identity and, significantly, as an idea that continues to feed into the culture and practice of 'race' research itself. That is, the historical and political forces that have shaped contemporary society leave no stone unturned. Race, as others have argued, has resonance, and whether or not we choose to see it as a 'social construct' or as an instrument of categorisation and control which enables its corollary, racism, it demonstrably governs moments and lives. Research culture, even in the apparently enlightened fields of social science, is not free of this and, indeed, is built on the disadvantages that race has, and continues to afford.

FOUR

Anthros and pimps doing the God trick: researching Muslim young people

M.G. Khan

I came so far for beauty, I left so much behind, my patience and my family, my masterpiece unsigned. (Leonard Cohen, 1993)

These are lyrics from Cohen's song, 'I came so far for beauty'. It is unwise to try to explain a poem as any explanation falls short of what actually lies in it. Poetry is a beautiful way to scream, a means to simultaneously hide and reveal, an alchemical process through which anger, frustration, feelings of brutalisation, marginalisation, of being unheard may be expressed, through which essence finds form. It asks for alchemists, individuals who can experience all the aforementioned traumas and yet engage with society, apparently free of any semblance of their effect. This is the alchemy asked of any marginalised group or individual, and it is a real *jihad* (struggle). Maxine Greene, in an article entitled 'In search of a critical pedagogy' (1986, p 428), writes that poets 'remind us of absence, ambiguity, embodiments of existential possibility'. She goes on to suggest that poets will not give us answers but can awaken us to a greater reflectiveness and give play to our imaginations, and maybe broaden the scope of what is possible for us in our lives. Hoping against hope, maybe this chapter may find words for what I feel about Cohen's lines – 'I came so far for beauty, I left so much behind' – in relation to trying to make sense of/express the exchanges between British Muslim democratic idealism/naivety (Khan, 2013), and the Muslim experience of being researched in the post-9/11 context. The title of this chapter is taken from three notions all expressing something of the feeling and experience of being researched: anthros – Floyd Red Crow Westerman (1982); the God trick by Donna Haraway (1991); and research as pimping by M.G. Khan (2013).

'Theyification'

Academic knowledge generated out of research on any marginalised community rarely finds itself in verse, careful as it is about the validity of its methods to secure the expertise of the researcher and the factualness/correctness of its data for potential generalisability.

The following examples of texts aim to express the feeling and impact of being researched. The first example is the lyrics of a song entitled 'Here come the anthros' by Floyd Red Crow Westerman (1936-2007) a Sioux actor, political activist and musician:

> And the anthros still keep coming
>   Like death and taxes to our land;
>   To study their feathered freaks
>   With funded money in their hand.

> Like a Sunday at the zoo
>   Their cameras click away –
>   Taking notes and tape recordings
>   Of all the animals at play.

> [...]

> And the anthros bring their friends
>   To see the circus, watch the show.
>   And when their pens run dry,
>   They pack their things and go.

The second expression of the experience of being researched was a piece entitled 'Ethical pimping' that I wrote, and which was published in *Muslim News* in 2007 in their 'From another shore' column, while I was chair of the Muslim Youthwork Foundation.

I grew up in the 1980s in Balsall Heath, Birmingham; it was a well-known and busy red-light district where kerb crawlers often left little room on the pavement. The exchanges taking place were obvious to even the youngest among us, and made us witnesses to the exploitation of lives that were visible in all the ways ours was not. Even to a child it was hard not to notice young women grow very old, very quickly, and all that was vulnerable and fragile giving way to survival and bare life. The traffic has slowed down somewhat since the prostitutes and the pimps were driven out, but the lust for and trading on 'experience' has resurfaced in different guises on the kerbs of our neighbourhoods, and with it, a new kind of pimp. A new type of go-between, extortionist and entrepreneur has emerged living off the exploitation of 'experience' and trading on its current hyper-inflated political and academic currency: the researcher. Some will find this analogy between dissonant experiences and exploitations unpalatable or downright objectionable. Some may see it as merely metaphorical. But exploitation is exploitation, whether of another's body or experience. My assertion that research can become a form of pimping is not one that I make without experience or observation, and by doing so I put myself under the same charge. As a former youth worker there were often and in recent years an increasing number of phone calls from consultation companies, research houses, 'think tanks', government departments and researchers hoping I'd procure them 'ten Somalis', 'five Kashmiri vegetarians', or just generally 'your yoooth'. As an academic, the demand to 'capture and analyse the Muslim experience' has never been greater. Articles, surveys, questionnaires, focus groups, charting and polling all aspects of Muslim life proliferate in a manner suggestive of the colonial survey groups of old charged with mapping terrain, territory and tradition. For the 'Aden survey group' of old, read 'British Muslims' today.

The rawness and directness of the experience finds expression through poetry in the case of Westerman – the terms used to name this experience, anthro/pimp, generate reactions of denial, anger, rejection, hurt and in some cases, recognition. The pieces recast the educational and ethical intentions, and safeguards, that legitimate the intention and the outcome of the research. In terms which are Freirian (Freire, 1970) acts of naming an experience, and an oppressor, Westerman writes 'hide your past away.' His lyrics call for a preservation of knowledge and experience that should only be possible to know through belonging. The hiding of the 'valuable' from the 'educational' intentions of external scrutiny speaks of an experience that the words of T.S. Eliot do well to describe from 'The love song of J. Alfred Prufrock':

> And I have know the eyes already, known them all
> The eyes that fix you in a formulated phrase,
> And when I am formulated, sprawling on a pin
> When I am pinned and wriggling on the wall,
> Then how should I begin
> To spit out all the butt-ends of my days and ways?
> And how should I presume? (Eliot, 2004, pp 14–15)

Floyd Red Crow Westerman's is a poignant statement of the feelings of the objectified as people and culture. I have sat in on research meetings where nothing unethical could be felt about attaching recording microphones to children in madrasahs, so that what they talk about could be researched. There has been a 'theyification' of me in other research exercises in which much of what was me in terms of community, religion, ethnicity was extracted as indicative of the generic characteristics of an externally defined 'they'. Thus, there is a process of 'theyification': a researcher's creative act of power in rendering me into something that existed outside the room, something they brought in as a priori knowledge of me. Haraway (1991) describes her experience and those of feminists in challenging the entrapment of the claims of objectivity, thus: 'We have used a lot of toxic ink and trees processed into paper decrying what *they* have meant and how it hurt *us*' (p 183).

The Turkish language uses three words to differentiate the distance of an object to the person: *bu*, *su* and *o*. The *bu* is the near, the *su* the nearby, and *o* the distant. In these exercises it was the *o* that was being used as the something beyond reach. It was an example of the impact of language in the subliminal transformations involved in the 'othering' processes. The process of disconnecting experience and knowledge from its 'belonging space' is possible to trace simply by looking at the language being used in research – experience becomes data, places and relationships become research sites, and people become focus groups, respondents. This is the process of disembodiment that leaves the researched without body and view, according to Haraway. For MacIntyre this is not just the expression of a discipline, but evidence that the discipline is the expression of a wider culture, and therefore the researched should be wary of its intentions and practices. These are moves not about truth but about power, and not just any power but about 'objective power.' According to MacIntyre:

> Our culture has one idiosyncratic feature that distinguishes it from most and perhaps all other cultures. It is a culture in which there is a general desire to make social life translucent, to remove opacity, to reveal the hidden, to unmask.... A secret in our culture has become something to be told. And social science research cannot hope to avoid being in part an expression of this same tendency. (MacIntyre, cited in Lee, 1993, p 18)

To name this experience is not easy; it is not meant to be offensive – it is a reflexive necessity for those who research Muslim young people, whether they define themselves as Muslim or otherwise. The dilemmas are not any less if you are a Muslim researching Muslims; in many cases they are more. How to respond to them is not something that is easily comprehended and understood, and therefore is not without its issues. Nevertheless, the challenge of the subject is often received by researchers as offensive, and as questioning professional practice and personal relationships. Thus the researched's experiences, feelings and expressions often get crushed under the weight of the indignation of the researcher.

The wariness of the researched to research as the handmaiden of imperialism and colonisation is often dismissed as something of the past and not the present (Asad, 1973). Yet initiatives by the US Military, such as Project Camelot in 1965, saw clearly the importance of research in understanding indigenous structures, sensitivities and sensibilities in which interventions can be made to achieve military objectives – they demonstrate the importance of social science research to the imperial intentions of subjugation and control. Talal Asad (1973) captures this in the following:

> Bourgeois disciplines which study non–European societies reflect the deep contradictions articulating this unequal historical encounter, for ever since the Renaissance the West has sought both to subordinate and devalue other societies, and at the same time find clues to its own humanity. Although modern colonialism is merely one moment in that long encounter, the way in which the objectifiers understanding of these modern disciplines has been made possible by and acceptable to that moment needs to be considered far more seriously than it has. (Asad, 1973, p 104)

The creation of the 'other' as the 'object' is aided and abetted by first having some knowledge of the people or the place. Edward Said (1993) refers to the rise of ethnography, a research approach that normally entails direct engagement through participant attention to a group to codifications of difference naming a causal relationship between research and domination (Lee, 1993, p 18). In Orientalism, Said (1978) refers to the deliberate creation of interest, whether commercial, religious, cultural or military that merges into the notion of, for example, 'British self-interest' that then needs to be defended culturally and militarily. Linda Tuhiwai Smith (2012) critiques the relationships between imperialism, research, knowledge and truth regimes. For many, Islam is still symbolic of the 'Far East,' the different, the alien, but there is also now a 'Near East' captured by notions of 'Londonistan' or 'Bradistan' (Phillips, 2006).

There are long trajectories of naming and knowing that have defined the 'Orient', and by association, Islam, as something 'depraved, evil, licentious and barbaric, ignorant and stupid, monstrous and ugly, fanatic and violent' (Sardar, 1999, p 2). Sardar names these as the very traits used to civilise the Muslim world and to strip it of its wealth by colonialists. In the contemporary world the strong continuity of Orientalist modes of representation of Muslim peoples are still very apparent in media coverage (Karim, 2000; Poole, 2002; Poole and Richardson, 2005), and the many expressions of the 'War on Terror' have been woven into discourse and policies that have branded Muslims as alien to British life and security (Husband and Alam, 2011). Cities and towns where there is a visible Muslim presence have become sites of acute anxiety, and intrusive scrutiny from the state.

Is there a defensible, ethically viable external gaze?

The search for beauty, the different, and the idealist intentions to know compromises and endangers the researched more than the researcher, the powerless more than the powerful, since it is the cultural repertoire of the observer that informs the enquiring gaze. At the same time, it leaves us with the questions as to whether there can be a 'virtuous concern', an innocent curiosity or an ethical position of engaged curiosity. Is the idea of virtuousness already overly laden with notions of morality, and who are these notions determined by? Can I, in the pursuit of knowledge, beauty, the different, pursue an idealist wish *to* know, to comprehend, 'the other'? Can I have not only an innocent gaze on someone else's life, but in fact a virtuous concern with understanding (see, for example, Husband, 1996, 2009)? Husband proposes that there should be a universal *right to be understood*, which would be a necessary compliment to the existing political salience given to individual rights to communicate: to utter, to publish, to broadcast. This would require individuals to proactively develop a positive disposition toward seeking to be open to *the other*. This is a perspective that has more recently been given support by Dobson's (2014) advocacy of a capacity to *listen for the other*, to, in an open and appreciative way, anticipate a positive appreciation of difference.

I question whether this is possible, and my scepticism is given credence by Haraway when power-charged differences are present that would: 'like to insist on the embodied nature of all vision, and so reclaim the sensory system that has been used to signify a leap out of the marked body and into a conquering gaze from nowhere. This is the gaze that mythically inscribes all the marked bodies, that makes the unmarked category claim the power to see and not be seen, to represent while escaping representation' (1991, p 188).

This is Haraway's notion of the 'God trick', the scientific claims of objectivism, of seeing everything but from nowhere, that the struggles over how the world is understood are struggles about how to see. Yet the aforementioned aspirations to understanding could be said to be at the core of some of the current claims made for cosmopolitanism: of a shared universality plus difference (Appiah, 2006).

The Qur'an itself names difference and the need to know as a divine decree, as the following verse seems to suggest:

> O mankind! We created you from a single (pair) of a male and a female and made you into nations and tribes that ye may know each other. Verily the most honoured of you in the sight of Allah is the most righteous of you. And Allah has full knowledge and is well acquainted. (Surah Al-Hurriat 49-13)

This verse is a reminder of the need for wariness of absolute assumption of bad faith, or at least of hegemonically compromised intent, on the part of all researchers. Yet fears, and for that matter, anger in relation to the latter, are difficult to eradicate. The verse suggests a dialogue: a two-way process of knowing an equal relationship in which something of the self can be revealed by the other. This desire of a giving and receiving relationship is poignantly stated by Chief Dan George in his most famous work 'My heart soars' (1974):

> Everyone likes to give as well as receive.
>   No one wishes only to receive all the time.
>   We have taken much from your culture ...
>   I wish you had taken something from our culture ...
>   for there were some good and beautiful things in it.

At the heart of the thought of the Jewish philosopher Emmanuel Levinas (Peperzak et al, 1996) are descriptions of the encounter with another person, an encounter given a primordial importance by tracing his philosophy to the encounter between two human beings rather than between God and the human being. His notion of the 'face-to-face' is one that youth workers will recognise, as would the responsibility that this face-to-face encounter engenders.

Experience suggests that research on Muslims has often focused on the proximal, them: their families, peers, neighbourhoods. This research often reifies public policy discourse and maintains the focus on Muslim young people, which informs a public policy that targets change in *them*, rather than focusing on the meta-narratives and meta-structures that bear down on them through policy. The reification of government policy occurs when the discourse generated within government departments in the unequal, and the occasional less than rational, dialogue between ministers, their departmental staff and their advisers is taken unquestioningly, or pragmatically, as an objective language of concerned policy, where the concepts that come to be the anvils on which policy is beaten out are taken as unproblematic. For example, Field (2003) and Arneil (2007) provide a revealing account of the enthusiastic importation of the conceptual language of social capital from the US, when in fact that concept was both problematic in its foundational definition and doubly problematic in its application in the UK (Husband and Alam, 2011). The hegemonic power of government to set the terms in which we come to locate other people's lives as objects of 'benign' state policy is one of the most potent and potentially oppressive forces shaping research and its interpretation. Funding tends to follow policy, rather than the other way round, and does this not make all research political?

Something of this process can be seen in the emergence of a new category of problematic Islamophobic behaviour – namely, the insidious offence of being an 'apologist'. The Muslim Youthwork Foundation designed a series of posters that sought to capture the experience of being young and Muslim in the 'Preventing Violent Extremism world'. One of the posters, titled 'How much can you carry?' (see opposite), captures the labels being generated by the wholesale labelling of the Muslim community as a terrorist threat.

This poster was designed and produced in 2008, but there is not much that can be taken off it as most of these labels continue to exist actively today. The CONTEST strategy published in July 2011 named a new kind of offender, 'the apologist'. While this policy seems to ignore the supremacist narrative that informs the racism of the English Defence League (EDL), it defines Muslim extremism as grounded in a supremacist narrative. The EDL is therefore a reactionary manifestation of the Muslim presence. This discourse has evolved and become a potent legitimation of oppressive action, rather than any demonstrable willingness to listen to Muslim grievances, and with this new label, the

ability of young Muslims to name underlying, structural inequalities that inform the experience of young British Muslims in Britain and Muslims internationally is effectively constrained.

It can also be argued that many of those Muslims who have engaged with government have done nothing more than help reify this discourse, acted as much needed representatives and experts with whom dialogue can be shown – in the case of New Labour, as a pragmatic ethical preoccupation with evidence-based 'collaborative' policy, while holding final editorial control.

The interest in access to young Muslims is an ethical concern for youth workers who not only act as gatekeepers but often as mediators and negotiators with and between structures for young people (Imam, 1999). Imam, writing in 1999, touches on the questions of primary loyalty with which black youth workers were/are often faced. This role as mediator and gatekeeper, and the ethical issues of exposing young people to unequal power relations that are inherent in participating in research, in the context of a highly politicised and visible discourse informing government policy towards Muslims in Britain and 'Muslim lands' abroad, is ethically loaded for the worker and the young person. It questions the role of consultation as a maker and shaper of policy, and it all too easily positions the researcher/consultant as a reifier of policy.

As somebody involved in the initial dialogue with the Department for Communities and Local Government in the establishment of the Young Muslims Advisory Group, these ethical tensions were very clear to me as a Muslim outsider (of government) youth worker. It seemed to me that this was not so clear to insider Muslim government civil servants.

The Young Muslims Advisory Group started life conceptually as the Young Muslims *Consultative* Group, that is, a group that government consults with on issues affecting young Muslims, whose name was later changed to the Young Muslims *Advisory* Group. For a government seeking approval, to have an advisory group is much more preferable than a consultative group. This change of title may have made the young people feel more significant *if* they were involved in this change, but it is definitely more in the government's interest to claim to have people who advise rather than people who they simply consult about their ideas. This is but one example of the ethical dilemmas faced by young Muslims in consultation processes in terms of exposure to unequal power relationships where there is comparatively little control of the image and the word – that is, how they are presented and what they say.

The strength of the discourse around Muslim young people and terrorism compromises the presence of young Muslims in areas of wider policy debate; it generates a suspicion to consultation processes that exacerbate the absence of this voice in broader policy issues. It is no surprise that the cumulative effect of these kinds of experiences can generate a research resistance, with individuals and groups feeling both over-researched and under-resourced, without any real tangible benefit in return. This experience generates an attitude that is ambivalent, at best, to the idea of research. The research in itself may not be a cynical anthropological exercise, but it can feel like one.

This feeling can be the strongest from communities that already feel the impact of social, economic and political marginalisation: there is a class and political dimension to the accommodation of research support and research resistance. The experience of being researched, however, generates a necessary concern with the 'critical question', that is, 'who is it critical to?' and 'what purpose does it serve?', and latterly, 'what's in it for me?' This invites a challenging of the objectification of people, places and relationships. It brings to the surface questions that you want to ask of yourself and your communities.

The post-9/11 research interest on Muslim young people has come from a variety of sources including universities, think tanks, local authorities and central government – some named as research, others as consultation or mapping – and many youth workers have played an important role, especially as *border pedagogues*, as they often are, that is, operating at the edge of communities, on the interstices of community life. This is the location of the encounter because this is where people live and develop a sense of belonging. It is the place where credentials for access are most critical, and where researchers' claims to insider expertise are most significant. It is not a place of being one or the other, but it is the place of difference and the acting out of indifference, and this is the place that youth workers often inhabit. Knowledge that comes second nature and relationships that are a normative part of their personal and professional worlds have considerable value to researchers who have an interest in both the people and the space. Young people will meet researchers on the strength of their being vouched for by youth workers, and this places significant responsibility on youth and community workers.

The credentialisation of researchers through their own, or borrowed by association with others, claims to being trustworthy and simpatico to the researched is itself a major area for exploration. The credentials of 'credentialisers' are themselves only as good as their last case of support for an incoming researcher. The trust question that is invoked is rarely tested in terms of the researcher's 'performance' as a researcher within the community, since often their findings are not published until 18 months or two years later, and may never become known to the researched – one of the benefits of disembodiment. In an era where the Research Excellence Framework (REF) process has made impact such a key element in the evaluation of research output, it remains noticeable how little accountability researchers have to the people who were the essential core of their research. Impact is typically measured in relation to the take-up of research findings by the powerful, not in terms of the significance it had for the researched, or the consolidation of an ongoing commitment between the researcher and the researched.

Lave and Wenger's (1991) notion of peripheral participation is extremely useful to understand the relationship between knowledge, relationships and peripherality for youth workers. 'Youth work knowledge' emerges from the interrelationship between all three of these elements. This is the locale of visibility and invisibility for youth workers. Youth work more often than not exists on the periphery, involved with those on the periphery, marginalised and alienated in terms of identity, socioeconomics and/or geography, or with those who just don't seem to fit in with the ideas and expectation of the centre. It is the reality of power-charged difference. The connection between relationships, locale and knowledge are eloquently described by Lave and Wenger, describing knowledge as something that is both inseparable from practice, but that is integrated in the life of communities, their values systems and ways of doing things. For youth workers and community workers, this locale is a position of privilege and responsibility, and many who are conscious of this can come across as obstructive and objectionable to voyeurs and those outsiders who would put their community under damaging scrutiny. Researchers may view research as something that broadens knowledge, improves understanding and that can make a positive difference in people's lives. It may be something that is a 'social good' carried out more often than not by well-meaning people, but how it is used can be unexpected.

There are two distinct issues that shape the impact of research on marginalised communities. One arises from the potential misfit between the self-defined good intentions of the researcher and their de facto practice. The extensive literature on institutional racism, and the growing literature on the implications of implicit prejudice (Dovidio et al, 2005) indicate that we should not look for the presence of malign intent as a necessary precursor to the reproduction of discriminatory practice. Expressed good intentions provide no inoculation against the reproduction of analyses based on cultural ignorance and ideologies of superiority. Second, it is undoubtedly the case that the structural relationship between those who create research and those who utilise it introduces a critical fracturing of control over its interpretation.

The unexpected use of research is anecdotally illuminated by George Smith who was the co-director of the Social Disadvantage Research Centre at the University of Oxford from the 1990s to 2005. Their work on the development of 'multiple deprivation indices' was meant to inform how government could target resources to need geographically – therefore the inquiry from the Council of Mortgage Lenders (CML) to use the indices to grade risk geographically was not the first expected. A system that was meant to develop profiles that could inform government grants to the most needy could also be used by the CML to weight lending and risk through geographical profiling.

It is revealing that while government, through consultation exercises, mapping exercises, special advisers, pet organisations and research exercises, seeks knowledge of young Muslims, young Muslims do not necessarily return the compliment of seeking this knowing of themselves from government, consultation reports and qualitative research papers. I do not think this is solely down to being able to access sites where the research is published, or the kinds of language that it is published in that could exclude people from understanding what has been said about 'them', or get to see how their words have made their way back through policy or practice intervention. In some cases it could simply be that their participation was an act of reciprocity between them and the 'mediator figure' rather than any relationship or engagement with the researcher or the topic, and therefore the matter is concluded with the completion of the interview.

Manuel Castells (1997) seems to suggest that young Muslims may be asking different questions which he describes as being about a search for 'meaning identities' in the context of the impact and impositions of global capitalism, and its demands for adaptive role identities to meet its needs for an adaptive labour force and maximising profits. Or the questions are about relationships, which is the dominant issue preoccupying the Muslim Youth Helpline. Muslim societies have been the subject of research interest long before its most current manifestation of 'researching Muslim young people'.

The following typology gives a broad-brush idea for some of the possible motivations for researching Muslims and Muslim young people in Britain or Europe today:

• a governmental approach in developing evidence-based policy;
• a historic exercise rooted in suspicion, fear, interest in Islam;
• a necessary activity in the act of colonising people or places;
• revealing knowledge that can 'make a difference' in how Muslims can be known, accommodated and related to;
• knowledge for the sake of knowledge;
• an attraction or interest in the exotic, the mysterious, the unknown;
• to know something of the self through the other;
• an interest in what has been lost in the self (community) but existing in the other;
• an engaged wish to contest exploitative and racist formulations of understandings of the marginalised.

Much of the above is indicative of the potentially highly political nature of research, its intention, reception and interpretation. Experience suggests that being Muslim does not equate to an automatic understanding or sensitivity; nor can one assume that not being a Muslim equates to an inability to understand this dynamic. The impact of the claims that can emerge from any of the above nine intentions derive their validity and force by a claim to objectivity rather than identity. Therefore the scientific observer, according to Haraway, seeks the position not of identity but of objectivity.

Muslim as an identity label is expressed and experienced through a variety of cultural practices that are informed by, for example, ethnicity, gender, race, geography, language, kinship, sexuality, and importantly, class. As somebody born in a Muslim family, my journey and experience as a Muslim or Muslim researcher (an insider) and being researched may not be the same as that of an English white Muslim. For example, he/she will have grown up with a different experience of racism to me. He/she may well have been exposed to and internalised stereotypical and racist messages of the 'other', but not the experience of being at the butt end of them, yet we may share aspects of the experience of Islamophobia as Muslims. But at the same time, I will not share the experience of the non-Muslim reaction to 'one of your own' turning to Islam. It is important to acknowledge that the 'Ummah' is not a level playing field. It is a place where privileges attached to race, gender, age, class, and sexuality can also, and do, get played out despite a rhetoric that seeks to resist. Such, however, is the power of the label Muslim that I, for example, am immediately viewed as an insider in a world partitioned by the labels 'Muslim' and 'non-Muslim', ignoring the myriad of differences that exist within this identity label that will influence my 'in group' location and perception by others. The experiences and depths of feelings evoked are dependent on context, and one's class location alone can bring to the surface powerful feelings/reactions, as Sayer explains:

> We are evaluative beings, continually monitoring and assessing our behaviour and that of others, needing their approval and respect, but in contemporary society this takes place in the context of inequalities such as class, gender and "race" which affect both what we are able to do and how we are judged. Condescension, deference, shame, guilt, envy, resentment, arrogance, contempt, fear and mistrust, or simply mutual incomprehension and avoidance, typify relations between people of different classes. (Sayer, 2005, p 1)

The insider/outsider paradigm in any research activity implies something static, a viewpoint on what is being observed, but within this lies the assumption that you can see more the further away you are, and you see less the closer you are. The insider's perspective in this model can be referred to as subjective, partial, that is, not generalisable, emotional, courageous even, all of which can be 'nicely' dismissed as methodologically/scientifically compromised. But the imposition of an insider/outsider paradigm is not always able to convey the movement that happens in the course of any question of looking for an answer. Those on the outside can move inwards and those on the inside can move outwards, and the feelings that this movement generates can be revealing of the *realpolitik* of the landscape being researched. Feelings, whether gratefulness, acceptance, respect, anger, frustration, revelation, disappointment, or confidence, themselves become useful insights. Vickers (2002) quotes Ranjan and Clegg (1997) about the dangers of conducting insider researcher in a society (and I would add, a community) politicised and pathologised such as Muslim communities in the UK.

As an insider the dilemma is in saying how 'you are feeling it and understanding it' personally and professionally, even when this challenges the informal and formal negotiated settlements/understanding being built between respected researchers and the researched, and between government and community institutions.

In this context, the recourse to methodological soundness for support can be perceived cynically, and can be seen as secondary to the values and principles that may inform your identity, and this is particularly significant due to the value base of traditional youth work pedagogy and the idealism of young people. The research approach taken can make casualties of both of these; equally it can provide the necessary conviction and strength to challenge these settlements.

Challenge of biography of the insider voice

There is a danger to the powerful and the powerless in revealing symbiotic relationships that are about securing and pacifying the powerful, of reifying a discourse being cultivated, that eventually, as Said (1978, p 94) observes, 'can create not only knowledge but also the very reality they appear to describe.'

In much the same way, funding reifies the policy discourse by a funding application process that asks researchers to demonstrate a connection to, and an awareness of, the consensual reality that it wishes to intervene in: Community Cohesion and Preventing Violent Extremism are excellent examples of this where Muslims may reject the wholesale labelling of the Muslim community as potential terrorists, but then have to affirm its presence or dangers in funding applications. This may then be viewed both as a pragmatic survival tactic, but also as an act of betrayal, of reifying and privileging a narrative that conflates terrorism with 'political Islam', of providing access to it to spaces that are personal and confidential, whether this is your neighbourhood, mosque or youth club. An irony here is that mosques have often been the most active participants in the Preventing Violent Extremism agenda.

The question being raised here relates to the viability of the voice of the researched being heard – and more than that, the possible risks of taking on the role of being a voice. It is not only an issue of speaking truth to the powerful, but may include ambiguous forays of intervening in the discourse of the oppressed. In both cases there is a claim to authorial integrity and legitimacy that may be condemned and rejected by the intended audiences. Although Vickers (2002) is writing here about insiders in organisations, the dynamic she describes is not exclusive to them, and she refers to the danger to the insider in challenging consensus:

> Frankly it can be dangerous to write about what goes on in organisations. Those of us who survive organisational life recognise that the speech of survivors can be highly politicised. Telling it like it was (or is) can threaten the status quo, and powerful political, economic, and social forces continue to pressure survivors either to keep their silence or to revise their stories. (Vickers, 2002, p 614)

In youth and community work, many enter the profession with a story that is rarely far from their own biography, a story that often has elements of resistance, challenge, inadequacy, and injustice in the context of family, education, work, or the criminal justice system. Part of the process of finding an identity as a pedagogue is the working out of these stories. This often means that these stories have to be put out, heard. For Muslims, many of these stories have been externally politicised by the events of recent years, and the opportunity to be 'heard' has become an increasingly difficult exercise due to the strength of the stereotyped 'Muslim imaginary'. It makes the task of finding the common humanness that Cottle (2002) describes here all the more difficult:

> Evoke the matter of our humanness along with those vexing questions involving our definitions of self at the very deepest levels of our capacity to reason and feel. The narrative possesses the potential to push us inward to those places that feel to us to be the farthest limits of our self knowledge. And painful and difficult as it may seem, this inward turning to ourselves may denote the best that we can do as sensate beings, for it may represent our attempts, however feeble, to make sense of the traces of meanings and sensations of our humanness, our own internal miraculous being. It may also be the best that we can do in our encounters with the traces of others, friends or strangers, as we seek to construct a sense of self. (Cottle, 2002, p 543)

There is a danger in the introduction of the personal narrative into the research process that the actual research becomes secondary, but this complexity seems to be highlighted as more of an issue for some researchers than others. In this chapter my reflections are not confessions about my fallibility that seeks to gain some form of authenticity through expressing this. They are my thoughts, feelings and reflections. These may be affirmed or rejected (Cottle, 2002), but for me, in order to express what I understand and observe, they need to be said.

> Academics may be among the best equipped to speak out, to share, to de-victimise the victim, to de-silence the wrongdoing, to lift the veil on the unspeakable and the undiscussed. What remains for researchers who choose to tell their stories is to know that they are truly writing on the edge – and there is no safety net. However, the reward and the excitement come from sharing with others and sharing with those who want to know. (Vickers, 2002, p 619)

It is no longer clear for me that academics are the best equipped to challenge social inequities, or see their vocation as 'speaking truth to power'. The Prevent agenda has a significant presence over the Muslim community, and the report by Mohammed and Siddiqui (2013), describing Prevent as part of a cradle-to-grave police state, where the understanding of human relationships and interdependencies is essential to interventions in them, can generate not only a research resistance but also a research suspicion, whereby the notion of 'pimping' and the idea of the 'God trick' are easily understood.

Leonard Cohen's poem, cited at the beginning of this chapter, is connected to this chapter because it names a lost idealism, in which Muslim activists were prepared to sacrifice time and effort that affected family, income, employment and reputation in order to engage with government post-Rushdie and post the 2001 disturbances, locally and nationally. This contribution was offered and given as an act of public service, sometimes with little public recognition, which sought a selflessness that left work 'unsigned' to service ideals and ideas of community and society. The personal and collective scars that have been accumulated over recent years as a consequence of the experience of the betrayal of this commitment must be recognised as having shifted the politics of research on ethnic relations in Britain with unmeasurable, and negative, consequences.

FIVE

Reflections of a research funder

Emma Stone

Introduction

On this occasion, it feels helpful to start with a personal introduction.

I joined the Joseph Rowntree Foundation (JRF) as a senior research manager in 1998, working on social care and disability. Before then, my focus had been China, not the UK. My early beliefs (I use the word deliberately) about research had been shaped by participatory methodologies, drawing from international development studies, UK disability studies and sociology. My preferences have been for words over numbers, the collective over the individual, and the embedded over the detached, combined with healthy unease about the relations between the researcher and the researched. My beliefs on what makes research good – and what makes research influential – have evolved, and I now value a wider range of methodologies and disciplines, although some preferences run deep.

Since December 2010, I've been the department's Director of Policy and Research. As I pull together my thoughts for this chapter, I'm struck that its content *is* different from the chapter I'd have written ten, five or even two years ago. In part that is about my personal journey, but it also reflects conscious shifts in our approach at JRF. These reflect changes in the external environment, as well as some important changes in what might be termed the relations of research production and use. I want to expose these as I address the questions that have been given to me to consider. Throughout this chapter, I've challenged myself to be open and frank. The occasional footnotes are reminders about JRF work that illustrate the point I am making.[1]

---

[1] JRF has a very comprehensive website. For more information about any of the programmes cited in this chapter, visit www.jrf.org.uk and get more information via the 'Our Work' pages or search facility. We have also provided contact details for the relevant programme managers and administrators for the programmes.

About JRF: heritage, identity and values

JRF is an independent endowed foundation, established in 1904 and based in York. Together with the Joseph Rowntree Housing Trust (JRHT),[2] our purpose is:

> To achieve lasting change for people and places in poverty; build communities where everyone is able to thrive; and contribute to a more equal society. Now and for future generations.

JRF aims to influence, inform and inspire social change – and one of the main ways we do this is through funding programmes of social research and development. As an endowed foundation, we are politically and financially independent. Importantly, we neither fund research for its own sake, nor seek impact for its own sake. We are values-led – and one of our values is that we value evidence, including the evidence that comes from rigorous social research.

1. We value *people and places in poverty*. We describe ourselves as 'on the side of people and places in poverty', and are committed to reducing poverty and social exclusion in the UK.
2. We value *community and communities*. We have a strong heritage of work that reflects our belief in community development and activism.
3. We value *evidence*. We believe that policy and practice and social change are better if informed by social research, practice and experience – including the experience of the people and communities themselves.
4. We value *working with others* – whether through formal or informal collaborations and joint work. We invest considerable time in building relationships, including with those we fund, making connections and enabling others to connect.
5. We value our *assets* – our financial and political independence, our skilled and expert staff, and our reputation. These help assure the credibility and usefulness of the work we fund.

---

[2] Joseph Rowntree Housing Trust (JRHT) was established in 1968 to take over responsibility for the housing operations of the (then) Joseph Rowntree Memorial Trust, which is now known as the Joseph Rowntree Foundation. JRHT provides housing and a variety of care, support and neighbourhood services in Yorkshire and the North East, and has a remit to innovate and develop new approaches.

I believe (and always have) that research *can* be useful, *can* inspire social change, *can* change the terms of debate and the way we understand the world, and *can* lead to practical solutions. But it never does so alone. This means that our work has to go beyond making research awards or publishing accessible outputs. It means that we, as JRF, have to be more than a funder; we have to be a *player*, an *influencer*, an *advocate* for evidence-based change.

In recent years, there has been a conscious effort to bring JRF and JRHT closer together so we can be more effective through using the experience, knowledge and networks from both. Together with JRHT, we are also a *builder and developer* of homes and communities in Yorkshire and the North East, a *registered provider* of housing and care services, and an *employer* with a payroll of over 750 staff. We're increasingly conscious of the value of drawing on all these facets of our identity to inform others and influence change. For me, this is about 'being the change you want to see in the world'. So, alongside our £2 million investment into a JRF programme on anti-poverty strategies for the UK, we are developing and testing our own approaches about being an 'anti-poverty employer' and 'anti-poverty landlord', and thinking hard about what 'anti-poverty communications' look like at a time when social attitudes towards recipients of welfare continue to harden. For us, the connection between our research and our own employment practice is well illustrated in our decision to become a Living Wage employer.[3] Similarly, our programme on dementia also includes a strand on our employment practice: what does being a dementia-friendly employer mean? Our research on environmentally sustainable design, behaviours and digital inclusion is wrapped around a major JRHT development with a mainstream developer (David Wilson Homes) in Derwenthorpe, York, where we're developing an environmentally sustainable community of 540 homes.

So, JRF is not a think tank, or a research institute, or a single-issue campaigning organisation. Nor do we see ourselves narrowly as a research funder. Many aspects of our work are similar to each of these, even more so as the roles of other organisations shift and stretch. Add

---

[3] JRF and JRHT use the outside London Living Wage that is based in part on JRF-funded research into Minimum Income Standards by the Centre for Research on Social Policy (CRSP) at Loughborough University; JRF continues to fund CRSP to work on Minimum Income Standards that uses focus groups of members of the public to determine what constitutes a minimum acceptable living standard in the UK. (This is not a poverty line but builds on well-known social surveys conducted by Seebohm Rowntree about poverty in York.)

into this the JRHT and the breadth of issues we are active on, and it is small wonder that we intermittently experience identity crises. Having such a multifaceted identity can be difficult for us, and confusing for others. But it is also a source of strength, challenge and insight. Where we can support better research/practice links or develop new routes to influence non-state actors (such as employers, finance and personnel professionals, commercial developers) as well as state actors, then this all adds to the contribution we can make to progressive social change.

Who sets the JRF agenda?

JRF sets its own agenda, working within the parameters of a founding memorandum.[4] Our agenda is neither set nor approved by the government, other funders or investors, or any one community of interest – including the academic research community. Such freedom is rare, and perhaps we do not use it as radically or powerfully as we might.

We have a decision-making hierarchy at the apex of which is the Board of Trustees and the chief executive. The senior executive team has extensive delegated authorities to make decisions within the parameters set by the Board and chief executive, and some authorities are further delegated to staff within the approved programmes. The strategic priorities for the next three years are set out in our second Strategic Plan (2012-14).[5] The plan itself was shaped by consultations with staff and external stakeholders. We built on what we already know and do. We commissioned an external team and held a large event to seek input and ideas from others and to push at our assumptions, ways of working and horizons. The strategic planning process was hard work, iterative, flawed (as these things often are!) but also successful in defining priorities including setting some new ambitions. It helps express what we don't do, as well as what we do (necessary for an independent funder with limited resources). But that said, we face the continuing challenge of how to prioritise within and across priorities. There is always much more that can be done.

Digging deeper: how we develop programmes

Far better people than I have published their thoughts on funding research, on grant-making more generally, and on doing and using

---

[4] The Founder's Memorandum (1904) can be found at: www.jrf.org.uk/about-us/our-heritage

[5] See www.jrf.org.uk/about-us

research to influence change. This chapter is a much more modest contribution – personal reflections, supplemented with insights from evaluations of JRF programmes, and focused on my own department's work. It is definitely not intended to suggest how others should work. Importantly, given the nature of this book, the sections that follow focus on our work as a research funder – but as noted above, this is only one part of what we do and how we work.

In this section, I explain how we develop programmes. When I first joined JRF in 1998, we worked through a small number of committees, each chaired by a trustee and serviced by JRF. This had strengths and weaknesses. One weakness was the constant production of a large number of mostly disconnected research projects, compared to the promise of building more coherent bodies of evidence, funded within single programmes, with ear-marked resources for non-research activities (anything from seminars to support for practice development) so as to make more explicit from the outset that these programmes were about contributing to social change. Arguably, another weakness was the under-use of talented, knowledgeable and skilled staff who were adept at straddling the boundaries of research, policy and practice, and well-placed to use JRF-funded research in order to contribute to change. Over the last 15 years there has been a determined and exciting shift from 'research manager' roles to designing, managing and leading programmes.

Having experienced both, I am convinced that programme-based working is more effective and increases the potential for impact. It does concentrate power more strongly in the hands of JRF executive and senior staff – a power and responsibility that we use with integrity and care. And that is why (and this really does take time) we are highly conscious of the need to involve others.

At JRF, we consult internally[6] and externally,[7] and often extensively.[8] This is because:

---

[6] JRHT; cross-department; trustee involvement.

[7] Through paid advisers, roundtables, bespoke conversations, on an 'as required' basis rather than via standing committees or groups (which we have used in the past).

[8] There are several recent examples where we have created a 'mini-programme' to scope a major new programme – with reviews, projects, consultations as part of the programme. For example: Poverty & Ethnicity; Dementia & Society; Housing for People on Low Incomes; and programmes on Risk (Ageing Society). They can take 12-24 months

- We are aware of the limits of our own knowledge and imagination, so we seek the expertise and ideas of others.
- We are aware of the limits of our resources so we want to be clear about our contribution, and avoid duplicating what others are doing.

We have always worked hard at involving and engaging others in designing and shaping programmes; it is an assumed and expected way of working. Constraints on time (ours and others) make this difficult, and there are added challenges where:

- It is new territory for us, and involves building new relationships and knowledge of relevant research, policy, practice and other actors in the field.
- It is new territory for us *and also* new territory for others, and involves trying to build relationships as well as connect across a range of different spheres, sectors and subjects.
- It is crowded or controversial territory, and requires a sound sense of the politics, actors, work already done and now underway, and identifying if and how we might contribute.

We have capacity for a limited number of programmes at any one time, so the stakes are high for programme development, as each programme reflects a major investment, including of staff time. Our standard template for programme proposals requires us to set out:

- What is the fit with our strategic priorities?
- What has been the decision-making route – who has been involved or consulted; what scoping work has been undertaken; what options have been ruled out?
- What are the aims and influencing goals? What change do we want to effect through our programmes? What is realistic? What is aspirational? What would success look like?
- How do we expect to achieve the programme's goals? What research, development, engagement or influencing work do we propose to undertake?
- Who are the potential partners, allies, audiences, decision-makers, opinion formers?
- What are the likely risks, blocks, obstacles? Where are the potential levers for change?
- What is the geographical and geo-political focus for the programme?
- What equality and diversity issues require specific attention?

- What are the plans for involving people with direct experience of the issues?
- What are the links, if any, with JRHT?
- What is the proposed governance and management for the programme?
- What is the timescale and the cost – including some indication of programme management costs? In what ways does this present value for money?
- How will we review, monitor and learn from what we do?
- What are the risks – and what actions or approaches have we included to mitigate these?

Everything that is set out in the programme proposal is premised on some sense (even if inadequate or evolving) of a 'theory of change'. I'm a firm believer in this not because I love the term (which I don't), but because it is a deeply practical tool that requires us to 'think out loud' and be explicit about how we see the world now, about what (including behaviours and whose behaviours) needs to change, about what specific changes we can effect directly, and what changes we can help bring about indirectly (such as working with partners or through intermediaries, or targeting specific actors who operate at the right level and in the right spheres of influence).

From experience, developing a 'theory of change' for a programme is a pretty challenging process to go through. But it does help us be clearer about where and how *we* fit, about who we might seek to work with or engage, about how our time and funding can best be used to be part of a wider movement to bring about change, and about whether and how research funding might be part of that. (And it might not, of course.) Theory of change is an unhelpful term in that it implies that there is a single theory or route to impact – although the reality of theory of change as a tool is exactly the opposite. There is no one right way. But because there is always more we could do than we have the power or resources to do, it helps to go through a structured process that makes us put our best thoughts out there about what we're trying to effect and how.

Programme development can take months. A key role is played by the programme manager who has to hold the ring on the whole process with expertise, tact and integrity, engaging with a diverse range of internal and external stakeholders – many of whom will have different, competing and contradictory views (and vested interests) about what JRF should do.

Where we are operating in territory that is very familiar to us, we can afford to consult with a smaller circle of experts to develop an agenda. We have also experimented with divesting greater power to others to set agendas, for example, in programmes on and involving people with disabilities and older people,[9] in some of our work in Bradford,[10] and programmes that are more development[11] than research. Increasingly, we fund time-limited scoping programmes – with budgets and staff time. Several of these have been influential in their own right, as well as instrumental in shaping JRF work, for example, the value of an evidence review to identify what is known and where the gaps are – creating a benchmark and resource that others can use; new connections and cross-overs made through convening people from different perspectives and sectors; and mapping issues, assets, needs and actors, raising awareness and stimulating practical responses. Some programmes incorporate subsequent stages of agenda-setting, building in review points before designing next steps.[12] At the time of writing, we are scoping two programmes: on Cities, Growth and Poverty; and a follow-on to our current programme on Climate Change and Social Justice. Alongside direct consultation, we've funded reviews of national and international evidence, and an independent evaluation of our current work on climate change and social justice. We have also just experimented with a new (to JRF) structured process of engaging a diverse group (policy, academics, activists) to identify the top 100 questions that, if answered, would be useful to poverty reduction in the UK. This – alongside a raft of evidence reviews, engaging people with experience of poverty, advisory and expert groups – will inform future stages of our own programme as well as, we hope, providing a research agenda that other academics and funders will use to inform their own work.[13]

This is all careful, consultative and collaborative work that depends on the integrity, skills and knowledge of JRF staff in navigating a way through a sea of options and opinions. It is worthwhile when the result

---

[9]   Older People's Programme; Independent Living Programme.

[10] Communities Bradford – where the priorities were defined through consultation with Bradfordians.

[11] Neighbourhood Approaches to Loneliness; Unheard Voices; Working in Neighbourhoods.

[12] How Much Does Money Matter?; Forced Labour; Risk, Trust and Relationships.

[13] This will be posted in full on the JRF website and submitted for peer review to a relevant journal. The process was facilitated by William J. Sutherland, University of Cambridge, and the Centre for Science and Policy.

is satisfyingly better than where you were originally heading,[14] or when the act of developing a research agenda proves *influential* in its own right as noted above,[15] or it proves to have been instrumental in developing the networks needed to deliver the programme.[16] It is in the nature of JRF's working ethos to seek to continuously be reflexive in responding to the lessons learned through our past and current work. Thus the account presented in this chapter is written about an organisation in permanent transition, and consequently changes in our practice and policy will necessarily modify this story over time.

Act and arts of research funding

This section is about funding research (although, as noted, JRF also funds practice projects, dissemination, engagement, and influencing informed by research that JRF has funded). I think we are good at funding research, proportionate to resources and in line with our freedoms. We are not, for example, bound by OJEU (the tendering process required by European Commission Directives for public sector procurement, where the value exceeds a threshold set in the *Official Journal of the European Union*). We have a good sense of what good funding practice means for us, and this is reflected in our internal guidelines.

JRF has three main routes for awarding research grants: open competition to respond to a call for proposals that is posted on the JRF website; limited competition to respond to a brief that is sent to a small number of relevant individuals or organisations; or direct approach to develop a proposal or enter into a form of partnership with JRF. Funding via open competition is our default as it reflects our commitment to wanting to widen and diversify whom we work with and fund. We supplement the website alert (anyone can sign up to receive funding alerts) with direct emails and social media. The limited and direct routes work well when time is of the essence; the

---

[14] Poverty and Ethnicity – and a shift from focusing on black and minority ethnic (BME) communities to ethnicity including majority white ethnicities, and much greater emphasis on intersectionality, including spatial and labour market dimensions.

[15] Dementia and Society – and the interest in dementia-friendly communities; Forced Labour – identifying an area neglected by others, and changing key concepts in the field.

[16] Climate Change and Social Justice – bringing together different sectors as well as perspectives.

budget is small; and/or it is a direct follow-on from previous work. We have a fourth route: the freedom to respond to good ideas while simultaneously discouraging unsolicited proposals. Any discomfort I have with this is balanced by a firm belief that we ought to use fully the freedoms we have as an independent funder. We have funded or part-funded some significant projects through this route.[17]

The briefs we issue set out the questions we expect proposers to address, while inviting proposers to build on the brief (for example, identifying additional or alternative questions). We are open to a range of methodologies as long as these are appropriate, ethical, can be undertaken by the team, and used to generate high-quality evidence to meet the brief. We set out the criteria against which proposals will be assessed, and secure independent external assessment (for example, an external adviser who is therefore excluded from submitting a bid) alongside internal assessment. Sometimes, we interview short-listed proposers. This takes time but we've found it helpful where the project is expected to be particularly significant for a JRF programme[18] and/ or JRF partners[19] and/or the team itself is required to involve multiple partners and we want to get a sense of the strength of the partnership.[20] Final decisions in approved programmes and up to set limits are delegated to senior managers.

We did experiment, over three years, with a much more open funding stream which we called New Insights – a responsive grants stream that invited expressions of interest for projects that fell outside specific JRF programmes but within or across our overarching interests. This has given us some 'gems' of projects that we would not otherwise have supported, but at too high a cost to make it worthwhile, either for JRF or for potential proposers for us to continue this process.[21] I make a habit of referring to this when I run workshops on 'Who we are,

---

[17] For example, Nuffield Foundation, Trust for London and JRF are jointly funding the London School of Economics and Political Science to conduct a major project into 'Social Policy in a Cold Climate'.

[18] Derwenthorpe evaluation framework; Risk, Trust, Relationships programme (both calls).

[19] Open call to evaluate three practice interventions funded by the Thinking Differently Partnership.

[20] Alternative Approaches – where shared value base was an additional reason for interviewing.

[21] For example, the number of expression of interests grew from 350 in 2008 to nearly 900 in 2010, but we only had resources for 6-10 projects in any given year, so the hit rate for applicants was far too low.

how we work, what we fund' in case there is a brilliant idea for how we can try and make this work better. I'm still searching.

Some academics are frustrated by the short timescale (compared to the UK research councils) for submitting a proposal to JRF. Our timescales are generally six to eight weeks. On the plus side, many applicants welcome the speed with which decisions are then made (often deciding within two or three weeks of the closing date).

Getting good funding proposals has become more important to us than ever. Our shift towards programme working is accompanied by greater ambitions to effect and inform real change – so every project counts in a way that wasn't the case previously. As a result, some of our 'asks' are high – but perhaps unreasonably so?

Connections and collaborations

As we recognise more deeply the complexity of people's lives and communities and of social problems and structures, we find that our calls for proposals require proposers to make many more connections across fields of knowledge, disciplines, sectors, issues, areas or population groups, networks and research competencies, and to work creatively and collaboratively with others.[22] This is not an unusual ask but it is still challenging.

Devolution and divergence

JRF works across the four nations/jurisdictions of the UK from a base in York. We take devolution seriously, and it stretches us. We have meeting space in London and advisers (but no staff or base) in each of Wales, Northern Ireland and Scotland. We are also affirming our identity in the North of England. What can and should we reasonably ask researchers to consider in a proposal to us, given the increasing political, public policy and practice divergence across the devolved administrations and across regions within England? There is no doubt in my mind that the traction in policy and practice of research can be increased where it is place-based (at different levels from neighbourhood to nation). Findings from independent evaluations of JRF work have repeatedly confirmed the scope for greater influence and engagement with policymakers in the devolved administrations than in the much more frequented corridors of Westminster and Whitehall.

---

[22] Forced Labour; Poverty and Ethnicity; Risk, Trust and Relationships; Climate Change and Social Justice (as examples).

Equalities and diversities

JRF has, at different times and in different areas, funded projects and programmes that focus on different aspects of diversity and equalities. Increasingly, our interests lie in the intersections between them. In the context of changing demographies across the UK, how much can we reasonably (proportionately, usefully, realistically) expect researchers to include or consider ethnicity, disability, age, life stage, gender, sexuality, faith, nationality, citizenship status, class, income, assets, rural/urban, north/south, and so on? Available funds constrain sample sizes, but there is also an issue of competencies, knowledge, and networks, as well as the elephant in the room of under-representation of minority groups and communities within academic communities and commissioners. A couple of years ago, we funded and took part in an investigation into the desirability and feasibility of developing guidance to help decide when and how ethnicity should be included in socially relevant research projects and peer-reviewed articles (Salway et al, 2011). The findings were informative and sobering, signalling a mixed response to receiving guidance from proposers and reviewers, and limited impact on improving the quality of research proposals.

Involvement and participation

Sometimes we are explicit about our expectations that proposals should be co-created or demonstrate participation and involvement of people with direct experience of the issues (for example, poverty, dementia, social tenancy, etc). These are challenging to develop, and to assess – as what appears to be a great proposal on paper may in reality mask a shallow approach that is more about securing funding than about genuine involvement. Over the years, and in different ways, JRF has sought to involve people with direct experience in informing decisions and advising or steering programmes, and in delivering programmes.[23] We are currently grappling with the best ways of involving people with

---

[23] For example, Older People's Programme (with an Older People's Steering Group); Independent Living Programme (with an Independent Living User Reference Group); the Neighbourhood Approaches to Loneliness Programme; participatory strands within bigger programmes (for example, with young people to develop a young people's charter on housing; with older people who have high levels of support need to provide a benchmark and vision for the programme; involving people with dementia and supporting a collective voice); and the Unheard Voices/ Change in Action programme.

experience of poverty in our anti-poverty strategies work, knowing that (by contrast to engagement with other social identities or movements, such as the disability movement) many people in poverty will not want or choose to be so defined or define themselves.

Costed solutions

We are increasingly conscious of the call that we make, and that others make of JRF, to fund projects that will generate costed policy ideas or costed practical solutions. I think three things about this. First, we need (and need researchers) to be part of the development of evidence-based or evidence-informed policy proposals and practical solutions. Second, we need to think carefully and creatively about our role in funding practice development and evaluations. There are pros and cons, not least the tensions that arise between a research funder with a primary interest in learning and sharing learning, and those whose hard work is being evaluated and who may be dependent on positive impact stories for future funding. One approach that seemed effective and influential has been to fund a systematic review of existing evaluations (as we did around poverty and education), but the benefits of this are in turn dependent on the quality and robustness of the evaluations being reviewed. Third, we need to be mindful about balancing the (real, felt, or constructed) need for evidence on costs and savings, with the reality that the blocks to change are seldom – in truth – a lack of research or evidence.

I am sometimes very sceptical of those within government, across any and all parties, who refer to the lack of evidence. There is always more we can know, but there is always more we know than is acted on. Do we (as JRF; as researchers and research centres who aspire to achieve change and who want to be influential and see impact) run the risk of being complicit in generating evidence that sustains dominant discourses that may themselves be fundamentally flawed? I know this does happen, even though I don't think it is a necessary by-product of being more focused on impact and influence. But it is essential for us to be alert to this, honest about it, and to try and hold in balance the imperative to speak to the now as well as having a keener eye to different futures.

It is clear to me that JRF is making more and heavier demands of researchers. We don't want to ask the impossible, but we are ambitious for research that can inform, influence and inspire change – as that is our charitable purpose. What does all this mean for the relations we have with researchers?

Relations of research production: the funder and the funded

The social relations of research production have more often been explored from the perspective of the researcher and the researched. But my task here is to share personal reflections about the relations between the funder and the funded, including any tensions between the necessary aspirations of academic research teams and those of the research funder.

It feels important to state clearly and truthfully: JRF values research and the researcher highly, whether based in universities, research institutes, consultancies or voluntary organisations. In my department, we love working with researchers, although we do find that we love working with some more than with others. (I guess that is the same for whoever is reading this chapter!)

We *depend* on researchers to generate high-quality evidence. As our ways of working have moved from committees to programmes – programmes with set budgets, time limits, ambitious goals for influencing policy and practice – so our dependency on researchers has increased. We continue to take pride in being a good funder: flexible, responsive and supportive of the researchers we work with, seeing ourselves as partners in a shared endeavour. However, we can no longer afford to be quite as supportive as we used to be (I understand some academics used to describe us a soft-touch, and perhaps some still do). There is a much bigger knock-on effect if a research project is delayed or poor quality, because it is seldom a stand-alone piece of work. Instead, it is embedded in a wider programme, which has its own drivers, plans and requirements, includes multiple projects and research teams, and requires coordination across multiple projects, research teams, internal colleagues, external allies, partners or targets for influence. Best-laid plans can be seriously thrown off course by a project that doesn't deliver to time, budget or quality.

As we've become more conscious of our dependence on researchers to deliver, so we have sought to strengthen our position. We are revising our terms and conditions of grant funding (again), so both parties can be clearer. Part of this will also make it easier (but not easy) for JRF to end a grant sooner, where this is necessary. This shift in our relationships with researchers reflects our shift to programme working.

We demand more of ourselves now to generate evidence that is useful, and to play a direct part (as well as indirect parts) in using that evidence to inform and influence change. We demand more of our staff, especially of programme managers whose role is no longer limited to managing research, but includes building influential networks, securing opportunities to inform policy or practice or debate, synthesising evidence and developing overarching messages. This has been a huge change for us. For many, including many of the researchers who are funded by JRF, this has been a welcome change, as it reflects a greater emphasis on working together to make a difference, and it comes at a time when university-based researchers especially are more conscious of the need to have, and be seen to have, impact. But it does bring dilemmas and discomfort too.

The most common areas of tension are:

- Where the research project is delayed, and this triggers knock-on impacts on the rest of the programme, including the potential for whole programme slippage where a project was key to informing a subsequent phase of work.
- Where the project is well researched and analysed, but poorly written – hence our terms and conditions of funding continue to allow for us to appoint external or in-house editors.
- Where the researcher's analysis and conclusions are inadequately substantiated by the evidence generated through the research or by the data.
- Where the researcher is unable or unwilling to answer the 'so what?' question, through proposing implications or recommendations for policy or practice that arise from the work.
- Where the researcher's view is that the evidence warrants much greater attention than JRF is either able or willing to give, especially in the dissemination phase. (As the extent to which JRF invests additional resources or capacity will need to be balanced against other projects and priorities, including from other programmes.)
- Where and how the research is described or referred to in relation to JRF's role.

This last question touches on the territory of ownership, as well as what makes for accurate communications as distinct from effective communications (let alone the extent to which any of us can control external communications). I'll explore this a little because it illustrates something of our relations with researchers as a *funder* as well as a *player*, *influencer* and *advocate*.

Our funding terms and conditions reflect the value we put on social research and the people who do that work. In a nutshell: the arising intellectual property from a JRF-funded project continues to rest (in almost all cases) with the lead researcher's organisation, or the individual where there is no organisation. The terms and conditions grant us extensive licensed rights so that, while we do not own the intellectual property, we have the right to use it and disseminate it widely. For us, this is essential if we are to live our purpose and use the evidence we fund to inform change. The evidence is to be widely shared, for the public benefit.

Where there has been more of a shift is in how we *communicate* about research we have funded and our relationship with it – how JRF *feels about, describes and uses* the research we fund.

JRF is more than a funder. We strive to add value (including intellectual value) to the work we fund, not least through the skills and knowledge of JRF staff. We do not do the research; we do not own the research; and we are careful to caveat each report we publish to signal that the views are those of the authors and do not necessarily represent the views of JRF as the funder. We rely on researchers, and on good relationships with them. At the same time, we have an active interest – indeed, our jobs require us – to use the research and evidence base we have funded to make a difference. And that does mean that we feel a sense of ownership of the programmes and the evidence they contain. It also places us in a unique position (which is valuable and also distinct from the position of each of the individual research teams funded within a programme) to be able to hover above the separate research projects, draw on and across them, and develop overarching messages. We are well placed to spot connections and contradictions, distil the learning, highlight the most significant findings, and identify recommendations for policy or practice. We involve others to help us make sense – and make the most – of the work funded in a programme, so as to inform what we promote or foreground when engaging with relevant audiences or stakeholders.

As a result, we sometimes find ourselves using the shorthand of 'JRF research' or 'JRF evidence' or 'our research' when we respond to government consultations, write blogs, send tweets, deliver presentations, or provide briefings. We continue to acknowledge authorship and use ready means to credit the authors (for example, hyperlinks to original research reports via blogs or consultation responses, including the Twitter handle of the researcher or institution in tweets about new publications). That said, the subtlety of referring to JRF-funded research is not always understood or replicated by others, not least busy journalists or commentators.

Many years ago, when the world seemed slower-paced, when we felt less overwhelmed by information or communications, and when there were fewer of us active in the business of producing policy-relevant research, it didn't feel necessary to think of JRF as a *player* or an *advocate* with a brand and an eye to our positioning. This is a different time. We have thought hard about the disbenefits of being perceived as left-leaning where this results in an automatic discount of research we have funded (which is not in anyone's interests). We have reflected on whether we achieved the right level (for JRF) of political independence from the previous government. At the same time, the shift to programme working has created a sense of responsibility for research generated in a programme, and a greater awareness of our own voice in making the research findings heard. We have pushed ourselves to be more confident about using the research we've funded in direct influencing activities, citing it and drawing out what we think it means for change. For us, this is about complementing and adding value to (not substituting or discounting) the direct influencing work of researchers themselves.

As with all relationships, this can get messy. JRF does not do research, so the descriptor 'JRF research' is inaccurate at best, and can be experienced as disrespectful by those who did the research. At the same time, I am conscious that some researchers feel let down that JRF has not done *more* with their research projects – and I suspect that appetite and expectations from researchers for JRF to do more active influencing from their work may grow as the Research Excellence Framework takes root.

But in among all the messiness, what I'm repeatedly struck by is how well the relationships between funder and researcher can work, and generally do work. This is about a shared endeavour: bringing high-quality social research to bear on achieving progressive social change, and working together – drawing on our different and complementary skills, knowledge, and networks, to ensure that research makes a difference.

Funding research to inform public policy and practice

JRF tries to pull off a difficult act in combining research funding with policy and practice advocacy. We want to be regarded as an influential and credible *player* that values high-quality *research* evidence, and takes pride in being evidence-based and investing in new research. We want to fund research that is sound, interesting and of high quality (and I think our vested interest in ensuring quality has increased as we have moved towards programmes, although the challenges of balancing the triangle of 'quality/time/cost' have also increased at the same time, making programme management more demanding and intensive than research management had been).

At the same time as wanting to be known for our commitment to evidence, we also feel we should offer more informed commentary, and inject ideas and fresh thinking. We want to be relevant and responsive to what is going on now – but without being seen to jump on the latest bandwagon. We know that social research, and the time required to do it well, can mean that there is a planned lag of 12 to 24 months between commissioning and publication (and that doesn't include the unplanned slippage that can result in an even longer lag).

In order to be a credible player in a fast-paced and difficult climate, we know we need to engage – actively and relevantly – with where people are (hence JRF on Twitter, blogs, Google Adwords as well as Select Committees, roundtables and private briefings).

The opportunities to influence from across the breadth of JRF programmes are vast and can feel overwhelming. Often our biggest constraint is not money but time ... our time, and also the time that other people have to work with or engage with us. For this reason, we have had to think more about *how* we seek to inform policy and practice, and *where* we see our contribution (direct and indirect contributions, for example, supporting or working with intermediaries who are better placed).[24] Activities that were once more than sufficient (publishing a report, mailing out a four-side summary) can now feel minimal.

Perhaps this reflects a sense that influence is best achieved (or rather, we can best see that it is achieved) where there has been direct *engagement*. And engagement is inherently relational, unpredictable and generally time-consuming.

If you want to engage with someone who has the power to shape or implement policy, then you need to be pretty confident you've got something worth engaging them with, something that will literally make their jobs easier. Many of the people we want to inform and influence are doing bigger jobs than they used to, with less support (including less support from in-house research or analysis teams), and with smaller budgets and greater demands.

We recently commissioned three independent reviews: two on our work to date in Bradford (where we are eight years into a 10-year commitment), and one on our work to date on Climate Change

---

[24] We have been using 'theory of change' as a tool to support our thinking and decision-making, and to help develop better frameworks so we can learn from what we do and evaluate or assess our impact.

and Social Justice. The lessons from both are rich and challenging – giving us both lots to feel good about as well as some fundamental truths about who we are, what we do and how we work. But there are interesting lessons about how the people we seek to inform use the research we fund.

There is real value when JRF funds research that is genuinely new and that fills a big gap in the existing knowledge, challenges assumptions, or opens up new lines of inquiry, action and thinking. In Bradford this was about research that challenged stereotypes about particular groups and communities in the district (unheard voices, ignored places). In the Climate Change and Social Justice programme this was about mapping social vulnerability and disadvantage onto maps of places that are highly susceptible to climate change (flooding, heat waves, etc). Sometimes, asking the question can itself start to shift the terms of debate, and the perspectives of those involved.

But we also know from these (and past reviews), that the policymakers and practitioners who tend to use and take up our research most are those who variously: (a) need to get up to speed on an issue that is new to them; (b) are seeking evidence that will help them make a case for change to others; (c) are hard-wired to be pro-research and champions of wanting to draw on research to improve their practice or policy development; or (d) are already on the journey.

As workloads in the public, voluntary and other sectors get bigger, and the pressures greater, we also know that the people who engage with us (and who we want to engage) are prioritising ruthlessly; have access via the internet and social media to more information than they can ever digest; and therefore lack what has become a luxury – the time to consider things that are not directly relevant to their in-tray, or that they can relate easily and with confidence to their work.

This links me back to earlier points about what it means to fund and undertake research that has practical application. In so far as any research project is narrowly conceived in ways that are tied to the immediate interests of policymakers or politicians or commissioners of services, then we run the risk of being complicit in sustaining dominant discourses that may run counter to progressive social change and may produce an inherently conservative nexus.

On the one hand, the research community (funders and researchers) need to find ways of answering questions like 'what would it cost?' and 'what would it save?' and 'what does it mean we should do in policy and practice terms?' And we need to be connected with dominant and emerging issues and ideas, so that we can contribute from an evidence base. But, as I suggested earlier, we also have to resist being captured and continue to fund (and seek to fund) work that problematises, disrupts and that privileges the perspectives of people and places affected by poverty and social exclusion. And we have to think carefully about who and how we use research to bring about change – and who the 'audiences' for such research are, or should be.

Informing government policy is only one way to effect social change, and it isn't always the most important way. Even where one can point to the impact of research on social policy, there can then be a significant gap between policy and its implementation into practice, and again, between practice and how it affects people and places. You can have sound and supportive policy interventions, but only partial and patchy evidence of this transforming practice on the ground.

One of the things we are more mindful of is mapping out the context, the players, the intermediaries, and starting to articulate more clearly our own hypotheses of what change we want to contribute to so that we don't automatically assume that the end goal is about changing central government policy. In doing this, we have also been challenged to pay more attention to the *behaviours* that may need to change and how (of policymakers, or practitioners, of employers, etc); the *capacity* of the relevant actors who could make change happen if they were able and willing (whether we are talking employers or community activists or civil servants or housing developers or supermarket chains); and the wider context into which research findings are shared and promoted, and change is advocated.

What role can we play in creating *more receptive conditions* so that the messages from research can be heard and heeded, and so that necessary decisions (especially difficult and long-term decisions) can be made? I am struck by the place of research and researchers as parts of wider movements for social change, by the power of research as a catalyst, or as fuel for social change. For me, this is not about party politics; it is more about a critical mass, consensus building, finding the common ground, and achieving a sense of what is acceptable and what makes, or remakes, 'common sense'. How we talk and communicate about issues, people and our research is very important here: the language we use, the statistics we cite, the case studies we convey, the imagery and illustrations. Also important are our starting points – who we partner with; who we listen to; whose ideas we run with; the questions we ask; the frameworks we use for our thinking and advocacy.

Conclusion

If nothing else, I hope I have conveyed that the question of how JRF seeks to contribute to progressive social change is a question that we continue to grapple with. As a research funder, and as a user of research evidence, and an advocate for evidence-based change, we have a vested and passionate interest in working well with the research community. For us, and for the time being, research into the root causes of poverty and social exclusion, and research that helps identify practical solutions to social problems, are a core part of what we do and how we work to achieve our core purpose. We were not set up to fund research for its own sake, but we believe firmly in its value, and its potential to spark, inform and shape social change.

SIX

The European Union Agency for Fundamental Rights: linking research, policy and practice

Ioannis N. Dimitrakopoulos[1]

Introduction

This chapter provides an introduction to the work of the European Union Agency for Fundamental Rights (FRA), and points out the centrality of research for the assessment of the respect, protection and fulfilment of fundamental rights, as well as the importance of such evidence-based assessment for informing policy. The account presented below provides a snapshot of the location and operation of the FRA within the political and organisational structure of the European Union's (EU) internal[2] human rights politics and practice. The aim of the FRA to provide objective, reliable and comparable data to assist EU institutions and member states in developing evidence-based policies on fundamental rights issues requires that it has both a means of remaining sensitive to those issues which are salient in current policy debates, and that it has a wider reach beyond the policy milieu in order to identify those issues that are currently below the horizon of political concern, but which should be given urgent attention. Research is thus central to the fulfilment of the FRA's mandate, and this places demands on the organisation to ensure that its research work is credible and policy-relevant, and to establish networks of communication that will enable the results of its work to reach the attention of those who shape policies, and those who devise the means of implementing them, at both EU and national level.

---

[1] Dimitrakopoulos is Head of the Department of Equality and Citizen's Rights at FRA. The opinions of the author expressed in this article do not represent those of the European Agency for Fundamental Rights.

[2] The FRA's mandate restricts its work to EU member states, although candidate countries and countries with a Stabilisation and Association Agreement with the EU may be included by decision of the relevant Association Council.

Background to the establishment of the FRA

On 15 February 2007 the European Parliament, the Council and the Commission, 30 years after they signed a joint declaration in Luxembourg to do their utmost to protect the fundamental rights enshrined in the constitutions of the member states and the European Convention on Human Rights (ECHR) '[…] in the exercise of powers and in pursuance of the aims of the European Communities' (OJEC, 1977), created the European Union Agency[3] for Fundamental Rights. Its prime objective would be to provide the '[…] institutions, bodies, offices and agencies of the Community and its Member States, when implementing Community law, with assistance and expertise relating to fundamental rights in order to support them when they take measures or formulate courses of action within their respective spheres of competence to fully respect fundamental rights.'[4]

The FRA succeeded the European Union Monitoring Centre on Racism and Xenophobia (EUMC).[5] Like its predecessor, FRA would fulfil its prime objective by collecting and analysing 'reliable, objective and comparable data' in EU member states, and possibly, under certain conditions, in other countries, such as those acceding to the EU. The specific areas of its work would be defined in a multi-annual framework decided by the Council of the EU, except for racism, xenophobia and related intolerance. Thus accurate, credible and relevant research lies at the heart of the FRA's activities.

The FRA conducts comparative research and its analysis is based on background material, such as secondary data, legal or policy analysis, as well as social fieldwork research. This material is collected mainly

---

[3] The decentralised EU agencies are independent legal entities under European public law, distinct from the EU institutions (Council, Parliament, Commission, etc). They have an important role in the implementation of EU policies allowing EU institutions, especially the Commission, to concentrate on policymaking. They also support cooperation between the EU and national governments in important policy areas, by pooling technical and specialist expertise from both the EU institutions and national authorities. See http://europa.eu/agencies/regulatory_agencies_bodies/index_en.htm

[4] Council Regulation (EC) No 168/2007 of 15 February 2007, establishing an EU Agency for Fundamental Rights, available at http://eur-lex.europa.eu/LexUriServ/LexUriServ.do?uri=CELEX:32007R0168:EN:NOT

[5] Council Regulation (EC) No 1035/97 of 2 June 1997, establishing a European Monitoring Centre on Racism and Xenophobia, available at http://eur-lex.europa.eu/LexUriServ/LexUriServ.do?uri=CELEX:31997R1035:EN:HTML

by FRANET,[6] a network of national focal points (NFPs) in each member state. NFPs are national-level organisations, such as equality bodies, human rights bodies, research centres or non-governmental organisations (NGOS), selected and contracted through international tender to collect data, and also to carry out qualitative fieldwork research, according to guidelines provided by FRA expert staff on a wide variety of fundamental rights issues ranging from the rights of the child to asylum, data protection, discrimination, etc.

The creation of FRA that sensu stricto is neither a national nor an international institution was preceded and followed by an intense debate about its functions and role, in particular vis-à-vis existing regional human rights mechanisms, such as the Council of Europe (CoE). Two parallel developments might have influenced this in different ways.

The first concerns an important paradigm shift in the conceptualisation of human rights that occurred after the end of the Cold War (see Kjærum, 2003). Human rights notions and conventions were, until then, used largely in a foreign policy context drawing attention to the human rights violations of 'others' and rarely mentioned in a domestic context. A new vision 'domesticating' human rights appears in the 1993 Declaration of the Vienna United Nations (UN) World Conference on Human Rights, urging governments to '[...] incorporate standards as contained in international human rights instruments in domestic legislation and to strengthen national structures, institutions and organs of society which play a role in promoting and safeguarding human rights.'[7]

The second concerns political and legal developments marking the gradual transformation of the EU from an economic community to a political union underpinned by democratic values and respect for fundamental rights (see Alston and de Schutter, 2005). In 1998, in a report prepared for the proposal of the Comité des Sages for 'a human rights agenda for the EU for the year 2000', Philip Alston and Joseph Weiler (1998) argued in favour of the creation of a 'European human rights monitoring agency' because '[...] monitoring is an indispensable element in any human rights strategy.' During the consultations for the establishment of the FRA in 2005 (EPEC, 2005), CoE Deputy Secretary General Maud de Boer-Buquicchio considered the type of motoring the FRA should carry out as 'advisory', limited to data

---

6   For more information, see http://fra.europa.eu/en/research/franet

7   Vienna Declaration, World Conference on Human Rights, Vienna, 14-25 June 1993, UN Doc A/CONF.157/24 (Part I) at 20 (1993) (www1.umn.edu/humanrts/instree/l1viedec.html).

collection and analysis – in contrast to 'normative' monitoring that assesses compliance with fundamental rights standards, a task for Treaty Bodies. A similar position was adopted by the CoE Parliamentary Assembly (PACE), which recommended that the FRA's activities should not duplicate those of the CoE, but be conducted in close coordination and cooperation, through '[...] mandatory provision for the full participation of the Council of Europe in the management structures of the Agency',[8] and this was reflected in the FRA's Regulation. By now the FRA has an impressive track record of close cooperation[9] with the CoE and the European Court of Human Rights (ECtHR) (FRA, 2011).

Underpinning these two developments one should also note the growing demand in the EU, at least since the 1990s, for the best available research-based evidence in order to inform policy development and implementation (Davies, 1999). In this light, the creation of the Agency can be seen as responding to the need to fill '[...] lacunae and gaps in the vindication of human rights in the field of application of Community law [...] because there is no agency which is empowered to provide or collect such information in a regular, on-going and systematic fashion' (Alston and Weiler, 1998).

Examining the obligations of duty bearers and the experiences of rights holders...

Traditional 'human rights monitoring' focuses on scrutinising and assessing duty bearers' compliance to international human rights norms, but provides little evidence about the rights holders' experience of the fulfilment of their rights. A need for robust evidence in the form of appropriately disaggregated statistical data in the human rights field (UN OHCHR, 2006) had been raised by UN Treaty Bodies since the 1980s in their efforts to improve the quality of concluding observations and recommendations affected by the quality of the available evidence. In this context, the use of quantitative indicators populated by statistical data for assessing the actual implementation of human rights in practice was seen as a necessary complement to

---

[8] PACE Recommendation 1427 (2005) *Plans to set up a fundamental rights agency of the European Union* (http://assembly.coe.int/Main.asp?link=/Documents/AdoptedText/ta05/ERES1427.htm).

[9] Overview of the cooperation between FRA and CoE (July 2011-June 2012) (http://fra.europa.eu/sites/default/files/fra-council-europe-coopoverwiew-july2011-june2012_en.pdf).

traditional human rights monitoring essentially conceived as a quasi-judicial exercise. As Navi Pillay, UN High Commissioner for Human Rights, stated in the Foreword to the UN's guide to measurement and implementation of human rights indicators in 2012, '[...] integrating human rights in [policy management and statistical systems] processes is not only a normative imperative, it also makes good practical sense. Failing to do so can have real consequences' (UN, 2012, p iii).

In this regard it is important to note that in its work, the FRA applies the Office of the High Commissioner for Human Rights (OHCHR) indicator model, which establishes three categories of rights-based indicators ('structural', 'process' and 'outcome') to measure progress in implementing human rights standards. In the EU context these standards are defined primarily in the European Union Charter of Fundamental Rights, the European Convention for the Protection of Human Rights and Fundamental Freedoms, and other international human rights instruments, in particular the UN Convention of the Rights of Persons with Disabilities to which the EU has been party since 22 January 2011. Structural indicators reflect the existence of legal instruments and basic institutional mechanisms to respect, protect, promote and fulfil fundamental rights; process indicators assess the actual efforts to do so in terms of specific policies, action plans and allocated budget; and outcome indicators measure the actual fulfilment of these rights, both individually and collectively.

Delivering policy-driven and policy-relevant research and analysis...

The FRA and its predecessor EUMC, has, to date, delivered a formidable body of evidence on a variety of fundamental rights issues including racism, homophobia, data protection, the rights of the child, access to justice, migration and asylum, and so on in the form of annual and thematic legal and social reports, case law databases and online data visualisation tools (see www.fra.europa.eu). The FRA's areas of work are defined by its multi-annual framework,[10] and its projects are approved by the Management Board in an Annual Work Programme. A key task of the Agency in fulfilling its objective to provide evidence-based advice is to conduct research, social, as well as legal. FRA's research differs from basic research conducted by research

---

[10] *Council of the European Union decision on the FRA's multi-annual framework for 2013-2017* (http://fra.europa.eu/en/news/2013/council-european-union-adopts-fras-multi-annual-framework-2013-2017).

institutes and universities in that it is policy-driven, addressing the needs of stakeholders, and also policy-relevant to produce the type of evidence that can be used to advise EU institutions and member states. This means that FRA staff engage systematically with key stakeholders at EU and national level to be constantly updated on legislative and policy developments. As a result, the Agency's findings and opinions are often cited and used mainly by EU institutions, such as the European Parliament, the Commission and the Council, but also by member states, as well as other human rights actors.[11]

Fundamental rights issues are not always characterised by consensus over either the definition of the problem area, or of its salience as a priority for action or funding. Thus the policy impact of the FRA's research activities does not rest entirely with the Agency; it also follows from the political debates and decisions on often contested fundamental rights issues. Given this context, the Agency's independence is ensured through the composition of its Management Board[12] made up of independent fundamental rights experts assigned by the member states, the European Commission and CoE, as well as through direct funding (in 2012, €20 million) allocated annually by the European Parliament and the Council. At the same time, in order to ensure that research underpinning the FRA's reports is robust enough to meet critical academic scrutiny, the Agency's Scientific Committee[13] – composed of 11 experts in legal and social research – works closely with staff to ensure scientific quality.

Based on objective, reliable and comparable data...

The Agency's legal analysis is conducted primarily in-house, and is based on information and analysis of EU and national legislation and case law provided by the FRANET network. It may concern a broader issue, such as the involuntary placement and involuntary treatment of people with mental health problems, or an opinion on specific thematic topics. The European Parliament, the Council or the Commission can ask the Agency for opinions on EU legislative proposals 'as far as their compatibility with fundamental rights are concerned'. To date,

---

[11] For several examples, see http://fra.europa.eu/en/about-fra/how-we-do-it/how-our-work-is-used

[12] For more information, see http://fra.europa.eu/en/about-fra/structure/management-board

[13] For more information, see http://fra.europa.eu/en/about-fra/structure/scientific-committee

the Agency has issued a number of such opinions, for instance, on the Commission's proposal for a Directive on the use of passenger name record (PNR) data for the prevention, detection, investigation and prosecution of terrorist offences and serious crime; on the proposed EU legislation on property consequences of registered partnerships; and on the Commission's proposal for a Directive on the freezing and confiscation of proceeds of crime, etc.

The social analysis conducted by the FRA is based on secondary and primary data collected across the EU and is subject to rigorous quality controls. According to the Agency's remit, data forming the core of its evidence should be 'objective, reliable and comparable'. The term 'objective' indicates that the information should be collected with scientific rigour. The term 'reliable' relates to an 'everyday' usage, rather than the meaning the term has in social science methodology; it implies that data should be accurate and not misleading. The term 'comparable' poses more problems, as it implies that data should be comparable between member states. However, there is little national data available on human rights issues, such as, for example, data on equality and non-discrimination, on data protection, on access to justice, on criminal or civil justice, etc. Even where such data are available from some countries, for instance, on hate crime, they are not comparable as they are collected on the basis of different legal definitions and according to diverging methodologies. The analysis of secondary data produced by the FRA is then *comparative*, describing, analysing and commenting on similarities and differences between member states, but the data on which the analysis is based are rarely *comparable*. This issue has often been raised in the Agency's past annual and thematic reports, providing insights into why data are not comparable, and into what would be needed to enhance comparability adding to public policy debates on better data. This has been particularly the case in the area of hate crime and equality statistics, where there is a gradual acknowledgement of the need for officially collected data which record ethnic and national origin, as well as religion and belief, alongside gender and age. Such data in statistical form can be drawn on as evidence to design better-targeted and more effective policies, and can also be useful in illuminating processes of indirect discrimination or in assessing the outcome of policies and actions. Thus, the cumulative research activity of the FRA has generated not only a significant body of robust evidence, but has also contributed to an necessary debate about the creation of common national frameworks of data collection that would facilitate more coherent and accurate comparative data.

The Agency's research network FRANET provides yearly reports setting out all available statistical and descriptive data on incidents and developments relating to racism and discrimination, and positive policy and practical initiatives. They collect several types of data, including statistical data from official, semi-official and NGO sources; data and information on hate crime and court cases; information on relevant legal provisions and case law; information on positive initiatives; and descriptive and analytical information from research activities, opinion polls, etc. These reports form the background material for comparative analyses which are mainly drafted in-house and are published 'without disclaimer', which means that the FRA takes responsibility for both the content and quality of its analysis and for its opinions and recommendations. The Agency employs expert staff with academic background, who specialise in legal analysis, qualitative and quantitative social analysis and statistics in the operational departments where research is carried out: 'Equality and citizens' rights' and 'Freedoms and justice'.

The Agency takes several steps to ensure the accuracy and quality of its data, scrutinising them in-house and by external experts with specialist knowledge. The analysis, blending legal and sociological evidence, is conducted with scientific rigour and quality-controlled at different stages, while the FRA's Scientific Committee guides the work to guarantee its scientific quality. In its research work the Agency collaborates also with other EU agencies, with the Commission, the CoE and with other international organisations, such as the Organization for Security and Co-operation in Europe (OSCE), the United Nations Development Programme (UNDP), the World Health Organization, UNICEF, and so on.

Enhancing data comparability across the EU for 'hard-to-reach' population groups...

Given the paucity of directly comparable EU-wide data on many fundamental rights issues, the Agency set out from early on to develop ways of producing its own primary data through large-scale fieldwork research involving quantitative surveys, as well as qualitative research. To date, the FRA has gained valuable experience in survey design, implementation and analysis on fundamental rights issues with different population groups, in particular, those often termed 'hard to reach' in survey research, such as minority ethnic groups and lesbian, gay, bisexual and transsexual (LGBT) people. The results of this work has been well received and widely referenced informing policy developments at EU and national level, particularly with respect to surveys on minority ethnic groups and sexual minorities. This type of survey-based research is very labour intensive because it has been undertaken in areas where no other comparable EU-wide research has been done, and also because FRA staff undertake the development of the survey instruments, for example, sampling, questionnaires, translations, as well as the analysis of the results and the drafting of reports.

EU surveys, for example, EU-SILC (Statistics on Income and Living Conditions) or the Labour Force Survey, and opinion polls, for example, Eurobarometer, target the general population. Surveying minority groups, for example, people with minority ethnic origin, with disabilities, and so on, requires different sampling techniques because their members often make up only a very small part of a general population sample in large EU surveys, which are therefore not able to provide data on their experiences.

A first example of this type of work was the EU Minorities and Discrimination Survey (EU-MIDIS) conducted in 2007-08 and published in 2009.[14] This was the first systematic large-scale attempt to survey selected immigrant, minority ethnic and national minority groups in all EU member states about their experiences of discrimination and victimisation. The survey design, including sampling and questionnaires, was developed by FRA staff who also participated in the training of interviewers and the actual fieldwork, which was undertaken by Gallup Europe. The survey was based on face-to-face interviews with 23,500 minority ethnic and immigrant people using the same standard questions. In addition, 5,000 people from the majority population living in the same areas as minorities were interviewed in 10 member states to allow for comparison of selected results. The survey asked respondents about their experiences of discrimination in nine different areas of life: when at work; when looking for a house or an apartment to rent or buy; by healthcare personnel; by social services personnel; by school personnel; at a café, restaurant, bar or club; when entering or in a shop; and when trying to open a bank account or get a loan. The survey also asked respondents about their experiences of criminal victimisation, including racially motivated crime, concerning theft of or from a vehicle; burglary or attempted burglary; theft of property not involving force or threat; assault and threat; and serious harassment. The publications based on the data produced by this survey were cited in EU policy documents

---

[14] For more information, see http://fra.europa.eu/en/project/2011/eu-midis-european-union-minorities-and-discrimination-survey

and referenced by EU institutions facilitating efforts to improve legal protection against discrimination. Reflecting the experience developed through EU-MIDIS, FRA contributed to the UN *Manual on victimization surveys* and the work of Eurostat in the area of survey research (UNODC-UNECE, 2010).

A second example, illustrating the value of robust statistical evidence for policymaking, is the FRA's Roma survey[15] published in 2012. In 2010 the European Commission's internal task force, in which the FRA participates, assessed how EU funds had been used for Roma integration in order to identify ways to improve their effectiveness. One of the major issues identified by the task force was the lack of data on the socioeconomic situation of Roma across the EU. In response, the Commission's DG Regional Policy provided funds to the UNDP and The World Bank for a household survey of Roma in central and eastern EU member states and the Western Balkans. In parallel, the FRA, building up on its previous experience with EU-MIDIS, and using its own funds, developed a household survey covering western and southern member states not covered by the UNDP/World Bank survey, such as Italy, Greece, Spain, Portugal and France, as well as central and eastern member states. The Commission, FRA, UNDP and The World Bank combined their efforts and collaborated closely, collecting data from a massive sample of 22,203 Roma and non-Roma respondents living nearby to allow for comparison of information on a total of 84,287 household members on a range of topics from living conditions and education levels to migration and experiences of discrimination, criminal victimisation and rights awareness.

The report based on data pooled from both surveys was prefaced by three EU commissioners, Viviane Reding, European Commission Vice-President, Johannes Hahn, Commissioner for Regional Policy, and László Andor, Commissioner for Employment, Social Affairs and Inclusion. Its impact was profound, as it fed directly to discussions in the Council and Parliament, and the Commission used the data in its assessment of national Roma integration strategies. Subsequently, the FRA was tasked in the Commission's Communication of May 2012 (EC, 2012) not only to continue collecting data to assess Roma inclusion efforts, but also to work directly with member states to develop monitoring tools to provide robust and comparative data on the situation of Roma across the EU. In response, the Agency set up a working party composed of government representatives, national experts, Commission officials, experts from other EU agencies, as

---

[15] For more information, see http://fra.europa.eu/en/survey/2012/roma-pilot-survey

well as international bodies, such as UNDP and The World Bank, pooling their knowledge and expertise on indicator development, data collection, monitoring and statistical analysis. In this way the FRA is engaging more directly with actors responsible for policy design and implementation in an effort to further develop their capacity to rise to the challenge of monitoring the impact of policies on a particularly disadvantaged population group, which is rarely captured by standard statistical tools.

A third example concerns the Agency's survey of LGBT people carried out in 2012 across the EU. Some 93,000 LGBT people responded to this online survey which collected data on LGBT people's experiences of hate crime and discrimination, as well as their level of awareness about their rights. This was the FRA's first online survey, and this methodology was selected because it is effective in reaching populations, such as LGBT people, who cannot practicably be identified and sampled through other means, such as door-to-door or over the telephone. The survey was available in the official languages of the EU, as well as Catalan, Croatian, Luxembourgish, Russian and Turkish. This was the first FRA survey to be published through a 'survey data explorer', namely, an online data visualisation tool[16] that allows web page visitors to view and analyse results as they want.

The Agency is currently completing other important large-scale surveys. One is also employing online methodologies exploring the experiences and perceptions of Jewish people on anti-Semitism, hate crime and discrimination in nine EU member states. The results were published on 8 November 2013.

The largest survey the Agency has yet conducted was completed in late 2013, and was published on 5 March 2014. It examines through interviews with a representative sample of more than 40,000 women across the EU their experiences of physical, sexual and psychological violence – including sexual harassment and stalking – by partners and others.

In future, the Agency plans to repeat surveys, in particular on migrants and minorities, including Roma, and on LGBT people, in order to assess trends over time, thus providing valuable insight to policymakers on the real impact of relevant legislation and policies.

While the FRA produces unique statistical data, it also conducts qualitative research. Without denying the political impact of quantitative data, qualitative work is also important because it provides a new dimension of deeper understanding of issues, which cannot

---

[16] See http://fra.europa.eu/DVS/DVT/lgbt.php

be gained from quantitative research. The inherent weakness with qualitative research is the small number of cases that can be studied that makes it more difficult, both to compare between countries and to draw generally valid conclusions. On the other hand, qualitative research is indispensable when dealing with certain respondents, such as irregular migrants or children, and when dealing with particularly sensitive issues, for example, child abuse. The Agency has conducted projects, for example, on the situation of irregular migrants and asylum-seekers, on separated asylum-seeking children and on people with psychosocial disabilities using qualitative research methods, such as personal interviews and focus groups. The FRA is currently concluding two major qualitative research projects: one on the treatment of children in criminal and civil justice procedures involving interviews with both adults and children, and one on the attitudes of public authorities on the rights of LGBT people. Such qualitative research is undertaken by specialists recruited by FRANET, with national focal points closely coordinated and managed by FRA staff.

Providing targeted and effective evidence-based advice...

Producing the necessary evidence is a key aspect of the FRA's work, but communicating it effectively to stakeholders is equally important. The research needs to target areas where decision-makers need evidence to shape their policies and legislation, and where the Agency has established that problems exist that policymakers should consider. Engagement with stakeholders is therefore a critical aspect of the work. The FRA engages and consults with stakeholders, for example, the EU and national officials, European Parliament members, national human rights institutions, ombudsmen and equality bodies, and civil society representatives on an ongoing basis and within all its projects to identify how best it can assist them in improving the EU's fundamental rights' 'performance'.

In addition, another operational department in the FRA responsible for communication and awareness-raising has been established and operates networks that meet regularly, such as the network of national liaison officers,[17] the network of national human rights bodies,[18] and the network of civil society organisations Fundamental Rights Platform

---

[17] See http://fra.europa.eu/en/cooperation/eu-member-states/national-liaison-officers

[18] See http://fra.europa.eu/en/cooperation/national-human-rights-bodies

(FRP)[19] that brings together annually over 300 NGOs working on different fundamental rights issues across the EU. Stakeholders participating in these networks are regularly informed about the Agency's work, explore synergies with their activities, and provide input to the FRA's Work Programme and Annual Report, helping to better tailor the agency's work to the real needs of European citizens.

In conclusion...

> If it is not counted, it tends not to be noticed. (Kenneth Galbraith)[20]

There is a growing acceptance of the Agency's added value in providing the kind of policy-relevant analytical input that can inform decision-makers in EU institutions and in national governments, especially when they lack a strong tradition of evidence-based policymaking.

There is also a general acknowledgement of the need to actually measure if human rights are more than ink on paper, if people experience reality differently in their daily life. Perhaps more importantly, there is a growing recognition by governments and by civil society that the fulfilment of fundamental rights requires direct engagement with the citizen.

Through its work providing policy-relevant and evidence-based advice, the Agency may also be contributing to what Olivier de Schutter has called a *fundamental rights culture* capable of transforming '[...] a "normative judicial" approach to human rights to an approach that sees the protection of fundamental rights as part of a broader effort to improve governance' (de Schutter, 2007, p 2).

In this light, the work of the FRA in the complex landscape of the developing European fundamental rights architecture produces results that help take the respect, protection and promotion of human rights one step further towards their actual fulfilment.

This becomes all the more pertinent today, a time of acute economic crisis, which, as the FRA's Annual Report 2012 highlighted, has wider implications for democratic legitimacy and the rule of law, and therefore also for the respect of fundamental rights. The EU, recipient of the Nobel Prize for contributing for over six decades to the advancement of peace and reconciliation, democracy and human rights, is therefore

---

[19] See http://fra.europa.eu/en/cooperation/civil-society

[20] See www.ohchr.org/EN/NewsEvents/Pages/DisplayNews.aspx?NewsID =13258&LangID=E

expected to ensure that its fundamental rights infrastructure will continue to guarantee a better level of protection for the population of the EU, particularly in such turbulent times as these.

SEVEN

The value of research for local authorities: a practitioner perspective

Stan Kidd and Tony Reeves[1]

Introduction

This chapter explores the purpose, status and utility of research in local authorities. In doing so, it examines the relationship between the types of research undertaken directly by councils and that undertaken by academics, policy think tanks and other 'outsiders', about councils and the wider local public sphere, and how related public policy problems are understood and addressed. It draws on examples of research about community cohesion and related policy fields in order to inform this exploration.

We write as practitioners operating at the strategic level in English local government. Although we have engaged as undergraduate and postgraduate students directly in academic research, we claim no expertise. Our stance is intentionally provocative, for while we come across academic research that we can appreciate as either having intrinsic intellectual value, or being instrumentally useful to praxis, this is unusual, given the heavy demands we face. Our working lives are circumscribed by the pressing exigencies of operating in a contested political environment, and in a dynamic urban setting characterised by myriad complex and interlocking social problems and public policy dilemmas. This requires us to combine, in Gramsci's famous maxim, 'a pessimism of the intellect and an optimism of the will' (Gramsci, 2005, p 175). It also results in a determined focus on making a difference to the lives of the people we serve, and as such, our appetite for intelligence is framed by an impatient demand for instrumental utility – information

---

[1]   At the time of writing, both authors worked for City of Bradford Metropolitan District Council. However, the views expressed in this chapter are personal, and do not represent the policies of the council.

needs to lead to effective action. Our aim here is to stimulate debate among academics and policy analysts about how research can have a more consistent and effective impact to deepen the understanding of policymakers about these complex issues, and to have a positive impact on the salience and quality of policymaking. We hope to do this while being honest about the practical and professional barriers that make the engagement of academic researchers on projects in real-life, contested settings sometimes problematic, although not insurmountable.

It is important to recognise at the outset that *academic* research is not routinely or systematically commissioned by councils, and that when this does occur, its output is only a small sub-set of a much wider range of knowledge and intelligence sources and tools that a 21st-century local authority needs to utilise, in order to make sense of the massively complex and dynamic adaptive system(s) operating in the public and private spheres of a place such as Bradford District. This process of continuous sense-making is paramount because its democratic leadership is predicated on Bradford Council being:

- the leading player in coordinating the increasingly networked governance of the District;
- able to safeguard or improve the sustainable wellbeing of the place and its people;
- able to influence key domains such as the local economy, communities, the environment, and population behaviour in ways that create conditions for other actors within these domains (as well as itself) to generate public or shared value.

Put all of this in a contemporary context of crisis, with:

- a deep and long-lasting recession having a disproportionate impact on post-industrial cities in the North which lack the knowledge capital of London and the South East;
- the prospect of a decade of spending reductions leading to year-on-year rationing of services at a time when demographic and social trends are placing increasing burdens on public services; and
- an extremely 'contested' local political environment whereby no political party has held a majority of council seats for over a dozen years;

then it is clear that while empirically robust academic research can be a useful tool for councils, it has its limitations.

Local authorities have a distinctive place in the delivery of the social contract that binds the people and the state. They sit between the central state, with its determination of wide-reaching strategic policy and its implementation at the level of cities, towns and neighbourhoods. Local authorities have a primary democratic function in identifying and seeking to serve the particular needs and common interests of their own citizens and stakeholders.

This purpose, to serve the needs and protect the interests of our communities, is what drives our broad intelligence functions and output, within which research of various kinds plays a role. On the one hand, we need high-quality, timely information that describes and codifies the deep characteristics of place, people and socioeconomic dynamics in order to frame and inform effective policy and decision-making, service delivery and other policy tools. On the other, we need a fundamental understanding of the impact of our own policy interventions and the impact of other exogenous phenomena on the people, place and domains of socioeconomic existence. These particular and reflexive drivers of intelligence and research, along with our fundamental duty to make a value-creating, practical difference to the wellbeing of a dynamic, complex and multiply challenged district, differentiates our research milieu and motivation from those of academia and policy think tanks.

Within a UK, and particularly English context of governance, the three-way relationship between national state, local state and citizens is characterised by a range of problematic dynamics and factors, both for us as the local government of Bradford District, and for researchers. Any social research in the place needs to take account of these factors, at least as part of the context-setting for a meaningful study of dynamic social phenomena.

First, it is widely acknowledged that political power and its attendant capability to control and allocate financial resources is more highly centralised and prescriptive in England than in almost all other developed countries (Commons Select Committee, 2012; LGA, 2013a). This is less so in the other countries of the UK where the devolution reforms of the past 15 years have resulted in significant and increasing degrees of autonomy, compared to the stark and circumscribed position of England's sub-national governance. It is also much less so in other EU states and Anglophone developed democracies, where the particularities of constitutional history and development have resulted, in most cases, in far greater autonomy, devolution and constitutional protection for sub-national tiers of government (see Scottish Office, 1998; Copus, 2010; Commons Select Committee, 2012, LGA, 2013a).

Local authorities continue to fulfil a wide and increasing range of statutory responsibilities – at least 1,293 duties, more than half of which have been added in the last 15 years (Commons Select Committee, 2012, p 8). Yet, the apogee of English local government's power was as far back as 1948, before the creation of the National Health Service (NHS) and the nationalisation of a number of utilities such as gas and electricity formerly under local control. In the 65 years since then, successive governments have progressively stripped local government of many of its functions, funding autonomy and governing capacity, while loading it with increasing duties and accountabilities to the centre, rather than to its citizens. These lost functions and capacities have been ceded to government itself, to less accountable public agencies, to the private sector and other bodies, resulting in a fragmented landscape of delivery and responsibility and, in Rod Rhodes' famous phrase, the 'hollowing out' of the (local) state (Rhodes, 1994).

Second, and alongside this centralisation and constitutional circumscription, local authorities, along with many other parts of the public sector, have been subject to continuous waves of public service reform over many years and several governments. These programmes of reform have affected almost every aspect of local authorities – governance and accountability mechanisms, functions, statutory duties and powers, funding, how they are regulated, and their relationships with central government, inspectorates, citizens and other parts of the public sector. During the last 30 years, these reforms have transformed public services from classic Weberian bureaucracies via an ideologically coherent and extensive set of changes intended to apply market and business-like principles and approaches, to create what scholars refer to as the 'New Public Management' (Hood, 1991). Hence, contracting out and contestability; performance management frameworks; 'Best Value'; multiple regulatory and inspection regimes; housing stock transfer; new executive arrangements; comprehensive performance assessment; community right to challenge; and other innovations too numerous to mention here, but on which there is a massive and heterogeneous academic literature.

Paradoxically, these reforms that were intended to inject economy, efficiency and effectiveness into public services characterised as unresponsive and self-interested, have, in turn, imposed their own costly burdens, bureaucratic overheads and perverse effects, while diverting accountability away from local people and towards commanding and controlling central government. Nonetheless, a great deal of effort and ingenuity has been expended in managing such reforms, and local government is widely acknowledged to have responded successfully to wave after wave of policy change, while managing to maintain the efficacy of core functions and improving performance. However, these programmes of reform have also had perverse impacts, in the sense that there has been little positive effect on overall productivity, while citizen satisfaction with local government has flat-lined.

Third, the impact of government austerity measures on reducing local authority funding has been heavy, and some would say, disproportionate. The original 2010 Spending Review imposed budget reductions of 28 per cent on local government in real terms, between 2011 and 2015. The 2013 Spending Review added a further 10 per cent of additional reductions in 2015-16 (IFS, 2012). Because of the protection afforded to other departmental spending, the effect is that local government (via the Department for Communities and Local Government) has taken, and will continue to take, a far higher proportion of reductions than other government departments.

According to the Local Government Association (LGA) (2013b), the average, real-terms reduction over the life of the government will be around a third, compared to average public spending reductions of about 10 per cent, while other, non-protected government departments will see reductions of about 15 per cent. This average cut of a third masks considerable variation between individual authorities. Because larger urban authorities in the North and Midlands, such as Bradford, rely more heavily on the elements of their revenue which derive from the general Revenue Support Grant (RSG) and specific grants, they will suffer greater reductions in budget – of as much as 40 per cent by 2015, with further cuts announced in the 2013 Spending Round for the following year (2016/17).

Figures for Bradford illustrate this in real financial and proportionate terms (Bradford District Council, 2014). Bradford's net budget for the 2013/14 financial year was £453.4 million. This is around £100 million (18 per cent) less than it was in 2011/12, with respective reductions made over the last three years of £44 million, £28 million and £29 million. Following the 2012 Treasury Autumn Statement and the 2013 Budget, Bradford Council is now planning to save a further £100-115 million (22-25 per cent) by 2016/17. This is a cumulative reduction of at least 40 per cent over six years.

An added complication in this relationship between the national and local state is the degree of policy and ideological difference or alignment in the intersection of national and local party political power bases. Where there is a convergence between the national party in power and the party with control of a local authority, there is a basis for synergy between the policy impulse from central government and its expression at the local level. However, there may be occasions when the de facto political differences between central and local government are ameliorated by the fact that they both share a common, wider ideological or policy position on a specific issue. Thus, for example, in recent years the national, and indeed European, retreat from any robust expression of multiculturalism has provided a common zeitgeist that has ameliorated potential party political, and national/local divergences on matters of minority ethnic policy. Similarly, at the level of urban policy, it would be reasonable to suggest that the penetration of Putnam's notions around civility (Putnam, 2000), and the acceptance of the centrality of the notion of *social cohesion*, has provided a further instance of an essentially uncontested framing concept for a wide range of urban policy interventions.

Nature of the place and its people

Bradford Council administers the fourth largest metropolitan area in England – a district that is home to over half a million people. It is characterised by diversity: huge contrasts of geography, wealth and built environment; communities of many cultures and ethnicities; and a place which typifies the complex range of socioeconomic, environmental and political problems and opportunities which is the stuff of contemporary public policy and public management.

Bradford District is a place of contrasts containing the major city of Bradford itself, towns such as Keighley, Shipley, Bingley and Ilkley, and a rural hinterland. Two-thirds of the district is green belt, ranging from the uplands of Ilkley and Haworth Moors to the green spaces between the main settlements.

Bradford is one of the fastest growing urban areas in the UK (using comparisons between the 2001 and 2011 Censuses), has the fastest growing elderly population in England, and is also one of the youngest cities in Europe. It is the most ethnically diverse district in the north of England, with over 80 languages regularly spoken, although around 83 per cent of the population consists of two ethnic groups – White British and Pakistani origin. Eleven per cent of the population are in the most affluent decile in the UK, and 40 per cent are in the least affluent decile. From a research point of view this ethnic complexity provides different and potentially contested ways in which to characterise the population and the community relations that result, depending on the purpose and design of the research and the value position of the researchers. Bradford District can be construed as either highly diverse – based on the total number of ethnic groups and languages and the resultant rich cultural diversity – or as essentially bi-cultural – based on the numerical and cultural domination of White (UK-origin) and Pakistani-origin groups.

The city has grown as a result of inward migration for around 200 years. In 1801 the population of Bradford was 15,000, and by 1901 it was approaching 200,000. This extraordinary growth was driven by the Industrial Revolution and Bradford's emerging role as the centre of the global woollen industry.

As a result of the legacy of an over-reliance on a single industry in the past (textiles), together with systemic failings in primary and secondary education over the last quarter of a century, Bradford District has a low-skilled, low-wage economy compared to other comparable places in the UK, despite economic diversification since the rapid contraction of the woollen industry in the latter half of the last century, Bradford being home to more big companies than any other northern city, and having a very healthy business start-up rate.

Given this context, the problems and opportunities of local government and local communities provide a domain of research for a range of players including academia, government, policy think tanks as well as local public management professionals. The interests, motivation and approaches of these players do not always or even often coincide, but where they can, the output may well have added value and salience, not just for the players themselves, but also for others in the wider public domain. A divergence or dissonance of motivation and approach can be one of the factors that are problematic for fruitful collaboration between the council and academics or other external researchers.

The contextual and relational features of English local governance, and the resultant problematic challenges facing local authorities described above, prescribe or circumscribe particular approaches to research that are essentially derived from the verities of complex praxis, are politically contested both within the local polity and in a local versus national perspective, and are limited by resource and time pressures that demand such research is useful to processes of policy development and delivery of service or wellbeing outputs and outcomes. In short, in such a pressurised and exigent context, research is only likely to have instrumental utility if it can be seen to generate information for action.

This can be contrasted with the very different milieus of both academia and policy institutes. In the former, the drivers for research are often derived from some need to test out theory or ideological hypotheses, sometimes without any necessary connection to interdependent policy concerns, or attendant political exigencies, accountabilities and pressures, whereas research in policy institutes and think tanks tends to lack longitudinal or historical context, and to have particular narrow research concerns, often related to lobbying for alternative policy/political positions, or which are critical of orthodox positions of both policy and practice.

Even when academic or policy institute research is more directly aligned to evaluating practical public policy concerns, it is not necessarily directed at specific local contexts, unless it has been commissioned by either local public bodies directly, or by agencies such as the Joseph Rowntree Foundation that undertakes place-based micro-research. In the latter case, the utility of such research to local authorities can be influenced by such factors as a consensus on the assumptions and data underpinning the research brief, a mutual commitment to the salience of the hypotheses under investigation, and an effective relationship between the researcher and the authority, as well as with other stakeholders in the research exercise. All of these factors need to be carefully managed while at the same time not compromising the efficacy and independence of the research. This involves a delicate balancing of the interests of researcher and stakeholders, and a keen focus on effective design, governance and the accommodation of a common purpose.

Although based in a different policy domain to the one that is the focus of this book, a local exemplar of such coincidence of research motivation and one characterised by effective design and governance is the Born in Bradford programme (see www.borninbradford.nhs. uk). Bradford has high levels of childhood ill health – asthma, obesity, infections, diabetes, and childhood disability. Born in Bradford has been set up to provide a city-wide approach to understanding and tackling these health concerns. It is following up 14,000 children from their time in the womb to adulthood. Leading academics from across the world are helping to unravel the complex interplay between our genes, environment and lifestyles. Born in Bradford involves all health professionals – from recruitment (midwives), follow-up (health visitors and GPs) and schools. This model provides an example of how researchers, practitioners and policymakers can work together to address major health challenges. Born in Bradford works closely with a wide range of partners and organisations and with families themselves in a model of longitudinal action research and coproduction in order to improve maternal and child health and to reduce infant mortality rates across Bradford District.

Bradford Council's purpose and policy context

Like all unitary local authorities, Bradford Council has a number of roles including the provision of a wide range of services, from education and social care, to waste management and environmental maintenance. It has a significant public protection or safeguarding role in areas such as environmental health and child protection, and strategic leadership and coordination roles in areas such as spatial planning, economic development and transportation. It has recently taken on local public health functions.

In addition, in recent years much more emphasis has been placed on the council's role in community leadership and 'place-shaping' (see Lyons, 2007). In a sense, this more recent strategic focus on the leadership and stewardship of the place reasserts the council's historical, core purpose to provide local *government*: a democratically elected autonomous entity designed to represent, advocate for, safeguard and serve the people and institutions of the district.

This reassertion can be seen as a corrective to the period during the 1990s and the early years of this century when New Public Management was in the ascendancy. Although the imposition of managerialism and market-like mechanisms has been instrumentally beneficial, it has been more than offset by the politically enfeebling impacts of fragmentation, and by the loss of coherence across the local state and public sphere. The notion of place-shaping was one concept among several others that attempted to reclaim the purposive centrality of local authorities' governance functions, and rebalance the functional duality away from *service provision* for *customers* and towards *democratic engagement* with *citizens*. Other emerging concepts that have attended to this consolidation of democratic leadership include public value theory, coproduction, and the application of systems thinking to public and social problems, which has resulted in policy initiatives such as Total Place and Community Budgets (see Benington and Moor, 2011).

As a council we are obliged through various statutory instruments, government guidance and regulation to promote positive relationships between different communities, and to ensure that equality issues are properly considered in all aspects of the council's work. These requirements include our overall community leadership role as well as in specific functions such as in education. We have general duties to promote economic, environmental and social wellbeing in the district, and various duties around securing the provision of decent housing for our citizens and reducing health inequalities.

In order to make sense of, and intervene efficaciously in, this complex statutory and policy context, as well as ensuring we operate effective democratic and representative governance, we need to maintain and continually update a mass of intelligence, in a wide variety of forms including research, about:

- the characteristics and needs of the place, its people and stakeholder organisations;
- the impact of external economic, social and legislative factors on the place, and its people and organisations;
- the impact of the council's policies, services, resources, along with those of other public bodies, and those in other sectors; and
- the reflexive interrogation and interpretation of policy frameworks being developed nationally, regionally and locally.

This broad intelligence requirement includes a thorough understanding of community cohesion and the dynamic and complex relations between diverse communities in the context of Bradford's history, geography and demography. This is important because it enables the council to be able to execute its functions successfully, and to have a positive impact on the lives of all of our citizens.

Managing 'social cohesion'

It is important to understand the rich range of this intelligence, some of which is not necessarily abstracted and used directly for policy analysis. Rather, near real-time data is exchanged or shared between front-line officers and managers, and collected through dialogue with citizens and community representatives, or through direct observation and experience, and sometimes codified in service statistics. This kind of intelligence allows public agencies to monitor community tensions and the health of relations, and influences community dynamics through the shaping of informal and formal interventions. This undergirding of front-line praxis with the dissemination of emergent, street-level intelligence is not easily distilled or abstracted for use by academics, or even by strategic leaders, but its value in maintaining safe community relations should not be discounted. Such street-level intelligence, which is essentially coproduced in the interactions between professionals and citizens, comes into its own when urban communities are confronted with crises. Recent examples from Bradford involving the effective management by the police, council officers and community leaders, of English Defence League (EDL) demonstrations (consisting largely of EDL provocateurs from outside the district) and attendant counter-demonstrations, have tested the quality and utility of such intelligence.

It is also important to understand the local evolution of the social phenomena under investigation alongside the parallel evolution of our understanding and policy responses to these phenomena. We need to remember that prior to 2001 and the disturbances in Bradford and other northern towns, the dominant narratives about such policy issues were not couched in the language and associated semiotics of cohesion at all, but rather in related concepts of community relations, community development, equality and discrimination, and multiculturalism. During the period leading up to the disturbances, our intelligence and policy responses were primarily local and not mediated through assertive national government policy, research and delivery.

After 2001 the policy paradigm shifted. Successive governments and national agencies commissioned research, issued white papers, strategy and guidance on the subject of cohesion/integration in ways which, from a local political perspective, 'nationalised' and generalised the issues and the policy responses which were sometimes unhelpful or sub-optimal. There were pros and cons to this shift. It can be reasonably argued that comparing and analysing the state of community relations and associated policy interventions across a range of English urban settings, and identifying more general factors and features, had value in evaluating causes, correlations and the effectiveness of responses across a richer field of evidence.

However, we would argue that while this was not without value, the extrapolation of universal conclusions and policy responses at the national level circumvented and undermined an appreciation of local context and characteristics which are essential for appropriate interventions in complex and specific community dynamics. Furthermore, not only was much of the early research (for example, Cantle, 2001) based on a somewhat shallow and partial understanding of the issues in dynamic urban environments such as Bradford, but it was also conducted in a milieu of moral panic framed by perceptions and narratives about the potential consequences of apparent urban decay, segregation and 'parallel lives'. This early value position – which, perhaps uncharitably, might be described as *dystopian myopia* – was challenged by the greater breadth and depth of subsequent government commissions such as the multilayered research that underpinned the Singh report (2007). It has also faced a challenge from a range of critical academic research, albeit within a contested and dynamic field (see, for instance, Harrison et al, 2005). However, it should also be borne in mind that between 2000 and 2007, our understanding of cohesion and its context had changed as a result of 9/11, the 7/7 London bombings and the policy panic relating to the migration of people from the European Union (EU) new accession countries ('A8'), and also came to be associated, in part, with the 'Prevent' (anti-terrorism) agenda.

Another affecting factor which needs to be understood in locating this early cohesion research in an ideological context is that it was commissioned by a national government which was critical of the effectiveness of autonomous local authorities, and was infused by a command and control mentality and a New Public Management orthodoxy which was framing a massive reform programme attempting to 'modernise' local governance and service delivery along fragmented and marketised lines (see Martin and Bovaird, 2005). This is not a partisan point (except in so far as we are committed to local government as a legitimate tier of autonomous democratic leadership for local communities) because the same orthodox worldview which progressively reduced the functional power and resources of local government has infected governments of every hue since at least 1979, from the turn to New Public Management.

This contextual account serves to demonstrate that research into complex social phenomena such as community cohesion needs to be explicitly understood as both contingent on the dominant narratives of current policy and governance orthodoxy, and circumscribed by the values, motivations and methodological approaches of the researchers themselves. For instance, Cantle (2001) was preoccupied with bonding and bridging social capital (see Putnam, 2000), which, in his normative characterisation, was entirely bad or good respectively.

Further, we want to provoke discussion about why some policymakers often seem to start from a viewpoint that there is a normative and stable state of 'Britishness' to which migrant communities are expected to conform. From a practitioner perspective we would argue that, on balance, society has been, and continues to be, enriched with each wave of migration, and we should therefore be exploring key community dynamics and seeking to identify the interventions that can positively influence these dynamics to promote cohesion in a deeper and more sustained way.

A recent government paper setting out a framework for integration, *Creating the conditions for integration* (DCLG, 2012), was a somewhat lightweight document that didn't really go near the issues faced by deprived communities in urban Britain. It did, instead, refer to the role of the church, and identified the Diamond Jubilee and the 'Big Lunch' as opportunities for people to celebrate 'British life' and thereby enhance integration between communities.

This approach, together with an almost total avoidance of the multiple issues faced by people in inner-city Britain at a time of economic crisis, spiralling youth unemployment, disinvestment in key public services and a programme of tough welfare reforms, suggested that government wants to advocate an idealised set of circumstances to be enjoyed by British citizens and to be aspired to by new arrivals. This idealised view of British life probably did exist in small towns and villages some decades ago, but certainly doesn't reflect our contemporary industrial cities, most of which have been built on migration for more than 200 years.

Cities are increasingly being viewed as dynamic systems (*complex adaptive systems*, in the literature) that are in a state of perpetual emergence, that is, constantly changing across a range of dimensions and not necessarily in predictable ways. While there are patterns and processes of behaviour and change that are common, the combination of factors which come together and relate reflexively to each other in order to shape a place are unique to that place. This is important because it suggests that an over-reliance on lazy 'desktop' analysis and over-generalisation at the national policy level means that many of the attempts of central government to have an impact on these issues are destined to fail.

Central policymakers, rather than prescribing a generic set of solutions, should try to develop broad policy frameworks that set the national context for bespoke local analyses and interventions. In essence, it is likely that the most progress will be made when the centre and localities better understand and respect each other's roles, and the former enables the latter to develop interventions and innovation appropriate to local circumstances.

On the subject of 'localism', central government rhetoric is strong, but action is almost always, and paradoxically, top-down and prescriptive, often acting as an impediment to, rather than an enabler of, local action. This government rhetoric also masks specific policies designed to bypass or marginalise local government, discounting its ability to enable and shape locally appropriate policy instruments. This reflects, perhaps, an engrained ideological hostility to the local state in favour of local voluntary action, and a somewhat over-optimistic faith in the capacity and resilience of local civil society to self-organise and respond to social or public problems. This is not to disparage the worth and appropriateness of civil society organisations and groups as important tools to add public value and solve local public problems. However, such local social capital is best deployed when it is subject to coordination and oversight by strategic bodies working collectively on the system under the aegis of the community leadership provided by a local authority. Networked governance is most resilient when it is underpinned by agreed frameworks of strategic coordination and leadership. These frameworks have been weakened by the coalition government through their removal of any statutory underpinning for local strategic partnerships, and a more laissez-faire and fragmented approach to the governance of local public agencies.

Government public policy also sometimes struggles to free up local authorities and other public agencies to join up planning and delivery in order to focus on prevention and early intervention, and address local socioeconomic and cultural problems as systemic. Although there have been noteworthy exceptions, such as the Total Place and Community Budget/Troubled Families initiatives, such integrated systemic approaches are still not being adopted widely, probably as a result of departmentalism in government, and a weakened coordinating role in the Cabinet Office, compared to the pivotal role it played in the previous government. It remains to be seen whether the unprecedented budget reductions currently being experienced by local authorities will act as an impediment, or the requisite stimulus to further innovation in such whole-systems thinking and action.

In summary, academic research about social phenomena such as community and social cohesion can play a value-creating role beyond its primary creation or exploration of theory when its purposes are aligned to the complex challenges facing communities themselves, and to those of the public agencies working on policies designed to ameliorate the negative effects of such challenges. These public agencies, aware of their own shrinking intelligence resources, need to recognise the potential informational value of independent academic skills and voices in helping them deepen their understanding of the problems they are trying to tackle.

Such mutual recognition of value requires a range of preconditions, outlined above, which include an orientation towards systems thinking and multifaceted action research, open acknowledgement of the constraints and opportunities of the politics and governance arrangements pertaining at the local level, and an admission by local authorities and other public agencies that, while their instrumental impatience for 'information for action' is understandable, given the resource constraints they face, a corrective commitment to longitudinal evidence, and experimenting with innovation in conditions of complex emergence, will bear fruit and result in more finely tuned policy outcomes.

Self-segregation

In order to develop some of the points made above, it will be useful to unpack some of the debate around *self-segregation* and its impact on local government policy and practice.

In 2001, many people used Herman Ouseley's report about race relations in Bradford to explain the causes of the riots that took place in the same year (not just in Bradford, but in several other northern English towns). The report was published five days after the riots, and was actually completed before them. It coined the term 'self-segregation' and described a city 'gripped by fear'.

A number of reports (see, for example, Cantle, 2001, p 1; Clarke, 2001; Ritchie, 2001) went on to describe some of the processes that emerged after the riots as 'white flight'. Cantle later established a mechanism for measuring the resilience and sustainability of communities that he referred to as the 'barometer of segregation'. Simpson and Finney (2010; see also Simpson and Finney, 2009) and others (see, for example, Phillips, 2006) have robustly challenged these 'myths', and provided evidence and analysis to demonstrate that Bradford and many other UK cities had become progressively less rather than more segregated, and that 'white flight' was, in fact, middle-class flight that, if it existed at all, involved the dispersal of black and minority ethnic (BME) families from the inner city rather than just a whites-only exodus.

A major problem is that some politicians on a national stage have selectively used research evidence to suit their policy or ideological agenda, without being too bothered about its enduring validity or contested nature, in order to draw ex-cathedra conclusions about what is happening in inner-city Britain. When this is exacerbated by the behaviour or cynical stance of certain elements in the media, it tends to lead one to the view that if you say something often enough, it becomes accepted as true.

Given our professional experience, which includes a background in housing and urban development, we would argue that the notion that some immigrant communities actively choose to self-segregate misunderstands how cities function, and discounts the degree to which choice is circumscribed by economic and social circumstance. One of the biggest factors determining where new arrivals choose to live is the functioning of the local housing market, and the roles played within this by institutional players. This happens in two main ways. First, most migrants arrive in Britain with a limited or even non-existent experience of social housing, and therefore move into the areas of cities with the lowest priced privately rented housing, most often in the inner city. Bradford has an unusually high proportion of privately rented housing.

In contrast, poor white families from long-standing communities understand better how to navigate the social housing system. They are much more likely to have grown up on housing estates, and until the last decade, points-based allocations policies often rewarded length of residency in a location and family ties in the area. As a result, poor white families tended to live on estates, almost always built on the periphery of our cities, and poor migrant families tended to live in inner-city private housing.

This separation is nothing to do with (proactive) self-segregation, but, reinforced by issues of bonding social capital within all poor communities (something in itself criticised as anti-cohesive activity by some commentators), can very easily be explained by developing an understanding of the dynamics at play in the local housing market. Over time, as migrants become economically empowered, people tend to move out of the inner city in increasing numbers to access better housing, schools and other desired amenities. The impact this has on the inner city is masked by growing populations within the inner-city communities, and so the 'desktop analysts' don't tend to understand the real dynamics taking place.

An improved knowledge of social housing, coupled with more flexible and appropriate housing management policy and practice, means that this divide between poor communities breaks down over time. This can be evidenced by the significant change in the ethnic mix of tenants of social landlords in Bradford in the past decade, and the outward movement of increasing numbers of more established migrant families from the inner city and their replacement, either by growing populations from these communities, or with the more recent arrivals such as Eastern Europeans. Drawing on census data, the proportion of Asian families living in social rented housing almost doubled in the 20 years to 2011, from 4.4 to 8.5 per cent. A contrasting picture is provided by looking at the number of non-British White households, a cohort that includes many Eastern European migrant families. The number of 'Other White' households in the district almost doubled between 2001 and 2011, from 3,300 to 6,300. Of this growing number of households, nearly half lived in privately rented accommodation compared to only 15.7 per cent in 2001.

Like many urban practitioners, we see some inner-city residential areas as 'zones of transition'. The fact that the transition process may take many years for some communities doesn't alter our view that what is occurring is entirely consistent with cities built on migration across the world over many decades and in some cases for at least 200 years.

The dominant rhetoric of both major parties that ethnic (self-) segregation is a key feature of urban Britain has been challenged by demographic geographers such as Danny Dorling (2007, 2012; see also Singh, 2007), who draws on large sample census data to show that shifts in patterns of settlement have led to more ethnic mixing which has been complemented by the significant growth in households of mixed origin, with twice as many people being of mixed ethnicity now compared to 2001. Dorling contends that what such rhetoric is masking is a more profound economic and class segregation and decline in social mobility, despite material improvements in child poverty and employment since 1997: 'the key cleavages that run across contemporary social maps of Britain and which are widening in one way or another...' are not those relating to ethnic, religious or migrant division, but those of property-related wealth and 'poverty, education, employment and disease' (Dorling, 2007, p 7).

It is appropriate to acknowledge that there is a substantial amount of credible research material that evidences the urban dynamics outlined above (Harrison et al, 2005; Phillips, 2006; Dorling, 2007, 2012; Simpson and Finney, 2009, 2010; see also Afridi, 2007; DTZ, 2007; Vertovec, 2007 – all of which were commissioned to support Singh, 2007). A major problem, however, and a real challenge to the utility of good academic research, is that those 'desktop analysts' who frame their research design and output in ways that accord with dominant policy narratives are often the people with the most influence over national politicians and who hold key positions in publicly funded bodies. Their cosmetic analysis often throws up straightforward conclusions which are much more accessible to journalists and others looking for sound bites to reinforce their, often fixed, views of the world.

We recognise here that our distinction between 'desktop analysts' and more considered academic research is somewhat caricatured, but we make the point in order to emphasise the care needed by policymakers to not only look beyond their own immediate view of the local world on which they are attempting to act, but also to look beyond those analysts who are in some way captured directly or indirectly by the powerful orthodoxies and resources of government. It behoves local democratic leaders and their professional policymaking officers to constantly search and question the assumptions with which they work, and to find alternative viewpoints and counter-factual evidence with which to triangulate their policy design. In this sense, the work of more independent and critical academics deserves attention from practitioners, even when there is no direct commissioning relationship.

Afridi's research (2007) examines interrelationships between cohesion, deprivation and equality, and seeks to relocate cohesion within a 'capabilities' approach to equality. It starts from a critique of recent cohesion thinking as narrow and too bounded by 'wider debates about multi-culturalism … immigration and poor integration', but also, since the London bombings, 'dominated by concerns about alienation and radicalisation, especially among young Muslims' (2007, p 5). Afridi argues that this limited understanding has had the perverse effect of creating intercommunity tensions and weakening cohesion because of 'the public perception that equality and cohesion strategies have been primarily concerned with addressing the needs of BME communities at the expense of White British communities' (2007, p 5). The starting point of Cantle's research was in response to apparent, fundamental interethnic conflict. This was understandable given the commission Cantle had been given. However, Afridi uses the benefit of hindsight, and a broader research canvas, to show that cohesion is better understood as effective interrelations between *all* people, and that other critical factors that erode cohesion relating to deprivation, economic inequalities, resource competition, and intracommunity weakness have only recently become understood enough to provide a more balanced and holistic conceptualisation of cohesion and integration.

In sum, successive governments have treated the concept of community cohesion as a recent issue and policy goal peculiar to Britain, and centred almost exclusively on ethnicity rather than on the pattern of urban dynamics that has emerged over centuries as the process of migration to urban areas has unfolded. The research approach adopted by Singh's Commission on Integration and Cohesion stands as an instructive corrective to such orthodoxy, in that multiple projects were commissioned using a range of different methodologies, scales and disciplines, which allowed a much more systemic analysis of the phenomena under investigation. From this deeper analysis, a more tailored and nuanced set of policy recommendations resulted.

Conclusion

The broad body of research across the fields of community cohesion, integration, community relations and wider urban community dynamics is contested, and needs to be understood within a context of competing policy orthodoxies, the purposes and research milieus of commissioning bodies, and its ideological and theoretical framing.

Within this contested and broad corpus, a significant and increasing sub-set of academic research suggests that Britain has become increasingly tolerant, less segregated, and that settlement patterns are influenced by the dynamics in the local housing market, cultural capital, economic power, the degree of social mobility and familiarity with the British housing system, among other key factors.

Unfortunately, some commentators, national politicians and therefore large numbers of people persist in believing that communities self-segregate and somehow choose to live parallel lives to 'the rest of us'.

If academics accept this picture as valid, it throws up a real issue about the relevance of such academic research in shaping public policy and its practical application. Further debate is needed about how to raise the profile and salience of social science research and the role academics play in holding policymakers to account for the evidential basis of their policy decisions. It may be that the sources of funding for research and the clients for specific projects may be complicating (and compromising) factors, but we are not qualified to comment on those issues.

The utility of academic output would be improved if more systemic approaches to understanding and unpacking these urban dynamics were explored. Soft systems methodologies and other types of systems thinking have been increasingly utilised to understand complex human activity and behaviours in other fields, and indeed to develop tools to help shape strategic responses to the issues emerging from the analysis. It strikes us that the increased use of systems thinking techniques in this field would merit further discussion and exploration. Additionally, there is something about the development of trust and working relationships between academics and local authorities such as Bradford that requires thought and effort.

It is undoubtedly true that, given local authorities' current operating environment, they need all the help they can get from academic researchers and the work of policy institutes and think tanks. However, for this to have maximum impact and salience for the authorities and places, it needs to be commissioned, designed and undertaken in ways that appreciate a number of contemporary realities, including:

- the massive resource pressures and constrained autonomy of local authorities, as a result of government responses to the financial crisis, and longer processes of public service reform, fragmentation and centralisation;
- the networked nature of contemporary local governance, whereby local authorities work through, and facilitate partnerships with,

other public, private and third sector agencies, who in turn work more closely with citizens and residents to coproduce public value outcomes;

- the authority's overriding need for research to have a practical impact or explicit evaluative value in relation to the needs and characteristics of populations and places, or the efficacy of policy impacts on such populations and places;
- a growing recognition of the interconnected complexity and reflexivity of most contemporary public policy problems, and therefore the need for research design to recognise this through using, wherever appropriate, a whole-systems approach to exploring the nature of such problems and the contingent and emergent nature of concomitant policy interventions;
- that undertaking research on or for local communities and/or local public agencies, including local authorities themselves, is necessarily political, contested and framed by competing worldviews, and therefore researchers operating within this milieu must be willing and capable of negotiating such terrain as part of their commission.

We would hope that such advice will not deter academic researchers from engaging in the muddy, messy fields of local authorities and their relationship with the local communities they serve, because, despite the challenges that these fields undoubtedly provide, contained within them are rich social research questions that desperately need answering. Research output based on a deep understanding and examination of fascinating places such as Bradford could be invaluable in addressing the most pressing policy dilemmas, despite the inherent difficulties of such research, which this chapter has tried to elucidate.

Bibliography

ABC News (2013) 'ARC wasting taxpayers' money says Hockey', PM, 5 September (www.abc.net.au/pm/content/2013/s3842173.htm).

Access and Equity Inquiry Panel, Australia (2012) *Access and equity for a multicultural Australia: Inquiry into the responsiveness of Australian Government Services to Australia's culturally and linguistically diverse population*, June, Canberra (www.dss.gov.au/our-responsibilities/settlement-and-multicultural-affairs/programs-policy/access-and-equity/access-and-equity-inquiry).

Alam, M.Y. (2006) *Made in Bradford*, Pontefract: Route Books.

Alam, M.Y. (2011) *The invisible village: Small world, big society*, Pontefract: Route Books.

Alam, M.Y. and Husband, C. (2006) *British-Pakistani men from Bradford: Linking narratives to policy*, York: Joseph Rowntree Foundation.

Alexander, C. (2006) 'Writing race: ethnography and difference', *Ethnic and Racial Studies*, vol 29, no 3, pp 397-410.

Alexander, J.C. (2013) 'Struggling over the mode of incorporation: backlash against multiculturalism in Europe', *Ethnic and Racial Studies*, vol 36, no 4, pp 531-56.

Afridi, A. (2007) *Community Cohesion and Deprivation: A discussion paper for the Commission on Integration and Cohesion*, London: Commission on Integration and Cohesion.

Ali, S. (2006) 'Racializing research: managing power and politics?', *Ethnic and Racial Studies*, vol 29, no 3, pp 471-86.

Ali, S., Campbell, K., Branley, D. and James, R. (2004) 'Politics, identities and research', in C. Seale (ed) *Researching society and culture*, London: Sage, pp 21-32.

Alston, P. and de Schutter, O. (2005) *Monitoring fundamental rights in the EU: The contribution of the fundamental rights agency*, Oxford: Hart Publishing.

Alston, P. and Weiler, J.H.H. (1998) 'An "ever closer union" in need of a human rights policy', *European Journal of International Law*, vol 9, pp 658-723 (www.jeanmonnetprogram.org/archive/papers/99/990101. html).

Anthias, F. and Yuval-Davis, M. (1993) *Racialized boundaries*, London: Routledge.

Anwar, M. (1979) *The myth of return: Pakistanis in Britain*, London: Heinemann Educational.

Appiah, K.A. (2006) *Cosmopolitanism, ethics in a world of strangers*, London: Penguin.

Argyle, M. (1967/1994) *The psychology of interpersonal behaviour*, Harmondsworth: Penguin.

Arneil, B. (2007) 'The meaning and utility of "social" in social capital', in R. Edwards, J. Franklin and J. Holland. (eds) *Assessing social capital: Concept, policy and practice*, Newcastle: Cambridge Scholars Press, pp 29–53

Asad, T. (1973) *Anthropology and the colonial encounter*, New York, NY: Humanity Books.

Asad, T. (1990) 'Ethnography, literature, and politics: some readings and uses of Salman Rushdie's The satanic verses', *Cultural Anthropology*, vol 5, no 3, pp 239-69.

Asare, B., Cairney, P. and Studler, D.T. (2009) 'Federalism and multilevel governance in tobacco policy: the European Union, the United Kingdom and devolved UK institutions', *Journal of Public Policy*, vol 29, no 1, pp 79-102.

Australian, Government of (2011) *The people of Australia: Australia's multicultural policy* (www.dss.gov.au/our-responsibilities/settlement-and-multicultural-affairs/publications/the-people-of-australia-australias-multicultural-policy).

Australian Government (2013) *Response to the recommendations of the Access and Equity Inquiry*, March (www.dss.gov.au/sites/default/files/files/settle/multicultural_australia/government-response.pdf).

Australian Social Inclusion Board (2009) *A stronger, fairer Australia*, Canberra: Department of Prime Minister and Cabinet (http://pandora.nla.gov.au/pan/142909/20130920-1300/www.socialinclusion.gov.au/sites/default/files/publications/pdf/report-stronger-fairer-australia.pdf).

Australian Social Inclusion Board (2012) *Social inclusion in Australia: How Australia is faring* (2nd edn), Canberra: Department of Prime Minister and Cabinet (www.afsa.gov.au/about-us/annual-report/annual-report-2012-13/downloads/how-australia-is-faring-report).

Back, L. (2007) *The art of listening*, Oxford: Berg.

Back, L. and Puwar, N. (eds) (2013) *Live methods*, Oxford: Wiley-Blackwell.

Back, L., Keith, M., Khan, A., Shukra, K. and Solomos, J. (2002) 'New Labour's white heart: politics and the return of assimilation', *Political Quarterly*, vol 73, no 4, pp 445-54.

Bagguley, P. and Hussain, Y. (2006) 'Conflict and cohesion: official constructions of "community" around the 2001 "riots" in Britain', *Critical Studies*, vol 28, pp 347-65.

Bagguley, P. and Hussain, Y. (2008) *Riotous citizens: Ethnic conflict in multicultural Britain*, Aldershot: Ashgate.

Banton, M. (1955) *The coloured quarter: Negro immigrants in an English city*, London: Cape.

Barzun, J. (1938) *Race: A study in modern superstition*, London: Methuen.

Baumgartner, F. and Jones, B. (1993) *Agendas and instability in American politics*, Chicago, IL: University of Chicago Press.

Beck, U. (1992) *Risk society*, London: Sage.

Becker, H.S. (2007) *Telling about society*, Chicago, IL and London: University of Chicago Press.

Béland, D. (2005) 'Ideas and social policy: an institutional perspective', *Social Policy & Administration*, vol 39, no 1, pp 1-18.

Bellotti, E. (2011) 'The social processes and production and validation of knowledge in particle physics: preliminary theoretical and methodological observations', *Procedia: Social and Behavioral Sciences*, vol 10, pp 148-59.

Benington, J. and Moor, M.H. (eds) (2011) *Public value theory and practice*, Basingstoke: Palgrave Macmillan.

Bhattacharyya, G. and Murji, K. (2013) 'Introduction: Race critical public scholarship', *Ethnic and Racial Studies*, vol 36, no 9, pp 1359-73.

BIMPR (Bureau of Immigration, Multicultural and Population Research) (1996) 'BIMPR projects and publications', *Bureau of Immigration, Multicultural and Population Research Bulletin*, no 17, pp 72-80 (www.multiculturalaustralia.edu.au/doc/bimpr_1.pdf).

Bloor, M. (2004) 'Addressing social problems through qualitative research', in D. Silverman (ed) *Qualitative research: Theory, method and practice* (2nd edn), London: Sage, pp 305-24.

Boese and Phillips (2011) 'Multiculturalism and social inclusion in Australia', *Journal of Intercultural Studies*, vol 32, no 2, April, 189-97.

Bolognani, M. (2007) 'Islam, ethnography and politics: methodological issues in researching amongst West Yorkshire Pakistanis in 2005', *International Journal of Social Research Methodology*, vol 10, no 4, pp 279-93.

Bolognani, M. (2009) *Crime and Muslim Britain: Race, culture and the politics of criminology among British Pakistanis*, London: I.B. Tauris.

Borofsky, R. (2005) *Yanomami: The fierce controversy and what we can learn from it*, Berkeley, CA: University of California Press.

Borrie, W.D. (Chair) (1975) *Population and Australia: First report of the National Population Inquiry*, Canberra: Australian Government Publishing Service.

Börzel, T.A. (1998) 'Organizing Babylon – on the different conceptions of policy networks', *Public Administration*, vol 76, Summer, pp 253-73 (http://ceses.cuni.cz/CESES-136-version1-1C_gov_networks_babylon_borzel.pdf).

Bourdieu, P. (1979/1984) *Distinction: A social critique of the judgment of taste* (translated by R. Nice), Cambridge, MA: Harvard University Press.

Bradford District Council (2014) *Medium-term financial strategy 2014-15 to 2016-17*, Bradford: City of Bradford Metropolitan District Council (www.bradford.gov.uk).

Brannick, T. and Coghlan, D. (2007) 'In defense of being "native": the case of insider academic research', *Organizational Research Methods*, vol 10, no 1, pp 59-74.

Briggs, A. (1984) *A social history of England*, London: Viking Press.

Briggs, J. (2013) 'Ending more of Labor's waste', *Labor=Waste* (http://laborswaste.tumblr.com/).

Browne, J. (2010) *Securing a sustainable future for higher education*, Report of the Independent Review of Higher Education Funding and Student Finance, London: Department of Business, Innovation and Skills.

Bulmer, M. and Solomos, J. (eds) (2004) *Researching race and racism*, London: Routledge.

Burawoy, M. (2005) 'For public sociology', *British Journal of Sociology*, vol 56, no 2, pp 259-94.

Burawoy, M. (2006) 'Introduction: A public sociology for human rights', in J. Blau and K.I. Smith (eds) *Public sociologies reader*, Lanham, MD: Rowman & Littlefield, pp 1-18.

Burawoy, M. (2007) 'For "public sociology"', in D. Clawson, *Public sociology: Fifteen eminent sociologists debate politics and the profession in the twenty-first century*, Berkeley and Los Angeles, CA: University of University of California Press, pp 23-64.

Campaign for the Public University (2011) 'Defence of public higher education', 27 September (http://publicuniversity.org.uk/2011/09/27/higher-education-white-paper-is-provoking-a-winter-of-discontent/).

Campion, M.J. (2005) *Look who's talking: Cultural diversity, public service broadcasting and the national conversation*, Oxford: Nuffield College, University of Oxford.

Cantle, T. (2001) *Community cohesion: A report of the Independent Review Team* (The Cantle Report), London: Home Office (http://resources.cohesioninstitute.org.uk/Publications/Documents/Document/DownloadDocumentsFile.aspx?recordId=96&file=PDFversion).

Cantle, T. (2008) *Community cohesion: A new framework for race and diversity*, Houndmills, Basingstoke: Palgrave Macmillan.

Carling, A. (2008) 'The curious case of the misclaimed myth claims: ethnic segregation, polarisation and the future of Bradford', *Urban Studies*, vol 45, no 3, pp 553-89.

Castells (1997) *The power of identity*, Oxford: Blackwells.

Chagnon, N.A. (1968/1997) *Yanomamo: The fierce people* (5th edn), Fort Worth, TX: Harcourt Brace Jovanovich.

Chesterman, C. (1988) *Homes away from home: Supported Accommodation Assistance Program Review: Final report of the National Review of the Supported Accommodation Assistance Program*, Sydney.

Chin, J. (2012) 'What a load of hope: the post-racial mixtape', *California Western Law Review*, vol 48, no 2, pp 369-97.

Clarke, T. (2001) *Burnley speaks, who listens?*, Burnley: Burnley Borough Council.

Cohen, L. (1993) *Stranger Music*, London: Random House, 297.

Cohen, P. (ed) (1999) *New ethnicities, old racisms?*, London: Zed.

Collini, S. (2012) *What are universities for?*, London: Penguin Books.

Collins, J. (1988) *Migrant hands in a distant land: Australia's post-war immigration*, Leichhardt, NSW: Pluto Press.

Committee of Review of AIMA (Australian Institute of Multicultural Affairs) (1983) Report of the *Committee of Review of AIMA – Report to the Minister for Immigration and Ethnic Affairs* (Vol 1), Canberra: Australian Government Publishing Service (www.multiculturalaustralia.edu.au/doc/multinst_4.pdf).

Commons Select Committee (2012) *Political and constitutional reform – Third report, Prospects for codifying the relationship between central and local government* (www.publications.parliament.uk/pa/cm201213/cmselect/cmpolcon/656/65602.htm).

Copus, C. (2010) 'English local government: Neither local nor government', in P. Swianiewitcz (ed) *Territorial consolidation reforms in Europe*, Budapest: Open Society Institute, chapter 5.

Cottle, T. (2002) 'On narratives and the sense of self', *Qualitative Inquiry*, vol 8, no 5, 535-49.

Coulthard, G. (2007) 'Subjects of empire: indigenous peoples and the "politics of recognition"', *Contemporary Political Theory*, vol 6, no 4, pp 437-60.

Council of the AIMA (Australian Institute of Multicultural Affairs) (1983) *Memorandum to the Committee of Review of AIMA*, Melbourne: AIMA (Australian Institute of Multicultural Affairs) (www.multiculturalaustralia.edu.au/doc/multinst_2.pdf).

Council of the AIMA (1986) *Future directions for multiculturalism – Final report of the Council of AIMA*, Melbourne: AIMA (Australian Institute of Multicultural Affairs) (www.multiculturalaustralia.edu.au/doc/multinst_3.pdf).

Dahya, Z. (1965) 'Pakistani wives in Britain', *Race*, vol 6, no 4, pp 311-21.

Davies, P.T. (1999) 'What is evidence-based education?', *British Journal of Educational Studies*, vol 47, no 2, pp 108-21.

DCLG (Department for Communities and Local Government) (2012) *Creating the conditions for a more integrated society*, London: The Stationery Office (www.gov.uk/government/publications/creating-the-conditions-for-a-more-integrated-society).

de Andrade, L.L. (2000) 'Negotiating from the inside: constructing racial and ethnic identity in qualitative research', *Journal of Contemporary Ethnography*, vol 29, no 3, pp 268-90.

de Schutter, O. (2007) *The new architecture of fundamental rights policy in the EU* (http://cms.horus.be/files/99907/MediaArchive/Presentation_110215_ODeSchutter_2FRAND.pdf).

Deakin, N., Cohen, B. and McNeal, J. (1970) *Colour and citizenship and British society*, London: Panther Books.

Dee, M. and Allred, J. (1980) *TUCRIC: The first year*, Leeds: Project Space Leeds.

Deegan, M. (2001) 'The Chicago School of Ethnography', in P. Atkinson, A. Coffey, S. Delamont, J. Lofland and L. Lofland (eds) *Handbook of ethnography*, London: Sage, pp 11-25.

Denham, J. (2001) *Building cohesive communities: A report of the Ministerial Group on Public Order and Community Cohesion*, London: Home Office.

Desai, R. (1963) *Indian immigrants in Britain*, London: Oxford University Press and the Institute of Race Relations.

DIAC (Department of Immigration and Citizenship) (1998/2012) 'Living in harmony' launch video (www.youtube.com/watch?v=2F9yM6OxPNo).

DIMA (Department of Immigration and Border Protection) (1997) 'Sub-program 1.1: Research and statistics', *DIMA Annual Report 1996-1997* (www.immi.gov.au/about/reports/annual/1996-97/html/prog1002.htm).

Dixon, J. and Levine, M. (eds) (2012) *Beyond prejudice*, Cambridge: Cambridge University Press.

Dobson, A. (2014) *Listening for democracy*, Oxford: Oxford University Press.

Dorling, D. (2007) *A think piece for the Commission on Integration and Cohesion*, London: HMSO (www.dannydorling.org/wp-content/files/dannydorling_publication_id2020.pdf).

Dorling, D. (2012) 'Ed, English and embarrassment', *The Huffington Post*, 14 December (www.huffingtonpost.co.uk/danny-dorling/ed-english-and-embarrassment_b_2299207.html).

Dorling, D. and Thomas, B. (2004) *People and places: A 2001 census atlas of the UK*, Bristol: Policy Press.

Dovidio, J.F., Glick, P. and Rudman, L.A. (2005) *On the nature of prejudice: Fifty years after Allport*, Oxford: Blackwell.

Downing, J. and Husband, C. (2005) *Representing race: Racisms, ethnicity and the media*, London: Sage Publications.

Drake, St C. and Cayton, H.R. (1945/1962) *Black metropolis: A study of negro life in a northern city*, New York: Harper & Row.

DTZ (2007) *Evidence on integration and cohesion: Phase Two*, Wetherby: Communities and Local Government Publications.

Du Bois, W.E.B. (1903/2007) *The souls of black folk*, Oxford: Oxford University Press.

Du Bois, W.E.B. (1970) *The selected writings of W.E.B. Du Bois* (edited by Walter Wilson, with an introduction by Stephen J. Wright), New York: New American Library.

Duggan, L. (2003) *The twilight of equality? Neoliberalism, cultural politics, and the attack on democracy*, Boston, MA: Beacon Press.

EC (European Commission) (2012) *Communication on national Roma integration strategies: A first step in the implementation of the EU framework*, COM(2012) 226 final, 21 May, Brussels: EC (http://ec.europa.eu/justice/discrimination/files/com2012_226_en.pdf).

Eliot, T.S. (2004) *Complete poems and plays*, London: Faber.

Encel, S. (ed) (1981) *The ethnic dimension, Papers on ethnicity and pluralism by Jean Martin*, Sydney, NSW: George Allen & Unwin.

EPEC (European Policy Evaluation Consortium) (2005) Preparatory study for impact assessment and ex-ante evaluation of Fundamental Rights Agency public hearing, Brussels: EPEC (www.eerstekamer.nl/eu/documenteu/verslag_van_public_hearing/f=/vgy0nmeq57ze.pdf).

Equiano, O. (1789/1999) *The life of Olaudah Equiano, or, Gustavus Vassa, the African*, Mineola, NY: Dover Publications.

ESRC (Economic and Social Research Council) (no date) *Partnering with business: How business-academic collaboration can drive innovation and growth*, Swindon: ESRC (www.esrc.ac.uk/_images/KE_brochure_web_tcm8-23749.pdf).

Estabrooks, C.A., Norton, P., Birdsell, J.M., Newton, M.S., Adwale, A.J. and Thornley, R. (2008) 'Knowledge translation and research careers: Mode I and Mode II activity among health researchers', *Research Policy*, vol 37, no 6-7, pp 1066-77.

Ewing, K.D. and Gearty, C.A. (1990) *Freedom under Thatcher: Civil liberties in modern Britain*, Oxford: Clarendon Press.

Exworthy, M. (2008) 'Policy to tackle the social determinants of health: using conceptual models to understand the policy process', *Health Policy Planning*, vol 23, pp 318-27.

Featherstone, M. (2004) 'Automobilities: an introduction', *Theory, Culture and Society*, vol 21, no 4/5, pp 1-24.

Fekete, L. (2001) 'The emergence of xeno-racism', *Race & Class*, vol 43, no 2, pp 23-40.

Fekete, L. (2009) *A suitable enemy: Racism, migration and Islamophobia in Europe*, London: Pluto Press.

Fhlathuin, M.N. (1995) 'Postcolonialism and the author: the case of Salman Rushdie', in S. Burke (ed) *Authorship: From Plato to the postmodern – A reader*, Edinburgh: Edinburgh University Press, pp 277-84.

Field, J. (2003) *Social capital*, London: Routledge.

Finney, N. and Simpson, L. (2009) *'Sleepwalking to segregation'? Challenging myths about race and migration*, Bristol: Policy Press.

Firth, R. (1936/1957) *We, the Tikopia: A sociological study of kinship in primitive Polynesia* (2nd edn), London: Allen & Unwin.

Flinders, M. (2013) 'The politics of engaged scholarship: impact, relevance, imagination', *Policy & Politics*, vol 41, no 4, October, pp 621-42.

Foot, P. (1965) *Immigration and race in British politics*, London: Penguin.

Forrest, J. and Dunn, K. (2006a) 'Racism and intolerance in Eastern Australia: a geographic perspective', *Australian Geographer*, vol 37, no 2, pp 167-86.

Forrest, J. and Dunn, K. (2006b) 'Constructing racism in Sydney, Australia's largest EthniCity', *Urban Studies*, vol 44, no 4, pp 699-721.

Foucoult (2008) *Foucault on Governmentality and Liberalism: The Birth of Biopolitics: Lectures at the Collège de France, 1978—1979*, by Michel Foucault, trans. Graham Burchell, Basingstoke: Palgrave Macmillan.

FRA (European Union Agency for Fundamental Rights) (2011) *Handbook on European non-discrimination law* (http://fra.europa.eu/sites/default/files/fra_uploads/1510-FRA-CASE-LAW-HANDBOOK_EN.pdf).

Freire, P. (1970) Pedagogy of the oppressed, London: Penguin.

Friedson, E. (2001) *Professionalism, the third logic: On the practice of knowledge*, Chicago, IL: University of Chicago Press.

Galbally, F. (Chair) (1978) *Migrant services and programs: Report of the review of post-arrival programs and services for migrants*, Sydney, NSW: Australian Government Publishing Service.

Gane, N. and Back, L. (2012) 'C. Wright Mills 50 years on: the promise and craft of sociology revisited', *Theory, Culture & Society*, vol 29, no 7/8, pp 399-421.

Gearty, C. (2007) 'Terrorism and human rights', *Government and Opposition*, vol 42, no 3, pp 340-62.

George, D. (1974) *My heart soars*, Toronto: Irwin Clarke.

Gibbons, M., Limoges, C., Nowotny, H., Schwartzman, S., Scott, P. and Trow, M. (1994) *The new production of knowledge: The dynamics of science and research in contemporary societies*, London: Sage.

Gilroy, P. (1987) *There ain't no black in the Union Jack*, London: Hutchinson.

Ginsberg, B. (2011) *The fall of faculty: The rise of the all-administrative university*, New York: Oxford University Press.

Giroux, S.S. (2010) 'Sade's revenge: racial neoliberalism and the sovereignty of negation', *Patterns of Prejudice*, vol 44, no 1, pp 1-26.

Glengarry Glen Ross (1992) [Film] Directed by James Foley, USA: New Line Cinema.

Glengarry Glen Ross scene (AREA Advisory) (2014) [Video online] (www.youtube.com/watch?v=v9XW6P0tiVc)

Goffman, E. (1959/1971) *The presentation of self in everyday life*, Harmondsworth: Penguin.

Goldberg, D. (2009) *The threat of race: Reflections on racial neoliberalism*, Oxford: Wiley-Blackwell.

Goldberg, D. (2010) 'Call and response', *Patterns of Prejudice*, vol 44, no 1, pp 89-106.

Goldberg, T.D. (2001) *The racial state*, Oxford: Blackwell.

Gomm, R. (2004) *Social research methodology: A critical introduction*, Houndmills, Basingstoke: Palgrave.

Goodin, R.E. (2008) *Innovating democracy: Democratic theory and practice after the deliberative turn*, Oxford: Oxford University Press.

Gore, T. (2011) 'Epistemic communities in universities', *Procedia: Social and Behavioural Sciences*, vol 10, no 1, pp 98-103.

Gramsci, A. (2005) *Selections from the Prison Notebooks of Antonio Gramsci*, Lawrence and Wishart Ltd: London.

Grassby, A.J. (1973) 'A multi-cultural society for the future', Paper prepared for the Cairnmillar Institute's symposium 'Strategy 2000: Australia for tomorrow', Canberra: Australian Government Publishing Service.

Greene, M. (1986) 'In search of a critical pedagogy', *Harvard Educational Review*, vol 56, no 4, pp 427-41.

Griffin, J.H. (1960) *Black like me*, London: Panther.

Griffith, J.A.G., Henderson, J., Usborne, M. and Wood, D. (1960) *Coloured immigrants in Britain*, London: Oxford University Press and the Institute of Race Relations.

Gunaratnam, Y. (2003) *Researching 'race' and ethnicity: Methods, knowledge and power*, London: Sage.

Hall, S. (ed) (1997) *Representation: Cultural representations and signifying practices*, London: Sage.

Hall, S., Critcher, C., Jefferson, T., Clarke, J. and Roberts, B. (1978) *Policing the crisis: Mugging, the state and law and order*, London: Hutchinson.

Halliday, F. (1996) *Islam and the myth of confrontation*, London: I.B. Tauris.

Hammersley, M. (2000) *Taking sides in social research*, London: Routledge.

Haraway, D. (1991) *Simians, cyborgs, and women; the reinvention of nature*, New York, NY: Routledge.

Harris, T. (1990) *London crowds in the reign of Charles II: Propaganda and politics from the restoration until the exclusion crisis*, Cambridge: Cambridge University Press.

Harrison, H.H. (1920/1997) *When Africa awakes*, Baltimore, MD: Black Classic Press.

Harrison, H.H. (1920) *When Africa Awakes: the 'Inside Story' of the Stirrings and Strivings of the New Negro In the Western World*, New York, NY: The Porro Press.

Harrison, M., Phillips, D., Chahal, K., Hunt, L. and Perry, J. (2005) *Housing, 'race' and community cohesion*, Coventry: Chartered Institute of Housing.

Hastrup, K. and Hervik, P. (eds) (1994) *Social experience and anthropological knowledge*, London: Routledge.

Henderson, R.F. (1975) *Poverty in Australia* (Vol 1), Canberra: Australian Government Publishing Service (www.multiculturalaustralia.edu.au/doc/henderson_1.pdf).

Hewitt, R. (2005) *White backlash and the politics of multiculturalism*, Cambridge: Cambridge University Press.

Hillyard, P. and Percy-Smith, J. (1988) *The coercive state: The decline of democracy in Britain*, London: Fontana Collins.

Hoggart, R. (1957) *The uses of literacy: Aspects of working class life*, London: Chatto & Windus.

Hood, C. (1991) 'A public management for all seasons', *Public Administration*, vol 69, pp 3-19.

Humphry, D. (1972) *Police power and black people*, London: Panther.

Humphry, D. and John, G. (1971) *Because they're black*, Harmondsworth: Penguin Classic.

Husband, C. (1996) 'The right to be understood: Conceiving the multi-ethnic public sphere', *Innovation: The European Journal of Social Sciences*, vol 9, no 2, pp 205-16.

Husband, C. (2009) 'Between listening and understanding' *Continuum: Journal of Media and Cultural Studies*, vol 23, no 4, pp 441-43.

Husband, C. (2010) 'Counter narratives to multiculturalism and the assimilationist drift in British policy: lessons from the era of New Labour', *Translocations*, vol 6, issue 2, Winter, pp 1-23.

Husband, C. and Alam, Y. (2011) *Social cohesion and counter-terrorism: A policy contradiction?*, Bristol: Policy Press.

IFS (Institute for Fiscal Studies) (2012) *Local government spending: Where the axe is falling*, London: IFS (www.ifs.org.uk/budgets/gb2012/12chap6.pdf).

Ikuenobe, P. (2013) 'Conceptualizing and theorizing about the idea of a "post-racial" era', *Journal for the Theory of Social Behaviour*, vol 43, no 4, pp 446-68.

Imam, U.F. (1999) 'Youth workers as mediators and interpreters: Ethical issues in work with Black young people', in S. Banks (ed) *Ethical Issues in Youth Work*, London: Routledge.

Jakubowicz, A. (2011) 'Anti racism reports released after thirteen years of suppression', *Cultural Diversity: Research* (http://bit.ly/1zbG23c).

Jakubowicz, A. and Buckley, B. (1975) *Migrants and the legal system: Research report*, Law and Poverty series research report, Canberra: Commission of Inquiry into Poverty.

Jakubowicz, A., Collins, J., Reid, C. and Chafic, W. (2014) 'Minority youth and social transformation in Australia: identities, belonging and cultural capital', *Social Inclusion*, vol 2, no 2 (www.cogitatiopress.com/ojs/index.php/socialinclusion/article/view/162).

Jessop, B. (2010) 'Cultural political economy and critical policy studies', *Critical Policy Studies*, vol 3, no 3-4, pp 336-56.

Joint Standing Committee on Migration [Australia] (2013)

JRF (Joseph Rowntree Foundation) (1904) 'Our heritage', York: JRF (www.jrf.org.uk/about-us/our-heritage).

JRF (no date) 'Neighbourhood approaches to loneliness: Unheard voices', York: JRF (www.jrf.org.uk/topic/loneliness).

Julien, I. and Mercer, K. (1996) 'De margin and de center', in D. Morley and C. Kuan-Hsing (eds) *Stuart Hall: Critical dialogues in cultural studies*, London: Routledge, pp 452-67.

Kalra, V.S. (2006) 'Ethnography as politics: a critical review of British studies of racialized minorities', *Ethnic and Racial Studies*, vol 29, no 3, pp 452-70.

Karim, K.H. (2000) *Islamic peril: Media and global violence*, Montreal: Black Rose Books.

Khan, M.G. (2013) *Young Muslims, pedagogy and Islam: Contexts and concepts*, Bristol: Policy Press.

Khan, S. (2006) 'Muslims!', in N. Ali, V.S. Kalra and S. Sayyid (eds) *Postcolonial people: South Asians in Britain*, London: Hurst, pp 182-7.

Khan, V.S. (1977) 'The Pakistanis: Mirpuri villagers at home and in Bradford', in J.L. Watson, *Between two cultures: Migrants and minorities in Britain*, Oxford: Basil Blackwell, pp 57-89.

Kipling, R. (1899) *The white man's burden* (www.fordham.edu/halsall/mod/kipling.asp).

Kjærum, M. (2003) *National human rights institutions implementing human rights*, Copenhagen: Det Danske Center for Menneskerettigheder [The Danish Institute for Human Rights] (www.humanrights.dk/files/Importerede%20filer/hr/pdf/n_h_r_i_h_fte_eng.pdf).

Klein, N. (2007) *The shock doctrine*, London: Picador.

Knorr-Cetina, K. (1999) *Epistemic cultures: How the sciences make knowledge*, Cambridge, MA: Harvard University Press.

Knowles, A. (2006) 'Handling your baggage in the field: reflections on research relationships', *International Journal of Social Research Methodology*, vol 9, no 5, pp 393-404.

Knox, R. (1862) *The races of men: A philosophical enquiry into the influence of race over the destinies of nations*, London: Henry Renshaw.

Kundnani, A. (2002) 'The death of multiculturalism', *Race and Class*, vol 43, no 4, pp 67-72.

Ladner, J.A. (ed) (1973) *The death of white sociology*, New York: Random House.

Lane, B. (2013) 'Coalition angers research community', *The Australian*, 6 September (www.theaustralian.com.au/higher-education/coalition-angers-research-community/comments-e6frgcjx-1226712215714).

Lave, J. and Wenger, E. (1991) *Situated learning: Legitimate peripheral participation*, Cambridge: Cambridge University Press.

Lee, R.M. (1993) *Doing research on sensitive topics*, London: Sage.

Lee, E. and Simon-Maeda, A. (2006) 'Racialized research identities in ESL/EFL research', *TESOL Quarterly*, vol 40, no 3, pp 573-94.

Lelohe, M.J. (1966) 'Bradford', *Race & Class*, July, vol 8, pp 30-42.

Lemke, T. (2011) *Foucault, governmentality, and critique*, London: Paradigm Books.

Lentin, A. (2012) 'Post-race, post politics: the paradoxical rise of culture after multiculturalism', *Ethnic and Racial Studies*, pp 1-19.

Lentin, A. and Titley, G. (2011) *The crises of multiculturism: Racism in a neoliberal age*, London: Zed Books.

Letherby, G. (2003) *Feminist research in theory and practice*, Buckingham: Open University Press.

Levitas, R. (2005) *The inclusive society: Social exclusion and New Labour*, Basingstoke: Palgrave Macmillan.

Lewins, F. and Ly, J. (1985) *The first wave: The settlement of Australia's first Vietnamese refugees*, Sydney, NSW: George Allen & Unwin.

Lewis, P. (2007) *Young, British and Muslim*, London: Continuum.

LGA (Local Government Association) (2013a) *Rewiring public services – Rejuvenating democracy*, London: LGA (www.local.gov.uk/web/guest/publications/-/journal_content/56/10171/4047947/PUBLICATION-TEMPLATE).

LGA (2013b) *Future funding outlook for councils from 2010/11 to 2019/20*, London: LGA (www.local.gov.uk).

Liebling, A. (2001) 'Whose side are we on? Theory, practice and allegiances in prisons research', *British Journal of Criminology*, vol 41, no 3, pp 472-84.

Liebow, E. (1967) *Tally's corner: A study of negro streetcorner men*, Boston, MA: Little, Brown & Co.

Long, E. (1774/2002) *The history of Jamaica. Or, General survey of the ancient and modern state of that island: With reflections on its situation, settlements, inhabitants, climate, products, commerce, laws, and government* (two volumes), Quebec: McGill-Queen's University Press.

Long, E. (1774/2002) *History of Jamaica, Volume II : Reflections on its Situation, Settlements, Inhabitants, Climate, Products, Commerce, Laws and Government. With Introduction by Howard Johnson*, Montreal: McGill-Queen's University Press.

Loomba, A. (1998) *Colonialism/postcolonialism*, London: Routledge.

Lyons. M. (2007) *Place-shaping: A shared ambition for the future of local government* (The final report of the Lyons Inquiry into Local Government), London: The Stationery Office.

Macpherson of Cluny, Sir William (1999) *The Stephen Lawrence inquiry: Report of an inquiry by Sir William Macpherson of Cluny*, London: The Stationery Office.

McGettigan, A. (2013) *The great university gamble: Money, markets and the future of higher education*, London: Pluto Press.

McGhee, D. (2008) *The end of multiculturalism: Terrorism, integration and human rights*, Maidenhead: Open University Press.

Madden, R. (2010) *Being ethnographic: A guide to the theory and practice of ethnography*, London: Sage.

Malinowski, B. (1922/2009) *Argonauts of the Western Pacific: An account of native enterprise and adventure in the Archipelagos of Melanesian New Guinea*, Garsington: Benediction Classics.

Marriott, J. (1999) 'In darkest England: the poor, the crowd and race in the nineteenth-century metropolis', in P. Cohen (ed) *New ethnicities, old racisms?*, London: Zed Books, pp 82-100.

Martin, J. (1978) *The migrant presence: Australian responses, 1947-1977 – Research report for the National Population Inquiry*, Sydney, NSW: George Allen & Unwin.

Martin, S.J. and Bovaird, A.G. (2005) *Meta-evaluation of the local government modernisation agenda: Progress report on service improvement in local government*, London: Office of the Deputy Prime Minister

Meekosha, H. and Jakubowicz, A. (1987) *Equal disappointment opportunity? A report to the Department of Community Services on programs for immigrants and their children*, Canberra: Department of Community Services.

Migrant Task Force Committee NSW (New South Wales) (1973) *First report of a task force established by the Minister for Immigration, into the immediate problems of migrants and recommendations for their resolution*, Sydney, NSW: Department of Immigration.

Milgiorino, P. (2013) 'Advocating ethnic interests', in A. Jakubowicz and C. Ho (eds) *'For those who've come across the seas...': Australian multicultural theory, policy and practice*, Melbourne, VIC: Australian Scholarly, pp 137-47.

Mirowski, P. and Plehwe, D. (eds) (2009) *The road From Mount Pelerin*, Cambridge, MA: Harvard University Press.

Modood, T. (2013) *Multiculturalism* (2nd edn), Cambridge: Polity Press.

Mohammed, J. and Siddiqui, A. (2013) *The Prevent strategy: A cradle to grave police-state*, London: Cage.

Monteiro, A. (2008) 'W.E.B. Du Bois and the study of black humanity: a rediscovery', *Journal of Black Studies*, vol 38, no 4, pp 600-21.

Morley, D. and Kuan-Hsing, C. (eds) (1996) *Stuart Hall: Critical dialogues in cultural studies*, London: Routledge.

Murphy, G. (2010) *Shadowing the white man's burden: US imperialism and the problem of the color line*, New York: New York University Press.

National Groups Unit, Department of Labor and Immigration (1974) 'Report on ethnic groups, study undertaken 1969 to 1974', Canberra (unpublished).

Nayak, A. (2006) 'After race: ethnography, race and post-race theory', *Ethnic and Racial Studies*, vol 29, no 3, pp 411-30.

Nowotny, H., Scott, P. and Gibbons, M. (2001) *Re-thinking science: Knowledge and the public in an age of uncertainty*, Cambridge: Polity Press.

Nowotny, H., Scott, P. and Gibbons, M. (2003) '"Mode 2" revisited: the new production of knowledge', *Minerva*, vol 41, pp 179-94.

Noxolo, P. and Huysmans, J. (eds) (2009) *Community, citizenship and the 'War on Terror': Security and insecurity*, Houndmills, Basingstoke: Palgrave Macmillan.

O'Brien, M. (1998) 'Postmodernism and British history', in J. Rees (ed) *Essays on historical materialism*, London: Bookmarks, pp 133-44.

OAIC (Office of the Australian Information Commissioner) (2013) 'Summary of version changes to s 93A Guidelines' (www.oaic.gov.au/freedom-of-information/applying-the-foi-act/foi-guidelines/summary-of-version-changes-to-s-93a-guidelines).

Oakley, A. (1981) 'Interviewing women: A contradiction in terms', in H. Roberts (ed) *Doing feminist research*, London: Routledge, pp 30-61.

OJEC (*Official Journal of the European Communities*) (1977), No C 103, 27 April.

ONS (Office for National Statistics) (2012) *Mid-year estimate*, Newport: ONS.

Orwell, G. (1946/1984) *Why I write*, Harmondsworth: Penguin.

Ouseley, H. (2001) *Community pride, not prejudice*, Bradford: Bradford Vision.

Paterson, J. (2011) 'How Tony Abbott should fight the culture wars', *Quadrant*, 1 November (https://quadrant.org.au/magazine/2011/11/how-tony-abbott-should-fight-the-culture-wars/).

Patterson, S. (1963) *Dark strangers: A sociological study of the absorption of a recent West Indian migrant group in Brixton, South London*, London: Tavistock Publications.

Peperzak, A.T., Critchley, S. and Bernaconi, R. (1996) *Emmanuel Levinas. Basic philosophical writings*, Bloomington, IN: Indiana University Press.

Pettigrew, T. and Tropp, L.R. (2005) 'Allport's intergroup contact hypothesis: its history and influence', in J.F. Dovidio, P. Glick and L.A. Rudman, *On the nature of prejudice: Fifty years after Allport*, Oxford: Blackwell, pp 262-77.

Phillips, D. (2002) *Movement to opportunity? South Asian relocation in northern cities*, End of Award report, ESRC R000238038, Leeds: School of Geography, University of Leeds.

Phillips, A. (2007) *Multiculturalism without culture*, Princeton, NJ: Princeton University Press.

Phillips, D. (2006) 'Parallel lives? Challenging discourses of British Muslim self-segregation', *Environment and Planning D: Society and Space*, vol 24, no 1, pp 25-40.

Phillips, M. (2006) *Londonistan: how Britain is creating a terror state within*, London: Encounter Books.

Phillips, R. (ed) (2009) *Muslim spaces of hope: Geographies of possibility in Britain and the West*, London: Zed Books.

Polyani, M. (1983) *The tacit dimension*, Gloucester, MA: Peter Smith.

Poole, E. (2002) *Reporting Islam: Media representations of British Muslims*, London: I.B. Tauris.

Poole, E. and Richardson, J. (2005) *Muslims and the news media*, London: I.B. Tauris.

Porsanger, J. and Guttorm, G. (eds) (2011) 'Working with traditional knowledge: communities, institutions, information systems, law and ethics', *Diedut, 1/2011*, Guovdageaidnu, Norway: Sami allaskuvla.

Putnam, R.D. (2000) *Bowling alone*, New York: Simon & Schuster.

Ramamurthy, A. (2006) 'The politics of Britain's Asian youth movements', *Race & Class*, vol 48, no 2, pp 38-60.

Ramamurthy, A. (2013) *Black star: Britain's Asian youth movements*, London: Pluto Press.

Ranjan, G. and Clegg, S.R. (1997) 'An inside story: Tales from the field - doing organisational research in a state of insecurity', *Organisation Studies*, vol 18, pp 1015-23.

Readings, B. (1996) *The university in ruins*, Cambridge, MA: Harvard University Press.

Reeves, F. (1983) *British racial discourse*, Cambridge: Cambridge University Press.

Reicher, S.(2012) 'From perception to mobilization: the shifting paradigm of prejudice', in J. Dixon and M. Levine (eds) *Beyond prejudice: Extending the social psychology of conflict, inequality and social change*, Cambridge: Cambridge University Press.

Rex, J. and Moore, R. (1967) *Race, community and conflict*, Oxford: Oxford University Press.

Rhodes, R.A.W. (1994) 'The hollowing out of the state: the changing nature of the public service in Britain', *The Political Quarterly*, vol 65, pp 138-51.

Ritchie, D. (2001) *Oldham Independent Review: One Oldham, one future*, Manchester: Government Office for the North West.

Runnymede Trust, The (1997) *Islamophobia: A challenge for us all*, London: The Runnymede Trust.

Ruthven, M. (1991) *A satanic affair*, London: Hogarth Press.

Said, E. (1978) *Orientalism*, Harmondsworth: Penguin.

Said, E. (1993) *Culture and imperialism*, New York: Alfred A. Knopf.

Salway, S., Barley, R., Allmark, P., Gerrish, K., Higginbottom, G. and Ellison, G. (2011) *Ethnic diversity and inequality: Ethical and scientific rigour in social research*, York: Joseph Rowntree Foundation (www. jrf.org.uk).

Sanghera, G.S. and Thapar-Björkert, S. (2008) 'Methodological dilemmas: gatekeepers and positionality in Bradford', *Ethnic and Racial Studies*, vol 31, no 3, pp 543-62.

Sardar, Z. (1999) *Orientalism*, Buckingham: OUP.

Sayer, A. (2005) *The moral significance of class*, Cambridge: Cambridge University Press.

SBS Television (1984, 1994) 'The Jobs for Women Campaign in Port Kembla, NSW' (www.multiculturalaustralia.edu.au/library/media/ Video/id/466.World-News-Women-at-work).

Scarman, Lord (1981) *The Scarman report: The Brixton disorders, 10-12 April*, London: Penguin Books.

Schmidt, V. (2010) 'Taking ideas and discourse seriously: explaining change through discursive institutionalism as the fourth "new institutionalism"', *European Political Science Review*, vol 21, pp 1-25.

Schwarze, T.T. (2002) *Joyce and the Victorians*, Gainesville, FL: University Press of Florida.

Scottish Office (1998) *The constitutional status of local government in other countries*, Edinburgh: The Scottish Office Central Research Unit.

Sennett, R. (1998) *The corrosion of character*, New York: W.W. Norton.

Shanahan, E.A., Jones, M.D. and McBeth, M.K. (2011) 'Policy narratives and policy processes', *Policy Studies Journal*, vol 39, no 3, pp 535-61.

Shaver, S. (2014) 'How a study lost its funding: Jean Martin and public knowledge of the refugee experience', *Journal of Sociology*, first published on January 20, 2014 doi:10.1177/1440783313518248.

Silverman, D. (ed) (2004) *Qualitative research: Theory, method and practice* (2nd edn), London: Sage.

Simpson, L. (2004) 'Statistics of racial segregation: measures, evidence and policy', *Urban Studies*, vol 41, no 3, pp 661-81.

Simpson, L. and Finney, N. (2009) 'Do ethnic minorities exclude themselves?', *Radical Statistics*, issue 99, pp 34-45 (www.radstats.org. uk/no099/SimpsonFinney99.pdf).

Simpson, L. and Finney, N. (2010) 'Parallel lives and ghettos in Britain: facts or myths?', *Geography*, vol 95, no 3, Autumn.

Simpson, L., Husband, C. and Alam, Y. (2009) 'Recognizing complexity, challenging pessimism: the case of Bradford's urban dynamics', *Urban Studies*, vol 46, no 9, pp 1995-2001.

Smith, K.E and Joyce, K.E. (2012) 'Capturing complex realities: understanding efforts to achieve evidence-based policy and practice in public health', *Evidence & Policy*, vol 8, no 1, pp 57-78.

Smith, K.E and Katikireddi, S.V. (2013) ' A glossary of theories for understanding policymaking', *Journal of Epidemiology & Community Health*, vol 67, no 2, pp 198-202.

Smith, L.T. (2012) *Decolonizing methodologies: Research and indigenous peoples*, London: Zed Books.

Singh, D. (2007) *Our shared future: Final report of the Commission on Integration and Cohesion*, London: The Stationery Office.

Solomos, J. (2003) *Race and racism in Britain* (3rd edn), Houndmills, Basingstoke: Palgrave Macmillan.

Solomos, J. and Back, L. (1996) *Racism and society*, Basingstoke: Palgrave.

Sparrow, J. (2013) 'Culture wars: battles against an undefined elite', *The Drum*, 28 April (www.abc.net.au/unleashed/4656520.html).

Staley, L. (2008) 'Evidence-based-policy and public sector innovation', November, Melbourne, VIC: Institute of Public Affairs (www.ipa. org.au/publications/1442/evidence-based-policy-and-public-sector-innovation).

Stephan, W.G. and Stephan, C.W. (1996) 'Predicting prejudice', *International Journal of Intercultural Relations*, vol 20, no 3/4, pp 409-26.

Stephan, W.G., Ybarra, O. and Bachman, G. (1999) 'Prejudice towards immigrants', *Journal of Applied Social Psychology*, vol 29, no 11, pp 2221-37.

Taylor, C. (2004) *Modern social imaginaries*, Durham, NC: Duke University Press.

Thapar-Bjorkert, S. and Henry, M. (2004) 'Reassessing the research relationship: location, position and power in fieldwork accounts', *International Journal of Social Research Methodology*, vol 7, no 5, pp 363-81.

Tierney, P. (2000) *Darkness in El Dorado: How scientists and journalists devastated the Amazon*, New York: W.W. Norton & Co.

Tileaga, C. (2007) 'Ideologies of moral exclusion: a critical discursive reframing of depersonalization, delegitimatization and dehumanization', *British Journal of Social Psychology*, vol 46, pp 717-37.

Tuhiwai Smith, L. (2012) *Decolonizing methodologies: Research and indigenous peoples*, London: Zed Books.

Turnpenny, J., Radaelli, C.M., Jordan, A. and Jacob, K. (2009) 'The policy and politics of policy appraisal: emerging trends and new directions', *Journal of European Public Policy*, vol 16, no 4, pp 640-53.

Tyfield, D. (2012) 'A cultural political economy of research and innovation in crisis', *Minerva*, vol 50, no 2, pp 149-67.

Uberoi, N. (1964) 'Sikh women in Southall', *Race*, vol 6, no 1, pp 34-40.

UN (United Nations) (2012) *Human rights indicators: A guide to measurement and implementation*, HR/PUB/12/5 (www.ohchr.org/Documents/Publications/Human_rights_indicators_en.pdf).

UN OHCHR (United Nations Office of the High Commissioner for Human Rights (2006) *Report on indicators for monitoring compliance with international human rights instruments*, HRI/MC/2006/7, 11 May, p 5

UNODC-UNECE (2010) *Manual on Victimization Surveys*, Available at www.unodc.org/documents/data-and-analysis/Crime-statistics/Manual_on_Victimization_surveys_2009_web.pdf

Vamvakinou, M. (Chair) (2013a) *Inquiry into migration and multiculturalism in Australia*, Joint Standing Committee on Migration, Parliament of Australia (www.aph.gov.au/parliamentary_business/committees/house_of_representatives_committees?url=mig/multiculturalism/report.htm).

Vamvakinou, M. (2013b) *Migration report* (www.mariavamvakinou.com/index.php?option=com_content&view=article&id=607:migration-report-committees-house-of-representatives&catid=2:speeches&Itemid=3).

Vertovec, S. (2007) *New complexities of cohesion in Britain: Super-diversity, transnationalism and civil-integration*, Commission on Integration and Cohesion, London: HMSO (www.compas.ox.ac.uk/fileadmin/files/Publications/Reports/Vertovec%20-%20new_complexities_of_cohesion_in_britain.pdf).

Vickers, M. (2002) 'Researchers as storytellers: Writing on the edge and without a safety net', *Qualitative Inquiry*, vol 8, pp 608-21.

Waisbord, S. (2013) *Reinventing professionalism: Journalism and news in global perspective*, Cambridge: Polity.

Walvin, J. (1971) *The black presence*, London: Orback and Chambers.

Watson, J.L. (ed) (1977) *Between two cultures: Migrants and minorities in Britain*, Oxford: Basil Blackwell.

Weh, L. (1987) 'Recent tendencies in the evolution of national law and practice in the field of asylum and refugees', in Council of Europe, *The law of asylum and refugees: Present tendencies and future perspectives*, Proceedings of the Sixteenth Colloquy on European Law, Lund, 15-17 September 1986, Strasbourg: Council of Europe, Publications Section.

Wenger, E. (2007) *Communities of practice*, Cambridge: Cambridge University Press.

Whyte, W.F. (1943/1993) *Street corner society: The social structure of an Italian slum* (4th edn), Chicago, IL: University of Chicago Press.

Wiener, R. (2002) 'A sociodramatist goes to work', in A. Chesner and H. Hahn (eds) *Creative advances in groupwork*, London: Jessica Kingsley Publishers, chapter 6.

Williams, E. (1944/1994) *Capitalism & slavery*, Chapel Hill, NC: University of North Carolina Press.

Williams, R. (1958) *Culture and society: 1780-1950*, London: Chatto & Windus.

Wilson, R.A. (ed) (2005) *Human rights in the 'War on Terror'*, Cambridge: Cambridge University Press.

Wilson, T. (2013) 'Paternalism: an unhealthy threat to freedom', 12 December, Melbourne, VIC: Institute of Public Affairs (http://ipa.org.au/news/3013/paternalism-an-unhealthy-threat-to-freedom).

Wise, T. (2010) *Colorblind: The rise of post-racial politics and the retreat from racial equity*, San Francisco, CA: City Lights Books.

Wright, S.C. and Baray, G. (2012) 'Models of social change in social psychology: collective action or prejudice reduction', in J. Dixon and M. Levine (eds) *Beyond prejudice*, Cambridge: Cambridge University Press, pp 225-47.

Young, I.M. (1990) Justice and the politics of difference, Princeton, NJ: Princeton University Press.

Yuen, N.W. and Ray, C.J. (2009) 'Post 9/11, but not post-racial', *Contexts*, vol 8, pp 68-70.

Index